THE CITY IN CHINA

New perspectives on contemporary urbanism

Edited by Ray Forrest, Julie Ren and
Bart Wissink

BRISTOL
UNIVERSITY
PRESS

First published in Great Britain in 2019 by

Bristol University Press
University of Bristol
1-9 Old Park Hill
Bristol
BS2 8BB
UK
t: +44 (0)117 954 5940
www.bristoluniversitypress.co.uk

North America office:
Policy Press
c/o The University of Chicago Press
1427 East 60th Street
Chicago, IL 60637, USA
t: +1 773 702 7700
f: +1 773-702-9756
sales@press.uchicago.edu
www.press.uchicago.edu

British Library Cataloguing in Publication Data
A catalogue record for this book is available from the British Library

Library of Congress Cataloging-in-Publication Data
A catalog record for this book has been requested

ISBN 978-1-5292-0547-3 hardcover
ISBN 978-1-5292-0549-7 ePub
ISBN 978-1-5292-0550-3 Mobi
ISBN 978-1-5292-0548-0 ePdf

Cover design by blu inc, Bristol
Front cover image: kindly supplied by Weng Fen. "On the Wall—Guangzhou (2)," 2002,
chromogenic color print, overall: 124 × 189 × 4.5 cm. M+ Sigg Collection, Hong Kong. ©
Weng Fen [2012.1089].
Printed and bound in Great Britain by CPI Group (UK) Ltd,
Croydon, CR0 4YY
Bristol University Press uses environmentally responsible print
partners

Contents

List of Tables and Figures

Tables

Figures

Notes on Contributors

Juan Chen is Associate Professor in the Department of Applied Social Sciences, Hong Kong Polytechnic University. She received her BA and MA (in Political Science) from Peking University, and her MSW and PhD (in Social Work and Political Science) from the University of Michigan, Ann Arbor. Her research centers around migration and urbanization, health and mental health, and help seeking and service use in the United States, Mainland China, and Hong Kong. Her work has appeared in *Social Service Review*, *Social Science & Medicine*, *China Quarterly*, *Habitat International*, and *Cities*, among others.

Ray Forrest has held full time posts at the Universities of Birmingham (UK), Bristol, and City University of Hong Kong. He was Head of the School for Policy Studies at Bristol from 2001 to 2005 and Head of the Department of Public Policy at City University from 2012 to 2017. He is currently Research Professor in Cities and Social Change in the Department of Sociology and Social Policy and Director of the Centre for Social Policy and Social Change at Lingnan University. He is Emeritus Professor of Urban Studies at Bristol, Fellow of the UK Academy of Social Sciences and Distinguished Professor at the Open University of Hong Kong.

Bettina Gransow is Associate Professor at the Institute of Chinese Studies, Freie Universität Berlin. Her research interests include the history of Chinese sociology, social risk analysis of Chinese infrastructure projects, migration, and megacity development in China from a space sociological perspective. She was guest editor of the Special Feature "Contested Urban Spaces—Whose Right to the City?" in *China Perspectives* (No. 2014/2).

Jeroen de Kloet is Professor of Globalisation Studies and Director of the Amsterdam Centre for Globalisation Studies (ACGS) at the University of Amsterdam and Professor at the School of Music and Recording Arts of the Communication University of China (Beijing), and is affiliated to the Beijing Film Academy. In 2010 he published China with a cut:

Globalisation, urban youth and popular music (Amsterdam University Press). Together with Yiu Fai Chow, he wrote *Sonic multiplicities: Hong Kong pop and the global circulation of sound and image* (Intellect, 2013), and, together with Lena Scheen, he edited *Spectacle and the city: Chinese urbanities in art and popular culture* (Amsterdam University Press, 2013). With Anthony Fung, he published *Youth cultures in China* (Polity, 2017), and with Esther Peeren, Robin Celikates, and Thomas Poell, he edited *Global cultures of contestation* (Palgrave Macmillan, 2018).

Zhigang Li is a professor of urban studies and planning at the School of Urban Design, Wuhan University, China. He has served as the Dean of this school since 2015. Before 2015, he worked at the School of Geography and Planning, Sun Yat-sen University, Guangzhou, China. As an urban geographer and planner, he works on the socio-spatial transformation of Chinese cities, with a focus on such topics as residential segregation, integration, satisfaction, migration, and related planning issues. He is known for his pioneering work on the study of African enclaves in China. His recent work concentrates on the migration of middle China, place attachments, and community planning.

Shuo Liu is Assistant Professor at the Department of Sociology, Hong Kong Shue Yan University. She graduated with a PhD degree in Sociology from the Chinese University of Hong Kong in 2009. Her main research interests include interpersonal relationships (*guanxi*) and the middle class in Mainland China. Her publications include "A middle-class community: Class formation and the building of a moral order" published in *Shehuixui Yanjiu*. Her current research interest focuses on consumption patterns among Chinese middle-class consumers.

Tai-lok Lui is Chair Professor of Hong Kong Studies, the Director of the Academy of Hong Kong Studies, and Vice President (Research and Development) at the Education University of Hong Kong. His publications include *City-states in the global economy, Hong Kong, China: Learning to belong to a nation*, and *Hong Kong: Becoming a Chinese global city*. He is also the co-editor of *Routledge handbook of contemporary Hong Kong*. His writings appear in academic journals like *Asia Pacific Viewpoint, Inter-Asia Cultural Studies, International Journal of Urban and Regional Research*, The *Sociological Review*, and *Urban Studies*.

Jan Nijman is Director of the Urban Studies Institute and Distinguished University Professor at Georgia State University. He holds a secondary professorship at the University of Amsterdam. His interests are in urban geography, urban history, the relationship between urbanization and development, and comparative urbanism; he has extensive research experience in North America, South Asia, and West Europe. His most recent (edited) book is *The life of North American suburbs* (University of Toronto Press, 2019).

Mary Ann O'Donnell is an artist-ethnographer who has sought alternative ways of inhabiting Shenzhen, the flagship of China's post-Mao economic reforms. O'Donnell creates and contributes to projects that reconfigure and repurpose shared spaces, where our worlds mingle and collide, sometimes collapse, and often implode. Ongoing projects include her blog, "Shenzhen Noted" and the Handshake 302 Art Space in Baishizhou. In January 2017, the University of Chicago Press published *Learning from Shenzhen: China's post-Mao experiment from special zone to model city*, which she co-edited with Winnie Wong and Jonathan Bach, and in December of that same year, she curated the "Migrations: Home and elsewhere" exhibition at the P+V Gallery for the seventh edition of the Shenzhen-Hong Kong Bi-City Biennale of Urbanism/Architecture. Her research has been published in positions: *East Asian Cultures Critique*, *TDR: The Drama Review*, and the *Hong Kong Journal of Cultural Studies*.

Shunxian (Cindy) Ou is a graduate student of Health Policy and Management program at the Johns Hopkins University, Baltimore. Her research interests include critical human geography and migration studies. In 2013 she graduated from Sun Yat-sen University, China, with a bachelor degree in Human Geography.

Julie Ren is Research Faculty at the Humboldt-Universität zu Berlin. She has previously held postdoctoral fellowships at the London School of Economics and the City University of Hong Kong. Formerly a Fulbright Fellow, she holds a BA from the College of Social Studies, Wesleyan University, a Master of Public Policy from the Hertie School of Governance and a PhD in Geography from the Humboldt-Universität zu Berlin. Her research focuses on comparative urbanism, urban theory, and cultural production through investigations of the intersection of artistic/cultural spaces and festivals, and cities of the majority world. Her most recent co-edited book (with Jason Luger) is *Art and the city: Worlding the discussion through a critical artscape* (Routledge, 2017).

Xuefei Ren is Associate Professor of Sociology and Global Urban Studies at Michigan State University. She is the author of *Building globalization: Transnational architecture production in urban China* (University of Chicago

Press, 2011), *Urban China* (2013, Polity Press), and co-editor of *Globalizing cities reader* (Routledge, 2011 with Roger Keil). She is a comparative urbanist and her current work investigates informal settlements, land security, and environmental governance in cities in China, India, Brazil, and the United States.

Zheng Wang is Lecturer at the Department of Urban Studies and Planning, The University of Sheffield. He holds a master's degree in Regeneration Studies (Cardiff University) and a PhD in Planning Studies at University College London. His research interests include the social cohesion and neighborly relations of rural migrants and marginalized social groups in Chinese cities. He is the winner of the 2017 Early Career Researcher Award by the Royal Town Planning Institute and his latest project, funded by the British Academy, explores the sense of community of residents who have been relocated due to urban development projects in Shanghai.

Bart Wissink is Associate Professor Urban Studies and Urban Policy at the Department of Public Policy at City University Hong Kong. He holds master degrees in urban planning and public administration (both cum laude) and a PhD in Social and Behavioral Sciences, all at the University of Amsterdam. His research projects explore enclave urbanism in five Asian city regions (Bangkok, Guangzhou, Hong Kong, Mumbai, and Tokyo), with special attention to comparative urban form, urban controversies, and social networks and the neighborhood. Bart Wissink has held visiting appointments in Bangkok, Hong Kong, Mumbai, Tokyo, and Paris. His most recent co-edited book (with Ray Forrest and Sin Yee Koh), *Cities and the super-rich: Real estate, elite practices, and urban political economies*, appeared with Palgrave Macmillan in April 2017.

Fulong Wu is Bartlett Professor of Planning at University College London. His research interests include urban development in China and its social and sustainable challenges. He has recently published *Planning for growth: Urban and regional planning in China* (Routledge, 2015). He is an editor of the *International Journal of Urban and Regional Research*. He was awarded 2013 Outstanding International Impact Prize by UK ESRC. He has previously taught at Cardiff University and the University of Southampton.

Rong Wu is PhD Candidate at the School of Geography and Planning at Sun Yat-sen University. She was previously the visiting doctoral student under the auspices of the Department of Sociology at the University at Albany, State University of New York in 2018. Her research focuses on urban space, and social and environmental psychology, with special attention to place attachment, civic engagement, and the neighborhood. Her most recent publication "Deciphering the meaning and mechanism of migrants' and locals' neighborhood attachment in Chinese cities: Evidence from Guangzhou" appeared in *Cities* in 2018.

Shenghua Xie is currently an associate professor at the College of Public Administration at Central China Normal University, China. He holds a PhD in Social Sciences from the University of Turku (UTU), Finland. He was previously a project researcher at the Department of Social Research at UTU from 2017 to 2018. He has focused his research on urbanization in China with a specific expertise in issues of rural to urban migration, social integration of migrants, and social protection in Chinese cities. His papers have been published in international journals such as *Cities* and *Health & Place*.

Acknowledgments

The chapters in this book were initially presented during the workshop "From Chicago to Shenzhen: 'The City' at One Hundred" which took place at City University in Hong Kong on June 6–7, 2016. This workshop as well as the preparatory work on this book were financially supported by the Research Grant Writing Fund of the College of Liberal Arts and Social Sciences at City University Hong Kong (project title: From Chicago to Shenzhen: 'The City' One Hundred Years On"; project no. 9618000)."

This collection also forms part of the background research undertaken for the project, "Frontier City: Place, Belonging and Community in Contemporary Shenzhen" (Grant No. 11608115), supported by the Hong Kong Research Grants Council.

The editors would also like to thank Ka Sik Tong and Weijia Wang at the Centre for Social Policy and Social Change, Lingnan University, for preparing the final typescript for publication.

Preface

In 2015, one hundred years passed since Robert Park published his seminal article "The city: Suggestions for the investigation of human behavior in the city environment" in *The American Journal of Sociology*. It provided an agenda for the nascent Chicago School of urban sociology, which came to shape urban research for decades to come. One hundred years later, much has changed, both in the urban world itself and in the urban research that reflects on those changes. Globalization and accelerated urbanization have involved a remarkable transformation in cities around the world, and nowhere as dramatically as in China. Chinese cities have undergone a transition marked by unprecedented scales and speeds, across economic, political, and social systems, and with extraordinary variations from ghost cities to urban villages and megacity regions. As a result, it is the Chinese city that is now under the spotlight—as was the American city a century ago.

In urban research much has also changed. The human ecology approach that Park and others initiated has lost most of its allure, and heated discussions on the parochialism of urban theory have dominated journal pages. Meanwhile, new urban forms, new urban economies, and new urban geographies have instigated new literatures and new research agendas. Enormous changes in China have resulted in a rapidly growing scholarship investigating the "great transformation" of cities in China, as well as the urban experience and the relevant policy responses to the challenges that cities face today. The emergence of this and related literatures on cities in a variety of social and cultural settings has resulted in pleas for a more worldly urban studies, encapsulating the experience of cities extending beyond the "West."

Against this background, this book invites specialists on urban China to reflect on the relevance of Park's article on "The city" for today—for cities in China, for urban research, and for questions about studying the social life of the city. After all, China's cities, with their unprecedented growth and massive urban–rural migration, today display characteristics that in certain ways are remarkably similar to America's cities like Chicago one hundred years ago. Again, radical urban changes are supported by technological innovations for transport and communication: the Internet, the high-speed train, and global logistics systems. Again, mass migration brings a diversity of urbanites together in unfamiliar settings; their mobility again uproots established traditional patterns of Chinese social life. But while many themes picked up by Park seem relevant today, at the same time the Chinese city has a radically different urban structure than the mid-century American city. And while the physical transformation of China's cities and the applied research developing its infrastructure and planning its resources are well charted, urban sociology is only starting to catch up with the dynamics and contours of Chinese urbanism. The aim of the book is therefore to take Park's essay as a point of departure to offer a critical reflection on both the research on urban China and the issues that Chinese cities face.

Coming from a diversity of specializations, the contributors engage with Park in different ways. The first half of the book considers Park more explicitly, discussing how Park's questions can be transplanted, and whether they should be. Chapters 1 and 2 offer reflections on Park in his time, providing some historical context for his work and reminding us of much earlier connections between his urban sociology and Chinese scholars. These explicit engagements reflect also on the nature of urban research and theory, particularly for urban China as illustrated in Chapters 3 and 4. Throughout, the questions of comparativism and commensurability are raised both theoretically and empirically by Chapters 5 and 6, and also in Chapter 1.

The second half of the book presents more distinct perspectives that reflect the varied and subjective directions that research on cities in China is now beginning to take. These chapters focus more on empirical investigation in order to reflect back on cities in China. They offer insights into urgent issues around new forms of urban inequality, and new approaches to studying the city. Chapter 7 scales back the lens to the neighborhood while Chapter 8 takes a cultural studies approach to the Beijing ring roads. Chapter 9 offers a rich empirical study of subjective well-being while Chapter 10 takes a qualitative approach to studying the "psychophysical" realm of rural migrant workers. Chapter 11 explores the way middle-classness is constituted and experienced in the Chinese city amid a broader process of social restratification. The final chapter concludes with thoughts on Chinese exceptionalism, arguing that instead of seeking out new dominant models or urbanisms, ethnographic approaches may offer more valuable and novel theoretical insights.

The book thus aims to offer readers a timely respite from the eruption of urban China research, to reflect on what the city in China contributes to urban studies more generally. Though Park was a starting point and inspiration for this volume, the contributors represent a range of perspectives that would disrupt any notion of a monolithic "Chinese School" that follows in the footsteps of Chicago. Indeed, the very idea of "following" in a developmentalist trajectory is roundly rejected throughout this volume. Yet many voices simultaneously reiterate that the experiences of displacement, segregation, or social class are not isolated.

This book is intended for a broad audience of urban studies scholars from geography and sociology, as well as policy makers and planners. These contributions will hopefully find an audience beyond China area specialists, as they provide a valuable addition to scholarship on urban theory, and the endeavor of theorization. For a constantly evolving field, *The city in China* serves as a reflection on how to engage with a giant of urban studies without an agenda of rehabilitation or rejection.

This book emerged from a workshop organized by the Urban Research Group at the City University of Hong Kong in 2016 with the theme, "'The City' One Hundred Years On." Contributors were asked to submit papers reflecting on the relevance of Robert Park for their research. Taking place over two days, the workshop also offered substantive discussion about issues around conducting research in urban China, and theory and discipline more generally, as well as issues of commensurability, methodology, and the institutional and historical settings of doing urban studies in the US and China. This book comprises revised papers from this workshop.

Robert Park in China

From the Chicago School to
Urban China Studies

Xuefei Ren

The Chicago School of urban sociology has been proclaimed dead many times in the last hundred years. The School, which proposed to study cities as an ecological unit through formal urban analysis, reached its zenith by the early 1930s (Park, 1915; Wirth, 1931). Then it gradually lost its influence, especially after Robert Park retired from the University of Chicago in 1933. In the second half of the twentieth century, the Chicago School was challenged and succeeded by other approaches to study urban life, such as the Marxist urban sociology spearheaded by Manuel Castells in the 1960s (Castells, 1977), the social network perspective to study urban subculture by Claude Fischer in the 1980s (Fischer, 1982), and the Los Angeles School declared by Michael Dear in the late 1990s, who elevated Los Angeles over Chicago as prototypical city of the 21st century (Dear, 2002). Considering the various criticisms launched throughout the 20th century, is there anything left to learn from the Chicago School?

This chapter examines past legacies and possible future contributions of the Chicago School to urban China studies. The Chicago School was not only influential in the US, but also helped to build the foundation of sociology in China in the early 20th century. Drawing on archival materials such as personal correspondence among Robert Park, Fei Xiaotong, and others, this chapter will first examine the relatively little known connections between Robert Park and China in the 1930s. Park was enthusiastic to expand urban research he had done in Chicago to Chinese cities. Park's comparative gesture can be borrowed in the field of urban China studies today, which has seen a tendency of exceptionalism, as scholars argue that Chinese cities are unique, and therefore, incomparable with cities in other countries. Drawing on examples of redevelopment in Guangzhou, Mumbai, Rio de Janeiro, and Chicago, the second half of the chapter demonstrates that Chinese cities are not as unique as specialists tend to argue. It suggests reviving Park's comparative spirit, because much can be learned by studying urbanization in China from a global and comparative perspective.

Robert Park in Beijing: Early connections

Robert Park was one of the first Western academics who helped to establish sociology as a discipline in China. Park visited China several times to participate in conferences in the 1920s. On retirement from the University of Chicago in 1933, he accepted an invitation to teach a semester at Yenching University in Beijing—today's Peking University. As with his teaching in Chicago, he told his Chinese students to use the city of Beiping (the former name for Beijing, commonly used up to 1949) as a social laboratory to understand the changing social relations in the turbulent years of 1930s' China. His ethnographic methods strongly influenced his students. Some wanted to do an ecological study of Beiping in the style of studies done in Chicago at the time, while others, such as Fei Xiaotong (费孝通)—one of the leading Chinese sociologists in the 20th century, took Park's message to heart and conducted extensive fieldwork in small towns and villages across China.

On November 15, 1943, Fei Xiaotong was sitting in Park's office on the fifth floor of the Social Science Building on the University of the Chicago campus, writing a letter to Park. Visiting the United States for the first time, Fei was attending the university on a scholarship from the US State Department through a program to promote cultural exchange with China. World War II was underway, and Yenching University, where Fei previously had studied and worked, had fallen under Japanese occupation. Fei's career to this point had been circuitous: he had spent five years in London studying under anthropologist Bronislaw K. Malinowski; then was recommended by his teacher Wu Wen-Tsao (吴文藻)—the head of the Department of Sociology at Yenching University at the time, to join the Yenching-Yunnan sociological station at National Yunnan University in southwest China, where he conducted a series of rural surveys; and then was sent to Chicago for a year to study new developments in sociology and social anthropology, and also to seek opportunities for collaborative projects with US-based scholars. In his letter to Park (Figure 1.1), Fei deeply acknowledged Park's continuing influence on his work and could not hide his excitement to visit the birthplace of the Chicago School of urban sociology. He wrote:

> This is from a student of yours when you were teaching in Yenching, China. At that time I was a small college boy and I remembered nothing outstanding that could attract your attention. But I was not the last one that had been very much inspired ... Today I am working in your office in Chicago. I am overpowered by a feeling of human fate. It is something like a dream, but the dream is in someway true ... A man coming from a folk society will certainly bewitched by the history behind the walls. I feel all the time I am working under your spirit. I hope your inspiration will be transferred into the work I am now engaging in.[1]

China was somewhat familiar territory for Park. Before he arrived in Beijing to teach in 1933, Park already had traveled to China several times for conferences and begun to show great interest in the country (Raushenbush, 1979). Park was actively corresponding with scholars based in China, advising them on how to study the changes in the traditional way of life. In a letter to Bernhard Hörmann, a German scholar of Chinese folk religions who was teaching at Lingnan University[2] in Guangzhou, Park stressed the need to carry out long periods of ethnographic fieldwork, to focus on social processes, and to map the location of social facts—all touchstone ideas of the Chicago School of Sociology (Abbott, 2002). Writing to Hörmann, in 1931, Park noted:

> I advise you to spend as much time as you can—say two or better, three years—in China getting the language and exploring the field in which you expect to write your thesis ... The theme you suggested—Chinese religion—and the manner of approach to the problem as outlined are both admirable ... A survey as you have suggested of the shrines of a definite locality is, in my opinion, the best possible way to begin ... It would be interesting to learn what were the circumstances under which they had their origin and to discover if you can what actual function they now perform in the life of the community.[3]

Figure 1.1: Letter from Fei Xiaotong to Robert Park, 1943, University of Chicago Special Collection

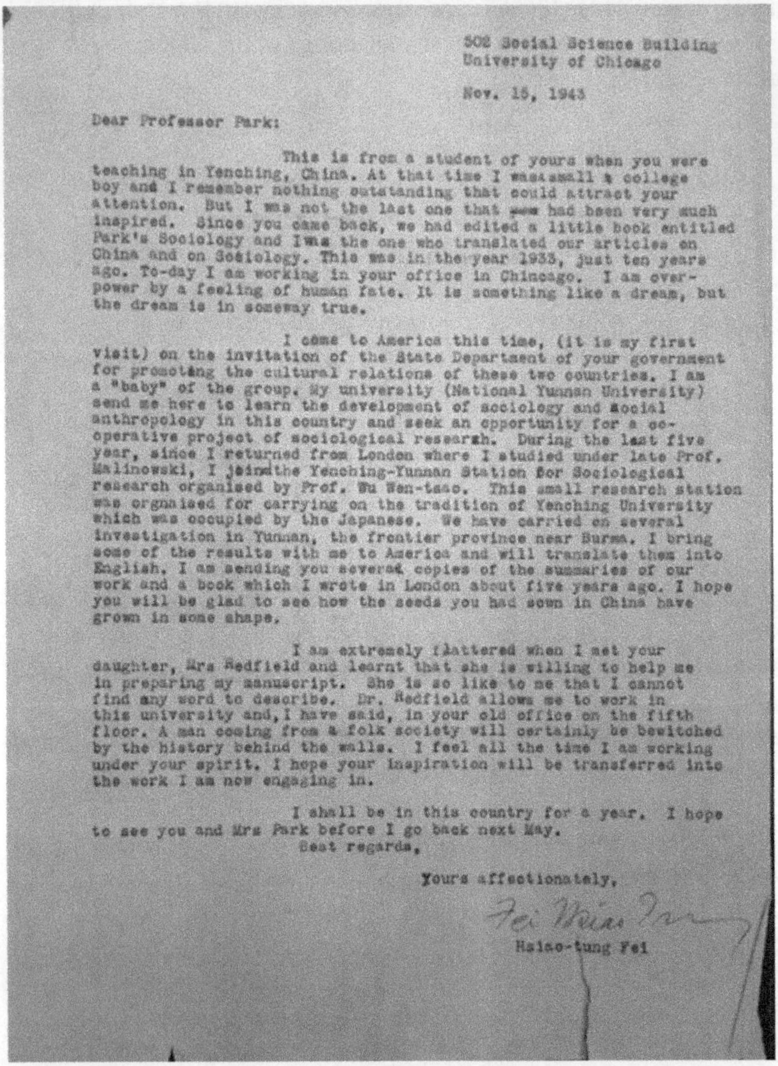

Source: Letter from Fei Xiaotong to Robert Park, November 15, 1943, the University of Chicago Special Collection, Robert Park papers, Box 13, Folder 15)

Park taught his students how to apply fieldwork methods to study urban communities, and this was an important first step to introduce sociology, a Western discipline, to study local Chinese society. At Yenching University, Park offered two classes—Collective Behavior and Sociological Research Methods, and the latter was especially popular among the Chinese students. Recounting Park's lectures, Fei Xiaotong noted that Park's methods class was the most exciting course for the graduating seniors and he still remembered how Park opened his first lecture, by telling students, "I am not here to teach you how to read books, but to teach you how to write books" (Fei, 2002). As Park had done with his students in Chicago, he encouraged his Chinese students to leave the classroom, go out to streets, and use the city as a laboratory to study social change. Park took students to pockets of Beiping unfamiliar to the elite students at Yenching University, including slums and the red light district of the Heaven Bridge area. Park told students that to understand Chinese society and social relations, the red light district was an excellent entry point, as it had everything in it (Fei, 2002). Later Fei Xiaotong recalled that he was overwhelmed by the visit Park led to the red light district. He was made to realize that the social relations that one would only find in novels were more vividly displayed in real life, and in a more complex way. It was not enough to just read *Dream of the red chamber* (Sun, 2005).[4]

Park also encouraged his Chinese students to conduct ecological studies of Chinese cities. In 1933 Fei Xiaotong and fellow classmates complied a book in Chinese entitled *Robert E. Park and his sociology* (Figure 1.2), which included Park's original essays and also chapters written by students who took Park's class (Park, 1933). In his introductory essay, Wu Wen-Tsao, the head of the Department of Sociology, identified Park's contribution in four dimensions: the pedagogical—the fact that Park trained many students who later became prominent scholars on their own rights; major sociological concepts devised to explain social events such as immigrant integration—for example, competition, conflicts, adaptation, and assimilation; his ethnographic fieldwork methods; and, lastly, his human ecology approach to study the city by emphasizing the location, population movements, and division of labor. One of Park's students, Chao Ching-Hein (赵承信), contributed a chapter on "Park and Human Ecology" (派克与人文区位学), in which he discussed the role Park played in developing the field of human ecology and also several ecological concepts by the Chicago School, such as position, mobility, natural area, and functional community.

After leaving China, Park continued in the following years to help recruit Chinese students to come to study in the United States. In a letter to J. Leighton Stuart, president of Yenching University at the time, Park expressed interest in setting up a program for Chinese students in Chicago, and suggested faculty members at US universities "getting acquainted with students who are planning to come to America some years before they actually arrive," so that the students can conduct fieldwork research in China and be well prepared for their dissertation research.[5] He believed that fieldwork-based sociological research would be helpful for young

Figure 1.2: The cover of an edited volume dedicated to Robert Park, compiled in 1933

Source: Book cover of Park, Robert E. (1933). 《派克社会学论文集》北平：北平燕京大学社会学会)

Chinese students, as they can "throw light on the sources and origins of their present problems," and Chinese students may "welcome any sort of information that may guide them in their efforts of reconstruction."[6] Park continued to read about China and wished he could have had more time to return to China to conduct comparative research. But he did not make it back to Beijing. Five months before he died in 1944, Park wrote a letter to his granddaughter who was at the time preparing to go to China,

> I think I would go to Beiping, if the Japanese would let me, and get acquainted with the city. Beiping is one of the most marvelous cities in the world. No one has ever given anything like an adequate account of it. There are three or four walled cities in one: there is the Chinese city, the Manchu city, there is the Forbidden City, and there is the more or less Europeanized city. Three of them have their own walls, one inside the other. Chinese walls themselves would make

an interesting topic. Beiping underworld, of which I gained some acquaintance while I was there, is a wonderful place. I got my acquaintance with it partly by visiting the Thieves' Market and partly by reading an account that the professional thief gave of his adventures in seeking to escape the police, but I can't begin to tell you the things I think are interesting about that city … the whole history of China is reflected in the geography of the life and customs of the people in Beiping but I think the way to study would be to take account of the human geography of the city first.[7]

Through his teaching and exchange with Chinese scholars, Park introduced sociology to China and sowed the seeds of sociological research there. He believed that sociological methods could be a great tool for students to understand social change and equip them in their effort to build a new Chinese society. Park also left his mark on Fei Xiaotong, the leading sociologist in China in the 20th century. In a career that spanned six decades from the 1930s to the 1990s, Fei absorbed the lessons of Park's teaching and treated small towns and villages across China as "social laboratories," and conducted systematic fieldwork research in dozens of small towns. This bottom-up, firsthand fieldwork later led to his well-known policy suggestion on "developing small towns (小城镇战略)," which was adopted by the central government as the official urbanization strategy in the 1980s (Fei, 1992).[8]

Learning from the Chicago School

Scholars are conditioned by the time and place in which they live. Revisiting the Chicago School today, we quickly notice its limitations. The Chicago School certainly missed a lot of things. Its central claim— that urbanism should be interpreted as personal life experience—is simply too narrow to capture the complexity of the urban society today. It did not pay attention to many topics salient for understanding urban processes, such as the role of governments, property speculation, the housing market, and transformations in the built environment. The individual-centered argument was rightfully challenged in the 1960s by Marxist urban sociologists, who proposed to study other processes central to understanding how cities work, such as collective consumption, class struggles, and political economy. Also, although called "urban ecology," the Chicago School ignored the real ecology—the interactions between the city and nature.

The Chicago School was also wrong about a lot of other things. Although deeply concerned with race relations, it viewed black migration just like other European migration, and did not delve into racial politics that deeply divided most American cities (Molotch, 2002). In Burgess's concentric model, African-American neighborhoods were labeled the "black belt," alongside other ethnic neighborhoods such as Chinatown, Little Italy, and the German Ghetto. Burgess's concentric model was developed solely on the basis of the 1920s Chicago, and the model did not fit the growth patterns of other cities at the time. This practice of projecting local processes onto the general and universal came under wide criticism in the 1930s. Even his Chinese colleagues questioned how much the insights from studying one single city could be generalized to other cities. For example, Wu Wen-Tsao summarized the questionable assumption of the Chicago School: it believes that if we can understand one city very well, then we can understand all other cities because cities have similar settlement patterns, life histories, and structures (Park, 1933: 9, author's translation).

If the Chicago School's ecological approach is problematic and outdated, is there anything left to learn from it? By revisiting the Chicago School's writings, I argue that perhaps it is not the research questions or methods that we should learn from the Chicago School, but rather its reflective stance toward systematically engaging with urban social inquiry. Specifically, two points merit consideration for urban China scholars—the effort to formulate a research agenda, and a comparative outlook.

In *The city*, the Chicago School scholars did not provide answers and prescribe theories, but instead they identified research questions central for understanding urban life at the turn of the century (Park et al., 1925). Park began by suggesting research on neighborhoods—the smallest units for social and political organization and population movement (Park et al., 1925). As a former journalist, he recommended studying the role of media in influencing human behavior. He also proposed studying social organization through community institutions such as family, church, and school, as well as social disorganization such as crime and prostitution. He made a list of urban occupations—the showgirl, the policeman, the peddler, the strikebreaker, the bartender—as he saw all these as "characteristic products of conditions of the city life" (Park, 1915: 586). These topics guided research by faculty and students at the University of Chicago from the 1920s to the 1940s, and led to the publication of many ethnographic studies of the neighborhood life in the city.

Just like Park and colleagues' *The city* that defined the research program for the Chicago School, we need to take stock and formulate a research agenda to guide urban China studies. At the turn of the 21st century, China has become an epicenter of the world's urbanization, propelled by market reform and an unprecedented scale of internal migration. Chinese cities today offer fertile ground to study urban structures and processes and, not surprisingly, the field of urban China studies has produced an impressive volume of scholarship since the 1990s. Scholars trained in various social science disciplines investigate the multifaceted transformation of Chinese cities—from the changing built environment, land development, and housing market, to neighborhood associations, informal settlements, poverty, and the role of the local state. After three decades of tremendous scholarly output, however, we might want to pause and ask ourselves: what is the object of our study? What research questions have been thoroughly examined? What questions are barely studied? Do we need to broaden our methodological choices? What are the main theoretical frameworks guiding our research? Where did they come from? What theoretical innovations have we made and can we make? A manifesto of this sort seems to be necessary, to avoid mindlessly chasing social problems and the newest developments.

Although Robert Park did not live to carry out any comparative research, we can learn from his comparative outlook by incorporating comparison in our research and teaching. Comparative studies are rare in urban China studies, as most scholars in the field seem to be only interested in China. This tendency of "introversion" has gotten even stronger in recent years, with the unspoken assumption that Chinese cities are unique, exceptional, and therefore, incomparable. Today, urban China scholars mostly write for each other and rarely shift their lens to compare and contrast Chinese cities with cities in other countries.

This inward-looking character of urban China scholarship can be explained by several factors. First of all, comparative research is demanding, even daunting, as one needs to spend years to acquire the language skills and knowledge of another country. Scholars based in China are often constrained by limited funding resources at their universities, which tend not to support international research outside of China. Moreover, urban China scholars are often lured by "low-hanging fruit," interesting developments wrought by China's fast urbanization—Special Economic Zones in the 1980s and 1990s, creative industries in the early 2000s, and then the post-2008 government-stimulus spending, local government debt, high-speed rail construction, and the eco-city boom. These developments have offered exciting materials for research, but empirical studies chasing the newest developments have rarely led to conceptualization and theorizing. Many see little pay-off to engage in comparative work that seeks to explain similarities and differences between A and B, as the stories of A and B are self-sufficient by themselves as narratives.

The unspoken assumption of exceptionalism and disregard of a comparative perspective is unfortunate. The Chicago vs. Los Angeles School debate can offer a valuable lesson in this regard. In the early 2000s, Michael Dear, an urban geographer based in southern California, launched the Los Angeles School of urban studies, by declaring that the Chicago School was dead and that Los Angeles was the prototypical city of the 21st century. Grounded in postmodern and Marxist political economy traditions, the LA School heralded Los Angeles as the city of the future, in which the periphery organizes the center, whereas Chicago represented the city of the past, in which the center organized the periphery (Dear, 2002). The LA School, however, did not go very far, as many of the empirical developments that were claimed to be unique to LA could be widely observed in other metropolitan regions in the US—such as suburban sprawl, edge cities, and gated communities. If the Chicago School took the local as universal, then the LA School veered in the opposite direction, treating certain general urban processes as locally specific. Some saw the inception of a Los Angeles School as another instance of academic rivalry and parochial exceptionalism (Molotch, 2002).

Similarly, extolling Chinese cities as new, exciting, and special—as did the Los Angeles School when touting its own city—will not take us very far. What we need instead are comparative perspectives to situate Chinese cities in a world of other cities (Ren, 2018a). A comparative approach can help us move beyond the parochial exceptionalist claim, and better understand the general patterns and local particularities of urban restructuring.

A brave new world: Comparing Guangzhou, Mumbai, Rio de Janeiro, and Chicago

Chinese cities are not as unique as specialists often argue, and much can be learned by comparing urban development in China to that in other cities in both the global South and North. To illustrate this point, this section draws on examples of my ongoing work on redevelopment in Guangzhou, Mumbai, Rio de Janeiro, and Chicago.

In the past decade, much ink has been spent on documenting the development of urban villages in China (Wang et al., 2009; Chung, 2010; Bandurski, 2016). Cities in the Pearl River Delta, such as Guangzhou and Shenzhen, are home to hundreds of urban villages that provide affordable housing to millions of migrant workers (Figure 1.3). As land prices go up, urban villages in the central locations are faced with increasing pressure to be removed. The Guangzhou city government, for example, has proposed redeveloping its 138 urban villages by inviting the participation of private developers. Redevelopment stands to benefit the usual stakeholders—the local government, private developers, and village landlords, whereas the majority of migrant tenants have little say in any decision making, regardless of how long they have lived and how much they have invested in their urban village. Urban villages often are viewed as a unique example of Chinese informal settlements, and scholars have documented in great detail how they came into being (Wu et al., 2013; Al, 2014; De Meulder et al., 2014).

Urban villages might be a unique product of China's dual-track land ownership structure, but the larger story of how they came into being and are targeted for removal is not unique. The sprouting of urban villages reflects the wide gap between supply and demand for affordable housing for the urban poor, a problem confronting cities throughout the developing world. In Mumbai, a city that suffers from severe housing shortages, between 50% and 60% of the city population lives in slums (Figure 1.4). As in Guangzhou, the surge in land prices has intensified the pressure to redevelop some of the best-located slums, and since the 1990s the state government of Maharashtra has pushed slum redevelopment through a model of privatization. Similar to Guangzhou, private developers are invited to partake in redevelopment—called "rehabilitation" in Mumbai—

Figure 1.3: Half-demolished Xiancun, an urban village in Guangzhou

Source: Photo by the author

and in return, are offered land to build market-rate housing. Although specific terms differ, the large picture is the same: the poor must be removed to make land available for those who can afford to pay more.

Figure 1.4: The "airport slum" in Mumbai, where residents live in precarious proximity to airport runways

Source: Photo by the author

The practice of "purging the poorest" (Vale, 2013) has been replayed in many other cities. In Rio de Janeiro, one quarter of its population lives in favelas (Figure 1.5), some of which occupied key locations for purposes of the 2016 Olympics. Certain favelas, such as those standing along the routes of BRT (Bus Rapid Transit) and Olympic venue sites, had to be removed to make way for infrastructural projects commissioned for the 2016 Games. In spite of the promise made by City Hall to upgrade and provide services to all of the city's favelas by 2020—as the social legacy of the Rio Olympics—demolitions and evictions took place in Vila Autodromo, Providencia, and some other favelas which have had the "good fortune" to be located on the chosen sites of Olympic infrastructures.

Property speculation and removal of the poor are not confined only to informal settlements in the global South; the global North needs to look no farther than the prosperous city of Chicago to see a textbook example of the poor being evicted from land that has become too valuable. Cabrini-Green, the city's best-known public-housing project occupying 70 acres of prime real estate near downtown Chicago, has been

Figure 1.5: Complexo do Alameo, a large cluster of favelas in Rio de Janeiro

Source: Photo by the author

gradually dismantled since the 1990s. On my morning commute in that neighborhood in 2016, I would count the number of cranes at nearby construction sites, erecting new buildings from hotels to high-rise condos. At one entrance to the housing project is a service shop for the luxury car brands Lamborghini and Perillo. Across from another entrance is a gorgeously restored loft building that flanks the Chicago River and houses the city's high-earning professionals. The majority of Cabrini-Green's former tenants—predominantly African Americans—have been dispersed and their buildings torn down; today only a few row houses still stand within the fenced-up compound. Built up on the site is "mixed-income" housing that promised to be accessible to former public-housing tenants, but in reality, strict selection criteria exclude most former public-housing tenants from returning.

The story of speculation and redevelopment runs through the redevelopment of urban villages, slums, favelas, and public-housing projects. The driving forces behind these processes are often similar, as are the winners and losers. For scholars writing about urban villages in China, it is not enough to focus only on local specific processes, but one should also be able to position urban villages in a comparative perspective and ask bigger questions. For example, in addition to documenting the growth dynamics of urban villages—the previous literature has done a great job on this—we should ask how urban poverty can be understood in relation to larger political and socioeconomic parameters, and how China compares with other countries in this regard (Ren, 2018b). By juxtaposing one city with another, we can get a better sense of both the locally specific processes and the common driving forces that produce precarious housing conditions for the poor.

Conclusion

After three decades of prolific research output, urban China studies is facing a crossroads, and critical reflection is needed on the field's next course of direction. This chapter has examined the Chicago School's influence on Chinese sociology, via Robert Park's teaching and his exchange with students in the 1930s in Beijing. If the Chicago School is to be reimported to China today, what is needed no longer are its ecological concepts, formal analysis of city growth, and developmentalist thinking. Instead, in the spirit that Park set out to delineate research questions in *The city*, we need to think ahead and identify the most salient questions and appropriate methods with which to study the Chinese city. Moreover, we can learn from Park's comparative spirit to overcome inward-looking tendencies. As the case of informal settlements and public-housing projects illustrates, the plight of the poor in the face of redevelopment is not unique to any single city. We need to move beyond parochial exceptionalism, open up the field of urban China studies, and widen our gaze to engage in comparisons. Only by positioning the Chinese city in a comparative perspective can we discover the underlying forces beneath urban restructuring in China and elsewhere under 21st-century capitalism.

Notes

[1] Letter from Fei to Park, November 15, 1943, the University of Chicago special collection, Robert Park Papers, Box 13, Folder 15.

[2] Lingnan University was a private college set up by American missionaries in 1888, and it was incorporated into today's Sun Yat-Sen University in 1953.

[3] Letter from Park to Bernhard Hörmann, November 9, 1931, Robert Park papers, Box 13, Folder 16.

[4] Also called *Story of the stone*, it is one of the four classical Chinese novels depicting life and romance in a wealthy family in the Qing dynasty in the 18th century.

[5] Letter from Park to J. Leighton Stuart, April 4, 1934, Robert Park papers, Box 15, Folder 3.

6   Letter from Park to Donald Slessinger, May 23, 1935, Robert Park papers, Box 14, Folder 6.

7   Letter Park to Lisa Peattie, October 18, 1943, Robert Park papers, Box 14, Folder 5.

8   This was, however, quickly reversed in the 1990s. Starting with the approval of Pudong new district in Shanghai in 1992, the central government swiftly changed the course to devote major investment in large cities instead of small towns.

References

Abbott, A. (2002) "Los Angeles and the Chicago School: A comment on Michael Dear," *City & Community*, 1(1): 33–8.

Al, S. (ed.) (2014) *Villages in the city: A guide to South China's informal settlements*, Hong Kong: Hong Kong University Press.

Bandurski, D. (2016) *Dragons in diamond village and other tales from the back alleys of urbanizing China*, Melbourne: Penguin Books Australia.

Castells, M. (1977) *The urban question: A Marxist approach*, Cambridge, MA: MIT Press.

Chung, H. (2010) "Building an image of villages-in-the-city: A clarification of China's distinct urban spaces," *International Journal of Urban and Regional Research*, 34(2): 421–37.

De Meulder, B., Lin, Y., and Shannon, K. (eds.) (2014) *Village in the city*, Zurich: Park Books.

Dear, M. (2002) "Los Angeles and the Chicago School: Invitation to a debate," *City & Community*, 1(1): 5–32.

Fei, X. (1992) 行行重行行:乡镇发展论述, Yinchuan: Ningxia People's Press.

Fei, X. (2002) 师承，补课，治学, Beijing: Sanlian.

Fischer, C. (1982) *To dwell among friends: Personal networks in town and city*, Chicago: University of Chicago Press.

Molotch, H. (2002) "School's out: A response to Michael Dear," *City & Community*, 1(1): 39–43.

Park, R. E. (1915) "The city: Suggestions for the investigation of human behavior in the city environment," *American Journal of Sociology*, 20(5): 577–612.

Park, R. E. (1933) 派克社会学论文集, Beiping: Yenching University Sociological Association.

Park, R. E., Burgess, E., and McKenzie, R. (1925) *The city*, Chicago: University of Chicago Press.

Raushenbush, W. (1979) *Robert E. Park: Biography of a sociologist*, Durham, NC: Duke University Press.

Ren, X. (2018a) "From Chicago to China and India: Studying the city in the twenty-first century," *Annual Review of Sociology*, 44: 497–513.

Ren, X. (2018b) "Governing the informal: Housing policies over informal settlements in China, India, and Brazil," *Housing Policy Debate*, 28(1): 79–93.

Sun, P. (2005) "从派克到费孝通－谈费孝通忆派克对中国社会学, 人类学的贡献," *Open Times*, no. 4. Available at: http://www.opentimes.cn/Abstract/788.html.

Vale, L. (2013) *Purging the poorest: Public housing and the design politics of twice-cleared communities*, Chicago: University of Chicago Press.

Wang, Y. P., Wang, Y., and Wu, J. (2009) "Urbanization and informal development in China: Urban villages in Shenzhen," *International Journal of Urban and Regional Research*, 33(4): 957–73.

Wirth, L. (1931) "Urbanism as a way of life," *American Journal of Sociology*, 44(1): 1–24.

Wu, F., Zhang, F., and Webster, C. (2013) "Informality and the development and demolition of in the Chinese peri-urban area," *Urban Studies*, 50(10): 1919–34.

2

"Bewitched by the History Behind the Walls"

Robert Park and the Arc of Urban Sociology from Chicago to China

Bettina Gransow

Introduction

The pace and extent of growth in Chinese cities since roughly the turn of the millennium have attracted the interest of scholars across a wide range of fields and disciplines. Archaeologists, historians, geographers, urban planners, sociologists, anthropologists, economists, political scientists, and specialists in cultural studies, literature, and film have produced many publications in response to this development.[1]

This chapter traces the links between the Chicago School of urban sociology founded by Robert Park and urban sociology in China, and examines their historical and disciplinary connections. It analyses four dimensions thereof: (1) personal relations between Robert Park and the Chinese students and colleagues who enabled his visit to China; (2) institutional embeddedness of the sociology departments at both the University of Chicago and Yanjing University within the funding structures and strategies of the Rockefeller Foundation in the 1920s and 1930s; (3) empirical fieldwork and comparative community studies in the form of Fei Xiaotong's research on small towns in China (early

1980s) and his conceptualization of rural urbanization, which built on his earlier classic rural community study and has influenced official Chinese urbanization strategies to the present day; and (4) theorization of China's "villages-in-the-city" (城中村) in light of previous debates inspired by the Chicago School on "cities within cities" (Park, 1915), the "slum" and "urban villages." I will use these four perspectives to follow the trajectory of urban sociology from Chicago to China, and to address questions of legacy, creative impetus, and possible limitations arising from Park's program vis-à-vis urban sociology in China today.

Park's research program in "The city"

When Robert Park arrived at the University of Chicago in 1914, the sociology pursued there hardly differed from self-reflective social work. Many of his colleagues came from families involved in Christian welfare work, or had otherwise come to sociology via social work. Their social analyses had a moral undertone. Park, by contrast, sought to develop sociology as a discipline rooted in neutral conceptual-theoretical understanding and empirical study of social realities (Christmann, 2007: 105). At this time he was already formulating his powerful research program *in nuce* in an article entitled "The city" (Park, 1915).[2] It is divided into four sections.[3]

In the first section ("The city plan and local organization") Park disagrees with the received idea that a large city is an artificial product of urban planning. He is far more interested in the "natural areas" that arise in unplanned ways as processes of human nature and that subvert the architectonic "block" and the administrative "district." The "natural area" stands for a cultural space with traditions, sentiments, and its own story, topographically localized and spatially defined to include especially "cities within cities," "colonies," and "segregated areas."

The second section ("Industrial organization and the moral order") looks at the potential offered to individuals as a space to live ("city air makes men free"). People can develop their special talents in cities. Park sees new vocations as a key object of research on cities (and compiles a list of interesting vocational types). The division of labor increases the interdependence among individuals—which on the one hand produces new forms of social solidarity based on shared interests (trade and labor unions, and so on), yet also requires instruments to restore equilibrium (markets, stock exchanges, boards of trade, economic reports). Critical psychological situations can arise when societies show a high degree of mobility, a position that Park backs up with reference to his dissertation

(*Masse und Publikum*—in German, 1904). He is interested in forms of collective behavior and social control.

The third section ("Secondary relations and social control") is also based on a dualistic system of space and behavior. Park calls for studying traditional institutions (family, school, church) and how they change under the influence of cities. Given the heterogeneity in cities, he considers consensus-building mechanisms especially important for arriving at a shared universe of discourse, via modern means of communication (newspapers, press, public opinion, density of communication among individuals).

The fourth section ("Temperament and the urban environment") is especially of interest because Park resolves the tension within the Chicago School between group segregation and individual mobility. Segregation (the city as a mosaic of small worlds) seems to provide precisely the condition for individual mobility (and therefore freedom). More so here than in the other sections, he addresses the specific qualities of cities in the sense of Georg Simmel, namely freedom for individuals and the opportunities thereby offered to eccentric or exceptional types.

"The City" therefore addresses basic questions on the interrelationships between urban space and behavioral patterns. As such, this "inaugural lecture" by Robert Park back in 1915 already contains the outline of what would subsequently form the cognitive identity of Chicago's urban sociology (Lindner, 1990: 109).

Emergence of urban sociology in Republican China

The 1920s saw the emergence of a new focus on Chinese cities, as the construction of roads in and among towns gave rise to the features of modern urban centers. Against this background, urban sociology emerged as a subfield of sociology, which was becoming established at both Chinese and Christian universities in the country at the time. While the Chinese institutions tended to adopt a more theoretical approach modelled on that in Japan, the Christian colleges focused more on empirical social research and social work.

Early urban sociological studies in Shanghai and Beijing grew out of the social reform activities of the YMCA, with the involvement of Chinese students. An early example of the connection between Christian social work and sociological studies dates to the 1910s. In the Yangshupu workers' quarter of Shanghai, the American Baptist missionary Daniel Harrison Kulp II from Brown University founded a community center in 1917 called the "Shanghai East Commune" (沪东公社) (Yang, 1987: 30–1), which was intended to fulfill three functions: (1) a social laboratory for students at Shanghai Baptist College; (2) a service center for workers' families in the quarter; and (3) a model of an industrial residential quarter (Gransow, 1992: 39).

The most well-known example of the link between urban social work and the launch of empirical social research in China is associated with John Stewart Burgess (1883–1949). A missionary sociologist, Burgess was instrumental in founding the (then rather small) department of sociology at Yanjing University in Beijing, and became its first dean in 1922. Together with Princeton-in-Peking,[4] he sought to convey the social gospel to Chinese students interested in social studies as a combination of Christianity and national renewal (Chiang, 2001: 36). S. D. Gamble and Burgess and published *Peking: A social survey* in 1921. Performed in close connection with the community program in the Dengshikou district of Beijing, the survey was intended to lay the foundations for a model program in social work, initially at the community level but later for the entire city (Gamble and Burgess, 1921: 26; Gransow, 2003: 503). This plan reflected the aims and methods of the social survey movement in the US and Britain at the time.

Sociology at Yanjing University and early contacts with the Chicago School

By the end of the 1920s, sociology was not only established at Chinese institutions but was also in the hands of the first generation of Chinese sociologists, who held leading positions at academic and non-academic facilities. Xu Shilian (Leonard Hsu), who had studied in Iowa, became the first Chinese professor at Yanjing University's department of sociology and social services in the mid-1920s. In Xu's eyes, sociology in China at the time had the following weaknesses:

• it was viewed as part of philosophy or psychology;
• it was confused with socialism and its practitioners were seen as social revolutionaries;
• the majority of its instructors made uncritical use of foreign teaching materials;
• its courses did not include systematic field research; and
• its coursework was unrelated to practice and could not be applied to the field of social services (Xu, 1925: 1–2).

From a political perspective, these views excluded Marxist approaches to sociology and instead were compatible with the policies of the Guomindang.[5] As for training, the biggest problem that Xu saw was the use of foreign textbooks. He called for the standard curriculum to include field studies, as well as for social service internships in partnership with welfare organizations (Xu, 1925: 3).

Xu Shilian became the chairman of the department in 1929, and visited European and American universities on a Rockefeller Foundation fellowship in 1931, including two trips to the University of Chicago. There he met university administrators and social scientists, including Robert E. Park. Xu intended to launch a joint project backed by the president of Yanjing University, Leighton Stuart, and discussed the idea of deepening institutional ties between the two departments and strengthening comparative research on social change in China and the US (Chiang, 2001: 52; Yan, 2004: 48), thus paving the way for Park's visit to China in the fall of 1932.

One of Park's students in Chicago was Wu Jingchao, who came to his sociology department as a graduate student in 1923. After studying with figures like E. W. Burgess and Robert Redfield, he wrote a master's thesis in 1926 on "Chinese immigration in the Pacific area" that examined mixed marriages in the Chinese diaspora. Building on this, he completed a PhD program in 1928 with a dissertation on "Chinatowns: A study of symbiosis and assimilation" (Wu, 1928). Wu Jingchao, whom many people later considered to be the founder of Chinese urban sociology, returned to China in 1928 and shortly thereafter published an introduction to the principles and methods of urban sociology (Wu, 1929).[6] Wu Jingchao used Chinese materials and emphasized the importance of field research (Sun, 1940: 166) – although he himself pursued no further field research beyond that for his dissertation. He introduced the Chicago School in China, but did not himself make use of Park's methods.[7] When Wu Jingchao returned to China from the US, he applied for a professorship at Yanjing University's sociology department, albeit without success (Yan, 2004: 124).[8]

In 1928, the sociology department at Yanjing University received funding from the Laura Spelman Rockefeller Memorial Fund (hereafter "Memorial"). This enabled it to have three professorships: for agrarian sociology (held by Yang Kaidao), for social work (held by Zhang Hongjun), and a third sought by two highly qualified applicants, namely Wu Jingchao as described above and Wu Wenzao who had studied sociology at Columbia University and concentrated on social theory and philosophy. According to Chiang Yung-chen, Wu Jingchao's lack of a Christian background could have led John Stewart Burgess to give the position to

Wu Wenzao, whom he had met while the latter was a doctoral student at Columbia University (Chiang, 2001: 55).

Wu Wenzao (1901–85) became dean of the sociology department at Yanjing University in the mid-1930s, replacing Xu Shilian, who had given the department a social work orientation. For reasons less political than methodological, Wu Wenzao and the faculty of the social anthropology wing of the sociology department at Yanjing University dissociated themselves explicitly from the social survey approach. They also did not support the dovetailing of science and social work, of university and administration. In the second half of the 1930s, Wu initiated a sea change in sociological research in China. He supported a systematic link between sociology and anthropology in China and saw the introduction of functionalist community studies as the appropriate way to Sinicize sociology.[9]

Wu Wenzao who himself belonged to the first generation of Chinese sociologists and became the *éminence grise* of Chinese community research, devoted sustained efforts in the 1930s to establishing a systematic link between sociology and anthropology. He sought to combine the field research of British anthropology with the Chicago School's approaches to community studies, emphasizing especially Radcliffe-Brown's idea of comparative sociology (cf. Kuper, 2003: 363). Given the extremely broad spectrum of social and cultural relations in China, he thought that comparative sociology should focus on juxtaposing different Chinese communities, starting with those in the coastal regions which at that point were under direct Western influence, and extending to those in relatively untouched areas in the interior of the country (Sun, 1940: 259). The aim was to base this comparative community approach on ethnographic studies of minority societies in border and colonial areas, studies by agrarian sociologists on village communities in the interior, and studies led by urban sociologists on emigrant and other communities in cities on China's eastern coast (Wu, 1982: 48; Gransow et al., 2005: 5).

As Wu Wenzao described it, comparative sociology therefore comprises agrarian sociology and urban sociology, social anthropology and cultural anthropology, and ethnology or folklore studies. The cornerstones of its conceptual matrix (概念格局) are the notions of community, culture, system, and function (Wu, 1944: 1–2). This type of program extended far beyond the possibilities of individual scientists, and Wu put a lot of energy into establishing a broader basis for implementing his ideas, by such means as acquiring funding sources and channeling targeted support to his students. The fact that this approach was only partially successful was due at first to the chaotic nature of the war period and subsequently to political restrictions.

In the period leading up to Park's guest lectures at Yanjing University, Xu Shilian, Wu Jingchao, and Wu Wenzao assumed key roles as academic intermediaries between sociology in Chicago and Yanjing. As an "academic entrepreneur," Xu Shilian was keenly interested in promoting joint research projects and in raising funds. In terms of content he belonged to the social work wing of sociology in Yanjing, and therefore shared little if anything with Park's approach beyond the drive to professionalize sociology. Wu Jingchao, who had studied with Park and other members of the Chicago School, had been instrumental in raising the profile of urban sociology and the Chicago School in China; he clearly either ignited or at least fueled Park's interest in China. And Wu Wenzao, who issued the invitation to Park, was the one with the greatest academic affinities with Park even though he himself did hardly any empirical work. As did Park, Wu believed in strengthening the position of sociology via a comparative approach to community studies and in increasing international academic cooperation to achieve this goal (Sun, 1940: 168–9).

At the same time, the sociology department of Yanjing University was receiving funding from the Memorial as of 1928 to support its academic and empirical pursuits. The following section will therefore look more closely at the Memorial, its strategy for promoting the social sciences, and the resulting effects on the sociology departments in Beijing and Chicago.

The role of Rockefeller funding in shaping sociology in Chicago and Beijing

Created by John D. Rockefeller, the Memorial existed from 1918 to 1929. In its early years, it focused on conventional charities such as Baptist churches, the Salvation Army, the YMCA, and the YWCA. With the appointment of Beardsley Ruml in 1922 as the new director, the Memorial underwent a process that Martin Bulmer described as a "transformation from an undistinguished social welfare charity into an instrument for the support of basic social science research throughout the world" (1984: 136). By strategically promoting social scientific centers inside and outside the US,[10] the Memorial wanted to support empirical approaches in economics, sociology, political science, psychology, anthropology, and history, in keeping with the motto of "making the peaks higher" (Chiang, 2001: 3). Ruml's strategy was to encourage professional social science expertise as a basis for social welfare, and he criticized the production of knowledge at universities as largely deductive and speculative (Bulmer, 1984: 137). In 1923 the Memorial awarded a grant to study local community problems to the department of sociology and anthropology and the department of political science and political economy at the University of Chicago. In sociology, the recipient was the urban research program of Park, Burgess, and their students. The Memorial continued to fund local community research at the University of Chicago for eight years (until 1932), with its commitments assumed by the Rockefeller Foundation following its merger with the latter in 1929 (Bulmer, 1984: 140).

Ruml's ideal of sociology can be described as an empirical approach based on scientific methods whose research results can be applied in practice, and whose character is interdisciplinary (Bulmer, 1984: 218). Generally speaking this was also the standard by which it assessed project applications from the sociology department in Yanjing. However, these applications were viewed far less favorably than those from Chicago. John Stewart Burgess, the first dean of Yanjing's sociology department, failed to receive funding in 1923 for a social reform program and training for social workers at a time when the Memorial's focus had already shifted from charity to academic social scientific research.[11] A proposal by his successor Xu Shilian to set up a social laboratory for field research at the Qinghe market grounds was only approved after a lengthy period of evaluation,[12] and a proposal submitted jointly by Xu Shilian and colleagues at the University of Chicago to establish a social scientific center at Yanjing University was also rejected.[13]

As Chiang Yung-chen observed, there was a major difference in the Rockefeller Foundation's promotion of the sociology departments in Chicago and Yanjing. "Instead of contributing to the ascendance of the new rising paradigm as it had with Chicago sociology, the Rockefeller Foundation helped neutralize its impact at Yanjing" (Chiang, 2001: 8). One might say, therefore, that by funding sociology at Yanjing University the Memorial (and since 1929 the Rockefeller Foundation) was promoting not a rising star but a setting one. In other words, when in 1928 the Memorial finally accepted Xu Shilian's social work–based proposal submitted years earlier, an innovative and rival direction was already on the rise with Wu Wenzao's approach, which as of the mid-1930s would make the Yanjing sociology department a center of functionalism and community studies and ground it in social anthropology (Fu, 1982: 273; Gransow, 1992: 116).

In the early 1930s in light of current events in China[14] and influenced by its vice president Selskar Gunn, the Foundation's China program was redirected to place a clear focus on rural reconstruction (Chiang, 2001: 64). Its agrarian priorities were displayed not only with respect to the sociology department at Yanjing University but also in its funding for the economics department at Nankai University. However, these two departments responded differently to the shift in emphasis from the city to the countryside and from industrial to rural development. While the economists could still appeal to the local business community for funding, the sociologists could not. They became even more dependent on the Foundation, and were soon facing accusations that their turn toward rural issues was fueled solely by the wish to retain its financial backing (Chiang, 2001: 66, 254).

Robert Park in China

Park had to interrupt an initial series of lectures in Shanghai, Nanjing, and Beijing in the autumn of 1929 for weeks on account of illness. When he returned to China in 1932 he gave more than ten major talks, not only at Yanjing and Qinghua Universities but also at the Chinese Political Science Association and the Beijing chapter of the Association of Sociologists. The main part of his stay in China, however, consisted of the two courses he led at Yanjing University, one on social research methods and one on collective behavior. "At Yenching University I found many students who had earlier studied in America and were now attempting to use the ideas and conceptions we had given them to understand and study their own society and civilization," he commented (Raushenbush, 1979: 134). His students included C. K. Yang and Fei Xiaotong who subsequently became famous sociologists. According to Yang Qingkun (C. K. Yang) Park told his students, "In this course I am not going to teach you how to read books, but I am going to tell you how to write a book." He also reported that "Park inspired the class to seek new knowledge from facts through scientific methods." Fei Xiaotong later wrote, "He met the need of the students by inspiring them in how to carry on field studies. He himself visited Heaven Bridge, the red-light area in Peiping, to demonstrate that useful knowledge can be derived from the life of even the lowest people" (Raushenbush, 1979: 133).

In the wake of Park's lectures at Yanjing University, the sociology department compiled a reader in Chinese consisting of transcripts and papers (*Park reader*, 1933), including a foreword by Wu Wenzao and three articles by Robert Park. Besides two articles on sociology and social concepts, Park also wrote one entitled "On China." It starts by considering cross-cultural research on Chinese civilization, India, the US, Europe, and Russia from a comparative perspective. Based on his own observations, Park then highlights differences between Beiping (now Beijing), exemplifying traditional Chinese society where everybody seems to fulfill his or her social role, and Shanghai, with a comparatively European urban lifestyle. He notes that his most important source for gaining an understanding of Chinese society is the information he gets from his students, whom he describes as coming from various provinces and representing the future of China (Park, 1933).

In his foreword, Wu Wenzao describes Park's thoughts on the position of Chinese civilization as a juxtaposition of American urban society and Chinese village society and expounds on them in such detail and affinity with his own comparative approach that he then proceeds to qualify his approach as follows: "Although my comparison does not derive from Park's original work, it is in fact based on Park's distinction between urban and village societies" (Wu, 1933: 11).

Other articles in the *Reader* acknowledge Park's contribution to American sociology and describe the development of the sociology department at the University of Chicago. They also present some important concepts in urban sociology and human ecology (人文区位学), such as symbiosis (共生), which had played an important role in Wu Jingchao's dissertation on Chinatowns in America. The reader includes an introduction to research methods and viewpoints in human ecology, and an article by Zhao Chengxin on Park's human ecology. Yang Qingkun writes about Park's research methods on urban society and explains what Park saw as the two major driving forces behind its development, namely the division of labor, and population mobility. Other sections concentrate on community studies and their methods, with special reference to field research (*Park reader*, 1933).

Park's greatest service to Chinese sociology doubtless lay in encouraging its field research and the community studies approach at Yanjing University. But he was also of the opinion, which was shared by the Rockefeller Foundation, that the priority in China at the time should be placed on the study of rural communities (Wu, 1933: 10; Yan, 2004: 48).

From Fei Xiaotong's rural community studies and small-town research to China's new-type urbanization plan

During a period in London (1936–38) under the direction of Malinowski, Wu Wenzao's famous student Fei Xiaotong (1910–2005) developed material for his subsequent *Peasant life in China* (Fei, 1939) which has since served as a textbook study of a Chinese rural community.[15] In this work, Fei describes the village of Kaixiangong (Jiangsu Province), the name of which he changed to "River Village" (Jiangcun), as a harmoniously functioning cultural unit with conflicts of external origin. Fei viewed social change here as the destruction of social harmony leading to confusion in social roles. The main problem he identified in Kaixiangong was a decline in rural income due to falling prices for rural products as a result of competition from world markets. He advocated raising rural incomes via a policy of reconstructing rural industries, in contrast to the Guomindang policy of reducing taxes on farmers (Fei, 1939: 285). With his subsequent study on three village communities near Kunming (Yunnan Province), Fei not only pursued a comparative approach to studying rural communities but also argued in favor of rural industrialization (Fei and Chang, 1945; Gransow, 1992: 125–9).

After sociology was banned in the People's Republic of China for several decades, Fei Xiaotong took up his earlier research again in the early 1980s, refined his theory of rural industrialization, and advocated the concept of rural urbanization as a suitable modernization strategy for China. With commune and brigade-run industries already underway in the 1970s, and especially so in the southern part of Jiangsu Province, a large number of small towns were starting to appear. The launch of modernization policies in the early 1980s accelerated this development. Fei's work on small towns, which began in 1983, advanced the hypothesis that under conditions of high population pressure and limited arable land, rural industrialization was the appropriate route by which modernization could lead to economic growth in China.

The small-town studies by Fei Xiaotong are outstanding examples of empirical projects during the initial phase of reviving Chinese sociology following the opening of the country in the early 1980s (Fei, 1984; Fei et al., 1986). Based on a functionalist analysis of local economic traditions, these studies sought paths of modernization that featured mutually adapted (spontaneous) micro- and (regulated) macro-developments. At the same time they were an implicit attempt to extract elements of a theory of adapted modernization from an empirical analysis of the revival of traditional economic activities. Fei's work also launched a number of studies on rural industry, conducted in cooperation with the World Bank.

Under the motto of 离土不离乡 (leaving the soil but not the land), Fei Xiaotong advocated interconnected strategies of rural industrialization and small-town urbanization in the countryside. But with its seventh Five-Year Plan (1986–90), the Chinese government presented a strategy of economic development based on the three zones of a developed coast, central provinces, and undeveloped western provinces, that is, a development strategy with a strong focus on the most developed and most urbanized coastal areas—which was diametrically opposed to Fei's urbanization strategy based on rural industrialization and developing small towns. Yet at the same time, the government's attempts to channel the flow of rural-to-urban migration into smaller cities did grant a certain significance to small-town development. However, this led to a situation in which the economic incentives offered by megacities exerted a greater attraction than state-propagated urbanization policies. Opinions have differed about the pros and cons of an urbanization strategy that promotes small towns versus one that focuses on big and megacities.

While large cities are seen as core centers of economic concentration and innovation that could be developed much more efficiently than small cities and towns in the countryside, their overload of social infrastructure (overcrowded kindergartens, schools, and hospitals, for example), congested traffic, and inadequate supply of affordable housing are arguments for controlling their further population growth (CDRF, 2013: 118; Zhang and Zhao, 2015: 256, 257). Small towns, on the other hand, are viewed as having limited capacities to promote urbanization because of their undeveloped industries, restricted employment opportunities, and poor public services. The costs of developing small towns are described as relatively high in terms of requisite resources (land, energy, job opportunities), environmental issues, and poor planning processes (using town planning to define the extent of township authority over village land) (Hsing, 2010: 166). In addition, small-town development as a primary mode of urbanization would not reflect China's administrative hierarchy. Putting too much effort into developing small towns would lead to upgrading their administrative levels and developing their own seats of government and political centers. Therefore neither extensive urban sprawl nor small towns are considered suitable primary residential locations for urbanization processes in China (CDRF, 2013: 130, 131).

Against this background and confirmed by General Secretary Xi Jinping's report to the 19th CPC congress in October 2017 (*China Daily*, 25 October, 2017), the most promising urbanization pattern is now thought to be city clusters with one or two megacities at their core. Plans call for the three urban clusters currently in existence (Pearl River Delta, Yangtze River Delta, and the Bohai hub including Beijing, Tianjin, and Hebei Province) to increase in number to 20. Small cities and towns around core cities (discrete, not conjoined) are intended to play a supporting role and expected to grow fast (CDRF, 2013: 132, 141, 142). The new-type urbanization plan (2014–20) also emphasizes the expansion of smaller cities (Guojia, 2014).[16] It seeks to guide both the flow of migration into smaller cities and the access by local governments to land resources by concentrating residential areas and expanding transportation infrastructures.

After Fei Xiaotong's research program in the 1980s, the role of small and mid-sized towns in (rural) urbanization became a comparatively understudied field.[17] With a huge variety of new towns and other new urban areas around cities, various forms of peri-urban transformation from rural into urban residency took place. These could be top-down urban expansion that subsumes villages, and/or bottom-up rural urbanization which might be formal or informal, that is, driven by hierarchical administrative policies or led by community initiatives whereby villagers sought to capture the value of their land. To give but one example, small cities provided an urban *hukou* registration as an incentive to rural workers and migrants during the 1990s, which was subsequently not well received because it is social *guanxi* that in fact actually facilitates access to services, jobs, and other resources (Hsing, 2010: 166; Carrillo, 2011: 155). More research is required in general on these and many different forms of rural urbanization. Also and especially, however, qualitative comparative community studies (possibly in combination with new digital forms of social research) could lead to a deeper understanding of the intended and unintended effects of these complex processes of transformation.

Urban village research in China: Theorizing villages-in-the-city

A core concept in current discourse on mega-urbanization and rural-to-urban migration in China is that of *chengzhongcun* (城中村), translated either as urban villages or more literally as villages-in-the-city. It stands for the end of natural villages encircled by rapidly expanding urban spaces. It also stands for the relatively independent self-government of collective villages, even when they are surrounded by the city and need to fend off various attempts by city authorities to incorporate what the latter sometimes view as "unruly" elements into their administrative systems. The concept of villages-in-the-city came to signify the introduction of market value into land and urban redevelopment. Not only agricultural land but also that used for industrial and residential purposes was converted to commercial space, and local governments, developers, investors, village committees (which sometimes themselves became real-estate companies), and former villagers started to negotiate prices and compensation. Last but not least, the concept of villages-in-the-city stands for settlements of rural-to-urban migrants who need affordable housing where they actually live although they lack the rights and privileges of permanent residents. There have been some early community studies on urban villages in Beijing and Guangzhou, by, for instance, Wang Chunguang (1995), Zhang Li (2001), and Lan Yuyun (2005).

To better understand mega-urban regions in China as problems of organized complexity, the concept of *chengzhongcun* can serve as an "unaverage clue" (Jane Jacobs) that reveals very basic yet also very complex processes and contradictions at a micro-level, which in turn reflect Chinese urban development at large (Jacobs, 1992: 440).

The perspective of community research offers three levels of comparison here: (1) between different types of urban villages within China; (2) between *chengzhongcun* and migrant settlements in other countries (for example, the *gecekondu* in Turkey); and (3) on a conceptual level between villages-in-the-city and earlier notions of "slum" and "urban village." I will focus solely on the third level here and begin by exploring conceptual historical links between the controversy over the term "slum" in connection with the Chicago School and between various contextualization's of the term "urban village." I will then examine why the discourse on urban villages in Chinese megacities has thus far displayed little reflection on this connection. And finally I will consider the extent to which Robert Park's research program outlined in "The city" (1915) can enrich current studies of urban villages in Chinese cities.

Slum—urban village—villages-in-the-city

In the history of urban sociology two community studies are of particular interest for the Chinese concept of *chengzhongcun*: the classic work by William Foote Whyte on the *Street corner society* (Whyte, 1993, first published 1943) in Boston's North End, and the critical study by Herbert Gans on *The urban villagers: Group and class in the life of Italian-Americans* in Boston's West End (Gans, 1982, first published 1962).

When Whyte conducted his community study of social networks and informal organization within an Italian immigrant community, he was still using the term "slum."[18] In fact, studying a slum was one of the main purposes of his work (Whyte, 1993: 281–2). Although he described "Cornerville" as a place marked by order, honor, and dignity, the term "slum" carried negative associations about the place and its people, with dilapidated buildings implying depraved qualities in the society (Lindner, 2004: 162). Whyte was later harshly criticized for the term, and Cornerville's inhabitants were offended because they—like many other people—associated the label with dirt, mud, filth, vermin, illness, and epidemics, above all with crime and a haven for criminals.

What was completely new about Whyte's study was that he analyzed informal social organization within the "slum" area. Previous sociological literature had equated slum districts with "social disorganization," so no one had endeavored to enquire into the hidden structures and groupings of informal social relations and organizations. When Whyte defended his doctoral dissertation at the University of Chicago, Louis Wirth, one of the authors of this earlier type of slum study and a member of the examining committee, attacked him sharply over the lack of a heretofore obligatory review of earlier studies (Whyte, 1993: 356). Wirth could not understand how to define a slum without including the idea of "social disorganization" and he wanted to provoke Whyte to address this but the latter resisted.

In the early 1960s Herbert Gans introduced the concept of "urban villager" to describe an Italian immigrant enclave in the West End of Boston. Gans criticized the use of "slum" as "an evaluative, not an analytical concept" (Gans, 1982: 350). He observed and criticized a tendency to comprehend low-rent areas by the physical condition of their buildings and then infer the character of the inhabitants from the dilapidation of their dwellings. Reflecting on the different class backgrounds and class-specific cultures of the various stakeholders in urban villages, he therefore urged taking the class and culture-specific behavioral patterns and values of working-class people as the starting point for planning processes in low-rent areas. This tradition of research on urban villages easily provides the basis for viewing villages-in-the-city as distinct, low-income, migrant workers' residential areas.

Another reason why Gans' study on urban villagers is worth rereading from the perspective of villages-in-the-city is that he discusses the problem of urban redevelopment projects and their intended and unintended impacts on low-income residential areas and their inhabitants. Gans did his field work in 1957–58 in an old part of Boston, which was the object of redevelopment, close to the city center. He argued that it is illusory to imagine that urban planning could be a suitable tool for establishing social communities, and that cautious and careful ways of renewing existing communities would be much more promising (Lindner, 2004: 167). These ideas have been increasingly taken up in recent literature on the redevelopment of *chengzhongcun* in China (such as Lan, 2011; Lin and de Meulder, 2012). Another version of this position is found in graffiti on dilapidated buildings in, for example, Beijing, which call for "harmonious demolition" (和谐拆迁).

While Gans was rejecting the use of "slum" as an evaluative concept, Jane Jacobs, whose critical study on urban planning (*The death and life of American cities*, 1961) had been published just one year before his *Urban villagers*, introduced the phrase "unslumming the slum." She argued that some slums are able to regenerate while others—which she calls perpetual slums that show no sign of economic or social improvement—run in vicious circles (Jacobs, 1992: 270). As indices for "unslumming," she suggests residents' attachment to their district, informal social control, and improvements to the interiors of residences (Jacobs, 1992: 272). For her, Boston's West End on the eve of its destruction which Gans described as a stable low-rent area was an "unslumming slum." But because developers' powerful interests and paternalistic approaches overrode those of slum dwellers and small businesses, the only choice was demolition. Gans and Jacobs agreed in their critical attitude toward urban planners and in arguing for soft and careful renewal of low-rent areas. But Gans was also very critical of what he considered Jacobs's romantic view of working-class life and the beauty of urban smallness (Gans, 2006: 214). Jacobs's ideas later inspired the urban village movement in the UK in the 1990s as championed by the Urban Villages Group.

Disconnected discourse on urban villages

Given the striking similarities between these contexts on the one hand and the formation of migrant communities in Chinese megacities and their vulnerability to redevelopment projects and gentrification processes on the other, we might ask why discourse on Chinese *chengzhongcun* has thus far not looked more closely at these earlier debates on slums and urban villages.[19] Possible reasons might include:

- Language and translation problems. The bulk of research on *chengzhongcun* is in Chinese.
- Many Chinese research articles focus on solving problems and advising policy rather than on providing historical, comparative, or theoretical perspectives.
- China's official self-representation as a socialist society without slums discourages the development of scientific attention to urban villages in the framework of slum research.
- A tendency toward single-disciplinary discourse means that interdisciplinary synergies are overlooked.[20]
- A focus on the "Chinese characteristics" of *chengzhongcun* seeks the particularities of Chinese urban villages rather than the traits they share with other migrant communities.

While there are various reasons for these weak or missing links in work on villages-in-the-city, comparative approaches to studying the formation of migrant communities internationally are on the rise. In his book *Arrival city* (2011), the journalist Doug Saunders describes migrant enclaves and how they serve as sites of arrival in cities all over the world, including in Shenzhen. Putting aside the common distinction between internal and international migration, Saunders highlights the fact that most migration worldwide flows from the countryside into cities, and especially into large cities. His fresh perspective on migration as rural to urban, whether internal or international, is a striking depiction of the needs of people in arrival cities and an eye-opener to the national and local governments that have to deal with these challenges.

Villages-in-the-city in comparative perspective

Reflecting on Park's research program as presented in "The city," the question arises as to what extent the village-in-the-city stands for "a locality with sentiments, traditions and a history of its own" (Park, 1915: 579). Such a characterization might be suitable for an original natural village, even after being encircled by an expanding city. It might also be suitable for the more homogeneous types of migrant enclaves. But does the community study approach still apply to heterogeneous urban villages with migrant populations from different provinces and backgrounds? Or would it be more fruitful to examine these urban villages not as a community but as a social group with a shared interest in affordable housing? While we can still find stimulating ideas on the interrelationships between urban space and behavioral patterns in Park's research program which could strengthen sociological research on urban village communities in big Chinese cities, it would also be worthwhile to think about Wu Wenzao's less well known research program of comparative community studies, including various types of rural and urban communities and their possible interconnections.

Conclusion

The development of urban sociology in China displays profound and long-term connections with the Chicago School and with Robert Park in particular. Xu Shilian, Wu Jingchao, and Wu Wenzao are three members of the first generation of Chinese sociologists who played an intermediary role between the Chicago School and emerging Chinese sociology in the late 1920s and early 1930s. A look at the sociology departments at the University of Chicago and Yanjing University in Beijing reveals the significance of financial support first by the Memorial and subsequently by the Rockefeller Foundation as part of a wider strategy to promote academic and empirically oriented social sciences. At the same time, the Memorial's funding strategies suggest that it deliberately wanted social science research in China to focus on rural issues instead of industrialization and urbanization strategies appropriate for the country.

Park's lectures at Yanjing University in 1932 impressed the students, among them Fei Xiaotong and Yang Qingkun who would acquire fame among second-generation Chinese sociologists. Fei Xiaotong visited Chicago a decade later. Sitting in what used to be Park's office on 15 November 1943, he wrote Park a letter acknowledging the latter's influence on his studies and describing himself as "a man coming from a folk society [who] will certainly be bewitched by the history behind the walls," and adding, "I feel ... I am working under your spirit [all the time]."[21] In a sense Fei Xiaotong fulfilled the research program of his teacher Wu Wenzao who sought to create comparative sociology by combining the Chicago School's approaches to community studies with field research à la Malinowski. Starting from his classical village community study of the 1930s and continuing with his small-town research program of the early 1980s (following decades in which sociology was banned in China), Fei Xiaotong refined his theory of rural industrialization as a modernization strategy suitable for China, by adding the concept of rural urbanization. His ideas of rural urbanization in situ were not without appeal to generations of Chinese political leaders searching for solutions to hundreds of millions of surplus rural laborers. They are mirrored (but only at a distance) in China's official urbanization strategy including its "National Plan on New Urbanization (2014–2020)," which aims to have over 60% of the entire population living in cities by 2020 and seeks to liberalize migration to small and medium-sized cities rather than to megacities.

What is special about China's rapid urbanization process is not only its speed and scale but also the attempt by Chinese governments at different levels to channel and shape it. As a consequence of official urbanization policy not being in harmony with the incentives that megacities have to offer in terms of jobs, services, and opportunities, a whole range of informal working and living conditions as well as informal institution-building has emerged in Chinese cities. Under these circumstances, the legacy of Park's research program, his methodology (and also his curiosity as a reporter) could still make a considerable contribution to urban sociology in and of China today.

Notes

[1] For an overview of research on Chinese cities, see Chen and Sun, 2006; Ma, 2006; Gu et al., 2012; He, 2014; Gu et al., 2015.

[2] A revised version of "The city" appeared in 1925 in a book edited jointly by Robert E. Park, E. W. Burgess and R. D. McKenzie. Only minor changes were made to the conceptual apparatus and research logic and are concentrated in the opening passage.

[3] This description draws partly on Lindner, 1990: 98–103.

4   An organization founded in 1898 by a group of Princeton undergraduates to
    support the YMCA in Beijing.

5   As of 1927, the Guomindang banned Marxist teachings at colleges and maintained
    a "black list" of undesired political writings that accumulated nearly 2,000 titles
    by 1937. To avoid censorship, Marxist works were published under neutral titles.
    An introduction to dialectical and historical materialism by Li Da, which Mao
    Zedong had recommended as an ideal teaching material, appeared in 1937 as *An
    outline of sociology* (Sun, 1987: 258, 275, 279, 384; Gransow, 1992: 61).

6   Wu's book presented E. W. Burgess's ideas on different urban zones, which fit in
    well with the large-scale master plans being drawn up at the time for Shanghai,
    Nanjing, and other Chinese cities (Lincoln, 2011). It appeared as volume 13 in the
    Outline of sociology series (社会学大纲) published by Sun Benwen and is divided
    into sections on urban economy, population, regions, and taxation processes.

7   According to Yan Ming (2004: 125), Wu Jingchao highlighted the social survey
    methods of Charles Booth as well as the comparative methods of William Sumner.

8   Wu Jingchao began teaching at Jinling College in Nanjing, was then at the sociology
    department of Qinghua University from 1931 to 1935, and subsequently worked
    for the Nanjing government, as of 1938 in the Ministry of Industry (Yan, 2004:
    124).

9   Many of Wu's students achieved international acclaim, among them Fei Xiaotong
    (*Peasant life in China*, 1939), Fei Xiaotong and Zhang Zhiyi (*Earthbound China*,
    1945), Lin Yuehua (*The golden wing*, 1944), Yang Qingkun (C. K. Yang) (*A Chinese
    village in early Communist transition*, 1959), and Xu Langguang (Francis L. K. Hsu)
    (*Under the ancestor's shadow*, 1948). On community studies in China see Fried 1954.

10 Including the London School of Economics and the sociology department at
    Yanjing University in Beijing.

11 While the Memorial supported the idea of a facility for social research in China,
    it wanted to fund a Chinese institution as opposed to a missionary university,
    and favored research over training (Gransow, 1992: 45–6). It therefore backed
    a department of social research at the China Foundation for the Promotion of
    Education and Culture, with Tao Menghe and Li Jinghan appointed as directors in
    1926 (Gransow, 1992: 59). With ever more frequent labor disputes and the rise of the
    workers' movement in the 1920s (until its violent suppression by the Guomindang
    in 1927), the department of social research did a series of sociological/economic
    surveys on the conditions of urban workers and their families. In the early 1930s
    it increasingly shifted its focus from industrial to village contexts, in keeping with
    the general development shown by the social survey movement in China. By 1933
    a substantial majority of surveys focused on villages, in the context of various rural
    reform projects as well as the retreat by the Communists to rural areas (Liu, 1936:
    43, 40; Gransow, 1992: 67).

12 When the Memorial awarded a grant to the department to promote sociological
    research in 1928, Xu could put his plans into action. Not far from the university,

he found a suitable spot on the grounds of the Qinghe market town to build a social laboratory and carry out social surveys. Despite the comparatively generous funding, however, the project quietly came to an end in 1934.

[13] Xu Shilian succeeded in submitting a joint proposal with colleagues from Chicago to the Rockefeller Foundation to establish a social science research institute at Yanjing University. But because the proposal lacked a genuine research focus and perhaps also because Yanjing University's sociology department did not seem to have accomplished much at its sociological laboratory in Qinghe town, the Foundation ultimately turned it down (Chiang, 2001: 52).

[14] Since the late 1920s, due primarily to the intensification of the agrarian crisis and the decline of rural trades in the face of foreign competition, a reformist rural reconstruction project emerged in response to the new Communist interest in the peasantry after the breakup of its united front with the Guomindang. Most prominent were the rural grassroots initiatives to reform the countryside led by Yan Yangchu ("scientific Dingxian model") and Liang Shuming ("philosophical Zouping model").

[15] For Fei, culture was not an expression of national essence, as it was for Sun Benwen, among others, but rather—entirely in accord with the social anthropological school—functionally conditioned, that is, he started with the assumption that specific cultural forms would disappear as they lost their functions. In order for culture to fulfill its function of adaptation, reforms must be based on a functional analysis of existing institutions or customs.

[16] This is evident already in the choice of words for the plan: 城镇化 (chengzhenhua) as opposed to 城市化 (chengshihua) where 镇 stands for small towns and 市 for cities.

[17] With a few exceptions such as Guldin, 1997; Carrillo, 2011; Hillman and Unger, 2013.

[18] Emerging as a spatial form and analytical concept in Victorian England, the slum was conceptualized by Friedrich Engels and his contemporaries as a by-product of industrial capitalism and its creation of an urban working class. Yet while Engels understood the slum to be the *consequence* of capitalist relations, most sociologists, at least through the first half of the twentieth century, have viewed the slum as the *source* of such social problems as immorality, vice, and dysfunctional family forms (Weinstein, 2014: 8, original emphasis).

[19] Exceptions are Wong et al., 2015 and Wang, 2016: 5–14.

[20] From a perspective of urban planning Him Chung (2010) stresses the differences between the two concepts of "urban village" and "villages-in-the-city." While he sees the concept of urban villages as closely related to the urban village movement in the UK he positions the two concepts at different stages of the urbanization process (Chung, 2010: 424). In addition, he describes the persistence of the villages-in-the-city in Chinese cities as a failure to integrate the rural area and its residents

into the urban system. He identifies villages-in-the-city only as former natural villages but not as a specific type of migrant communities.

[21] Robert E. Park—Addenda, box 1, folder 15 in Joseph Regenstein Library, Special Collections Department, University of Chicago, cited in Rolf Lindner, *Die Entdeckung der Stadtkultur: Soziologie aus der Erfahrung der Reportage*, Frankfurt am Main: Suhrkamp, 1990: 150. I thank Rolf Lindner for sharing Fei's letter with me. The letter also appears as Figure 1.1 in Chapter 1 of this volume.

References

Bulmer, M. (1984) *The Chicago School of Sociology: Institutionalization, diversity, and the rise of sociological research*, Chicago: University of Chicago Press.

Carrillo, B. (2011) *Small town China: Rural labour and social inclusion*, Abingdon: Routledge.

CDRF (China Development Research Foundation) (ed.) (2013) *China's new urbanization strategy*, Abingdon: Routledge.

Chen, X. M. and Sun J. M. (2006) "Sociological perspectives on urban China: From familiar territories to complex terrains," *China Information*, 20(3): 519–51.

Chiang, Y. C. (2001) *Social engineering and the social sciences in China 1919–1949*, Cambridge: Cambridge University Press.

Christmann, G. (2007) *Robert E. Park*, Konstanz: UVK Verlagsgesellschaft.

Chung, H. (2010) "Building an image of villages-in-the-city: A clarification of China's distinct urban spaces," *International Journal of Urban and Regional Research*, 34(2): 421–37.

Fei, H. T. (1939) *Peasant life in China: A field study of country life in the Yangtze valley*, New York: E. P. Dutton & Company.

Fei, H. T. and Chang, C. I. (1945) *Earthbound China: A study of rural economy in Yunnan*, Chicago: University of Chicago Press.

Fei, H. T. and Others (1986) *Small towns in China: Functions, problems & prospects*, Beijing: New World Press.

Fei, X. T. 费孝通 (1984) 小城镇,大问题: 江苏省小城镇研究论文选 (*Small towns, big problems: Collection of articles containing research on small towns in Jiangsu Province*), Huaiyin: Jiangsu People's Press.

Fried, M. H. (1954) "Community studies in China," *Far Eastern Quarterly*, 14: 11–36.

Fu, S. D. 傅愫冬 (n.d.) "燕京大学社会学系三十年" ("Thirty years of Yanjing University's sociology department"), in 北京市社会科学研究所社会学研究室编 (Beijing Institute of Social Sciences, sociological research department) (ed.) 社会学研究与应用 (*Research and application of sociology*), Beijing: Beijing Institute of Social Sciences, pp. 264–79 and Appendix, pp. 280–300.

Gamble, S. D. and Burgess, J. S. (1921) *Peking: A social survey*, New York: Doran.

Gans, H. J. (1982) *The urban villagers: Group and class in the life of Italian-Americans* (updated and expanded edition), New York: The Free Press, first published in 1962.

Gans, H. J. (2006) "Jane Jacobs: Toward an understanding of 'Death and life of great American cities,'" *City & Community*, 5(3): 213–15.

Gransow, B. (1992) *Geschichte der chinesischen Soziologie*, Frankfurt, New York: Campus.

Gransow, B. (2003) "The social sciences in China," in T. M. Porter and D. Ross (eds.) *The modern social sciences: The Cambridge history of science 7*, Cambridge: Cambridge University Press, pp. 498–514.

Gransow, B., Nyiri, P., and Fong, S.-C. (eds.) (2005) *Berliner China-Hefte /Chinese history and society vol. 28*, Münster: LIT Verlag.

Gu C., Kesteloot, C., and Cook, I. (2015) "Theorising Chinese urbanization: A multi-layered perspective," *Urban Studies*, 52(14): 2564–80.

Gu C., Wu L., and Cook, I. (2012) "Progress in research on Chinese urbanization," *Frontiers of Architectural Research*, 1(2): 101–49.

Guldin, G. E. (1997) *Farewell to peasant China: Rural urbanization and social change in the late twentieth century*, New York: M. E. Sharpe.

Guojia 国家新型城镇化规划 (National new-type urbanization plan) (2014–2020) of 16 March 2014. Available at: http://news.xinhuanet.com/politics/2014--03/16/c_119791251.htm.

He, Y. M. (2014) "Chinese urban history studies face the twenty-first century," *Chinese Studies in History*, 47(3): 73–99.

Hillman, B. and Unger, J. (2013) "The urbanisation of rural China" (Special feature), *China Perspectives*, No. 2013/3.

Hsing, Y.T. (2010) *The Great Urban Transformation. Politics of Land and Property in China*, Oxford: Oxford University Press.

Jacobs, J. (1992) *The death and life of great American cities*, New York: Vintage Books.

Kuper, A. (2003) "Anthropology," in T. M. Porter and D. Ross (eds.) *The modern social sciences: The Cambridge history of science 7*, Cambridge: Cambridge University Press, pp. 354–78.

Lan, Y. Y. 蓝宇蕴 (2005) 都市里的村庄: 一个'新村庄共同体'的实地研究 (*Villages in metropolises: Field research on a "new village community"*), Beijing: Sanlian shudian.

Lan, Y. Y. 蓝宇蕴 (2011) "论城中村改造对其非正式经济的影响: 以广州城中村改造为例" ("On the impact of redevelopment of urban villages on informal economies: The case of urban village redevelopment in Guangzhou"), 甘肃理论学刊 (*Gansu Theory Research*), 204(2): 77–82.

Lin, Y. L. and de Meulder, B. (2012) "A conceptual framework for the strategic urban project approach for the sustainable redevelopment of 'villages in the city' in Guangzhou," *Habitat International*, 36(3): 380–7.

Lincoln, T. (2011) "Chinese urban visions: The birth of urban sociology in China," paper presented at "East Asian Cities and Globalization: The Past in the Present," University of Warwick, July 9–10, 2011. Available at: https://warwick.ac.uk/fac/arts/history/ghcc/research/esrccitiesnetwork/activities/conference/papers/.

Lindner, R. (1990) *Die Entdeckung der Stadtkultur: Soziologie aus der Erfahrung der Reportage* (*The discovery of urban culture: Sociology from experience in newspaper reporting*), Frankfurt am Main: Suhrkamp.

Lindner, R. (2004) *Walks on the Wild Side: Eine Geschichte der Stadtforschung* (*A history of urban research*), Frankfurt: Campus.

Liu Y. R. 刘育仁 (1936) "中国社会调查运动" ("The Chinese social survey movement"), MA thesis, Yanjing University.

Ma, L. J. C. (2006) "The state of the field of urban China: A critical multidisciplinary overview of the literature," *China Information*, 20(3): 363–89.

Park, R. E. (1904) *Masse und Publikum: eine methodologische und soziologische Untersuchung* (*The crowd and the public: A methodological and sociological investigation*), Bern: Buchdruckerei Lack & Grunau.

Park, R. E. (1915) "The city: Suggestions for the investigation of human behavior in the city environment," *The American Journal of Sociology*, 20(5): 577–612.

Park, R. E. (1933) "论中国" ("On China"), in 帕克社会学论文集 (*Park reader on sociology*), Beiping: Yanjing University, pp. 1–6.

Park, R. E., Burgess, E., and McKenzie, R. (1925) *The city*, Chicago: Chicago University Press.

Park reader on sociology (1933) 帕克社会学论文集, Beiping: Yanjing University.

Raushenbush, W. (1979) *Robert E. Park: Biography of a sociologist*, Durham, NC: Duke University Press.

Saunders, D. (2011) *Arrival city*, Munich: Karl Blessing Verlag.

Sun, C. H. (1987) "The development of the social sciences in China before 1949," PhD dissertation, Columbia University.

Sun, Y. F. 孙以芳 (1940) "中国社会学的发展" ("The development of Chinese sociology"), BA thesis, Yanjing University.

Wang, C. G. 王春光 (1995) 社会流动和社会重构: 京城浙江村研究 (*Social mobility and social structure: Research on Beijing's Zhejiang village*), Hangzhou: Zhejiang People's Press.

Wang, D. W. (2016) *Urban villages in the new China: Case of Shenzhen*, New York: Palgrave Macmillan.

Weinstein, L. (2014) *The durable slum: Dharavi and the right to stay put in globalizing Mumbai*, Minneapolis: University of Minnesota Press.

Whyte, W. F. (1993) *Street corner society: The social structure of an Italian slum* (4th edn.), Chicago: University of Chicago Press, first published 1943.

Wong, T. C., (2015) "Developmental idealism: Building cities without slums in China," in T. C. Wong, S. S. Han, and H. Zhang (eds.) *Population mobility, urban management and planning in China*, Heidelberg: Springer, pp. 17–34.

Wu, C. C. 吴景超 (1928) "Chinatowns: A study of symbiosis and assimilation," PhD dissertation, University of Chicago.

Wu, J. C. 吴景超 (1929) 都市社会学 (*Urban sociology*), Shanghai: World Bookstore (世界书局).

Wu, W. Z. 吴文藻 (1933) "导言" ("Foreword"), in 帕克社会学论文集 (*Park Reader on Sociology*), Beiping: Yanjing University, pp. 1–14.

Wu, W. Z. 吴文藻 (1944) "社会学丛刊总序" ("Sociology Series, Foreword") in 马林诺斯基 文化论 (*Malinowski, On Culture*), Chongqing.

Wu, W. Z. 吴文藻 (1982) "吴文藻自传" ("Autobiography of Wu Wenzao"), in *Jinyang xuekan* (*Jinyang Journal*), 6: 44–52.

Xu, S. L. 许仕廉 (1925) "对于社会学教程的研究" ("Studies in teaching sociology"), 社会学杂志 (*The Chinese Journal of Sociology*) 4: 1–11.

Yan, M. 阎明 (2004) 一门学科与一个时代. 社会学在中国 (*A discipline and an era: Sociology in China*) Beijing: Qinghua University Press.

Yang, Y. B. 杨雅彬 (1987) 中国社会学史 (*A history of Chinese sociology*), Jinan: Shandong People's Press.

Zhang, L. (2001) *Strangers in the city: Reconfigurations of space, power, and social networks within China's floating population*, Stanford, CA: Stanford University Press.

Zhang, L. and Zhao, M. (2015) "Rural towns in China's rapid urbanization: A case study of Hubei province," in T. C. Wong, S. S. Han, and H. Zhang (eds.) *Population mobility, urban management and planning in China*, Heidelberg: Springer, pp. 243–58.

3

Moral Order in the Post-Socialist Chinese City

Generating a Dialogue with Robert E. Park's "The City"

Fulong Wu and Zheng Wang

Introduction

China is entering a new stage of slower economic growth and the government's attention is gradually moving toward the social challenges that have built up over the past decades of rapid urbanization. Millions of rural migrants now live in urban areas, and large cities such as Shanghai, Beijing, and Shenzhen continue to attract hundreds of thousands of migrants every year who tend to congregate certain urban neighborhoods (Chan, 2009; Yue et al., 2010; Wang et al., 2016). Both scholars and the Chinese government are greatly concerned about their integration into the city (Liu et al., 2013; Yue et al., 2013; Wang et al., 2016). Additionally, the early work of Whyte and Parish (1984) found that the social life of urban residents in socialist China consisted mainly of localized social networks. However, since then China's transition to a market economy and the rapid rate of urbanization have allowed residents to create a less territorially bound social network based on family, kin, and work ties (Hazelzet and Wissink, 2012). These fundamental changes to Chinese urban society now call for more understanding of how urbanization has affected the social life of Chinese urban residents. It is at this point in time that the works of Robert E. Park and the Chicago School seem to be more relevant than ever. One of Park's key arguments is that the city should not be merely regarded as a congregation of people but rather as an institution that has its own concept and structure (1915: 577). Studying the Chinese city from a human ecological perspective is therefore of great value. Urban China research is not an underdeveloped field and, especially, empirical studies on the political economic structure have proliferated since the late 1980s. However, it is important to stress that the growing number of studies adopting a structural political economy approach should not be interpreted as a critique toward the human ecology approach. Instead, after establishing a general understanding of the political economic structure of China, Park's work should inspire us to think again about the nature of the city and how to study the city as an institution rather than a collection of people affected by political economic forces. One major concern of the Chicago School was how the moral order of urban society has been influenced by the peculiar characteristics of the city. Park's (1915) and Wirth's (1938) argument that urbanism, characterized by the industrial organization of the city and impersonal relations defined by law and money, has replaced the traditional neighborhood social structure also resonate with the Chinese situation. Social class defined by different types of occupations may also play an important role in changing the moral order of the Chinese city. China's emerging middle class is able to retreat from state control by buying into gated private estates. Within these estates residents have started to rebuild their own social network and social order, which is primarily based on common interest and the shared social identity of homeowners (Pow, 2007; Li et al., 2012; Yip, 2012).

However, while this study acknowledges the continued relevance of Park's research, we also contest his argument that living in the city inevitably leads to the decline of the traditional moral order based on intimate local-based social relations (Park, 1915: 588). For the Chicago School the neighborhood played an integral role in studying the institution of the city as residents with similar characteristics and preferences concentrate in similar localities. China's urban landscape has also changed considerably due to the country's privatization of housing provision and findings indicate that the social life of residents differs considerably depending on the neighborhood type (Forrest and Yip, 2007; Wu, 2012; Wang et al., 2017b). Private commodity estates now dominate the housing market while older neighborhoods are facing demolition and redevelopment, raising concerns over the social cohesion among residents (Wu and He, 2005). On the other hand, migrant enclaves characterized by strong informality and little state control can equally be found in Chinese cities as well as organized work-unit neighborhoods, which continue to exist. Furthermore, China's position as the world's factory has attracted millions of rural migrants who move to cities in search of better jobs and livelihoods. Despite their importance in supplying the market with cheap labor, institutional limitations laid on them by the state prevent them from integrating into urban life. As a consequence in many cities, rural migrants are largely confined to living in urban villages among fellow rural migrants (Liu et al., 2012). In this study we argue that, unlike the Chinese urban middle class, migrants continue to rely on what Park (1915) may describe as the traditional moral order which is based on primary relations and local ties with neighbors (Liu et al., 2012; Wang et al., 2016; Wu and Logan, 2016). By taking a closer look at the different types of neighborhoods and their residents' social life and using the case of rural migrants, the purpose of this chapter is to explore the dynamics of the changing moral order of Chinese cities, why certain population groups continue to rely on primary and localized social relations, and what role the Chinese state has played. Our study will also draw on a 1,420-sized household questionnaire conducted in 2013 in Shanghai and argue that, especially, rural migrants who have moved from the Chinese countryside to the cities are still highly dependent on neighborly relations to survive in the city.

The chapter is structured as follows. The first section discusses how the deliberate marginalization of certain social groups by the Chinese state has forced them to rely on primary social relations. In the second part we take a closer look at the various neighborhood types and the community sentiments of different resident groups to substantiate our argument. Third, using the example of rural migrants we propose an alternative urban way of living in Chinese cities and the importance of the state in creating such a divergent path of urban moral order. Finally in our conclusion we try to reconcile the political economic and the human ecological approach in studying the city, arguing that Park's approach can help to connect the somewhat abstract concepts of political economic studies with the lived experience of urban residents.

Post-socialist Chinese cities: A new moral order in the making

For Park (1915: 577) the city is more than a simple congregation of people but rather it should be understood as an institution with its own concept and structure. Prior to China's economic reform, instead of the city itself, the work-unit (*danwei*) was the primary urban institution, replicating the social organization of the rural society into an industrialized economy. Similar to rural areas where residents were governed by village committees, urban residents and their social life were also organized around their respective work-units. However, there was a significant difference between the urban and rural in terms of institution. The urban area was under direct state control and within the system, while the rural part was largely a self-contained system outside the state's bureaucratic control. Nevertheless, the state also had strong control over the moral order of socialist urban China and the social relations of urban residents were largely neighborhood based (Whyte and Parish, 1984). The work-unit institution was abolished following the economic reform, which entailed the state's gradual retreat from the provision of housing and jobs. After the abolition of the work-unit system the importance of the city itself came into the forefront. From this perspective, it could be argued that Park's definition of the city as an institution only started to emerge after China's transition to a market economy.

One of the main concerns of the Chicago School and Park's research was the changing moral order in cities. Park borrows an old German proverb of "city air makes men free (Stadtluft macht frei)" (Park, 1915: 584) to describe the advantage and alluring characteristics of the city such as better chances of social mobility and individual freedom. However, Park was also concerned that the extension of industrial organization, which is based on "impersonal relations defined by money, has gone hand in hand with an increasing mobility of the population" (1915: 588). The division of the population into different vocational groups, rather than social groups, had broken down or modified the traditional social structure based on family ties and local associations and substituted them for organization of vocational interests (Park, 1915: 586). Wirth (1938: 13) further elaborates that the division of labor and the proliferation of different professions are driven by the "segmental character and utilitarian accent of interpersonal relations in the city." In short, the peculiar characteristics of the city exchanged the traditional moral order of urban residents, which is defined by shared sentiments and memories and based on primary and neighborhood relations, with secondary relations characterized by anonymity and personal interest. Figure 3.1 provides a simplified illustration of how the moral order differs between the city and the traditional village committee.

Such arguments by the Chicago School would also fittingly describe some of the processes in post-socialist Chinese cities. In the hope of breathing free city air filled with better living and job opportunities, millions of rural migrants moved to the coastal cities of China, which has gained the country its reputation as the world's factory. Due to the

Figure 3.1: The key differences between the moral order in the traditional rural society and the city

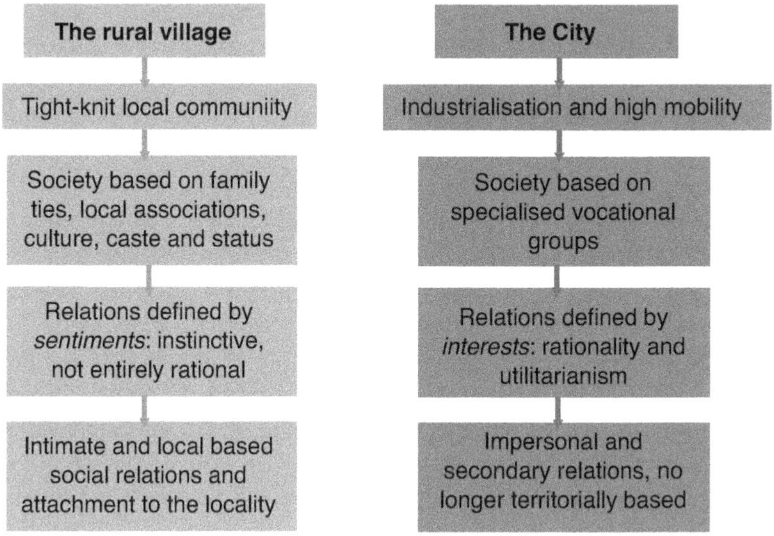

The rural village	The City
Tight-knit local communiity	Industrialisation and high mobility
Society based on family ties, local associations, culture, caste and status	Society based on specialised vocational groups
Relations defined by *sentiments*: instinctive, not entirely rational	Relations defined by *interests*: rationality and utilitarianism
Intimate and local based social relations and attachment to the locality	Impersonal and secondary relations, no longer territorially based

Source: Author's own creation

mass closure of state-owned enterprises, former work-unit employees formed another important source of labor needed for the increasing industrialization and privatization of Chinese cities. Slogans such as "walk out of workplaces and becoming a social man" were very common during this period of transition (Wu, 2008: 1094). Urban residents were no longer confined to their work-unit to provide employment and housing. Those who seek to move away from collective consumption areas monitored by the state now have the opportunity to live in private estates so long as they have the necessary finances. For instance, rural migrants who are not eligible for public housing but wish to retain more of their earnings now have the option to live in low-cost informal settlements such as urban villages, where state control is weak. China's middle class in particular has attained greater social mobility through the privatization of public services and housing provision, which has allowed them to access a wider social network that reaches beyond the confines of the neighborhood. The private housing market has also adapted well to the needs of the emerging middle class for higher security, comfort, and privacy by offering a packaged suburban lifestyle away from state surveillance and characterized by Western architecture (Wu, 2010c). Concurrently however, scholars have also detected the increasing transience and fluidity of urban social relations in China (Forrest and Yip, 2007). Although middle-class residents may prefer anonymity over intense neighborly interactions, the lack of neighborly relations does not seem to reduce their attachment to the locality. Instead, existing studies show that the neighborhood attachment of middle-class homeowners remains strong due to their homeowner status and common interest in defending their property against other stakeholders (Pow, 2007; Yip, 2012; Zhu et al., 2012).

The discussion so far largely follows the trajectory of moral change described by Park (1915). The industrial organization and commodification of services in urban China have given its residents higher mobility, which in turn has led to the decline of primary relations and attachment to the locality. Although Park's description captures an important aspect of social transformation in the Chinese urban society, Park's work has paid less attention to the role of state in affecting the moral order in cities. In China, the state has played a very significant role in affecting the institution of the city which in turn also has had an impact on the mobility of different population groups. In post-reform China, the demise of state control (tight citizenship) could be celebrated as a process of "empowering" to some population groups but other social groups such as rural migrants and the urban poor have benefited considerably less from this process (Wu, 2010a). Given these findings, it is therefore important to ask who has benefited from China's urban transition and how that has transformed their social life. Which population groups have benefited less and what are the implications of urbanization for their moral order?

In order to answer these questions, it is worth consulting the research methods proposed by Park (1915). For Park and the scholars of the Chicago School, the neighborhood is very useful in researching the nature of the city and its residents, as people with similar predispositions tend to congregate in similar areas. For instance, Park (1915: 583) refers to East London as a city consisting of one single class. The main differentiation of the Chinese city is based on the extent of state bureaucratized collective consumption, which is represented through different housing tenures (Li and Wu, 2008). Spatial segregation in Chinese cities is thus based on tenure and neighborhoods with different tenures have also attracted different social groups (Li and Wu, 2008). Neighborhoods therefore could provide important clues to reveal the extent to which urbanism as a lifestyle has penetrated the life of different urban population segments. In the following section we will discuss the various types of neighborhoods that can be found in Chinese cities and how they differ in terms of their varying ways of interpersonal relations and their sentiment toward the neighborhood itself.

Different neighborhoods, different sentiments

The shrinking of work-unit neighborhoods in post-reform China has led to the emergence of two new types of neighborhoods. One is the informal development of urban villages to accommodate rural migrants while the other is the formal development of commodity housing estates to accommodate the "new middle class." In addition, Chinese cities still retain a considerable share of work-unit compounds and traditional neighborhoods. These neighborhood types do not only differ from each other in terms of their architectural design and building density but more importantly in terms of their residential composition. It is important to note however, that the description of neighborhood types here does not apply equally to all Chinese cities since most evidence stems from major cities such as Shanghai, Beijing, and Guangzhou. The ratio of such neighborhoods also varies considerably across cities whereby cities such as Guangzhou and Shenzhen may have higher shares of urban villages than for instance Shanghai or Beijing (Wu et al., 2013).

Work-unit neighborhoods

These were introduced in the 1950s and represented the main form of housing production of the socialist city until the transition to a market economy in the 1980s (Li et al., 2012). These compounds incorporated workplace and residential life, as well as social infrastructure such as schools, medical care facilities, and markets (Zhu et al., 2012). Ma (2002) described such neighborhoods as rich in neighborly interactions and highly socially cohesive. To date, the governance in such settlements is still strongly characterized by state control and residential committees continue to play an active role in organizing and managing such neighborhoods. Work-unit compounds are still inhabited by residents working for the state or state-owned enterprises and increasingly also by retired work-unit employees. Since most residents are affiliated through their shared employer, they also have stronger social bonds with each other both as neighbors and as co-workers. Since residents are required to be work-unit members to live in these settlements, the residential composition remains fairly stable although there are also instances where more affluent residents have managed to purchase a private home and subsequently rented out their work-unit housing. It is therefore unsurprising that many residents are engaged in neighborly interactions and the trust among residents is also strong (Forrest and Yip, 2007; Wang et al., 2017a). Moreover, residents are very attached to the neighborhood, and the presence of a well-organized and active residential committee ensures that newly arrived tenants such as rural migrants can also be included in some of the neighborhood's social activities.

Traditional neighborhoods

These include old neighborhoods that were built prior to the communist government and are characterized by one- or two-story buildings, usually with shared kitchen and toilet facilities. The most prominent examples of such neighborhoods are Beijing's *hutong* or Shanghai's *nongtang*. During the socialist era, these neighborhoods were taken over by the state and distributed to work-units as a source of housing for its employees (Gaubatz, 1999). Due to the old age of the buildings and the state's lack of finance to maintain such buildings, many of these neighborhoods fell into disrepair. Following the emergence of commodity neighborhoods, most of its more affluent residents have moved out. The residential turnover of traditional neighborhoods is therefore very high and, especially, neighborhoods located in the inner city have experienced the influx of many rural migrants (Wang et al., 2017c). Currently most traditional neighborhoods tend to be inhabited by low-income residents. Overcrowding is also a major issue in such neighborhoods as two or more generations of a family would share the property. Traditional neighborhoods are governed by residential committees, which are the de facto state at the grassroots level. However, compared to work-unit neighborhoods which have the backing of the respective work-units, resources of residential committees in traditional neighborhoods are much more lacking and residents often need to rely on themselves, such as repairing shared communal spaces. Many of these neighborhoods tend to be located in the inner city and therefore also face demolition and redevelopment, which have important implications for residents' community sentiments and feelings toward the neighborhood. Long-term native residents feel a great sense of belonging and attachment to such areas and also frequently interact with neighbors (Forrest and Yip, 2007). Yet long-term residents do not necessarily wish to stay in the locality, stating poor housing quality and the influx of migrants as major reasons (Wu, 2012; Wang et al., 2017c). For the migrant residents who are newcomers to these traditional neighborhoods, their attachment to the locality is weak. Nevertheless they are very happy to remain in the neighborhood due to proximity to the public transport and the comparatively cheaper price (Wu, 2012). Neighborly interactions in traditional neighborhoods are often out of pragmatic necessity for migrant residents while native residents prefer to engage only with fellow locals

(Wang et al., 2016). The many shared facilities in such neighborhoods would serve both as a chance for encounter and neighborly interaction but potentially also as a source of conflict over its usage.

Private commodity estates

These were primarily developed following the housing reforms of the state, which essentially transferred the responsibility of housing production from the public sector to the market. Commodity estates now make up the primary housing source for urban residents as statistics show that in 2005 over 50% of Chinese urban households lived in commodity housing while less than 40% lived in work-unit compounds (Zhu et al., 2012). Commodity estates have proliferated in the suburban parts of cities (Shen and Wu, 2013) and inner-city regeneration sites (Wu and He, 2005) and distinguish themselves through their Western architecture style as well as privatized services such as green space provision (Xiao et al., 2016). Commodity housing residents are often of better socioeconomic status and are closest to what could be described as an urbanite in terms of their level of professionalization and their tendency to withdraw from local interactions (Li et al., 2012). Their preference for privacy and comfort also reflects their wish to lead a more urban and metropolitan lifestyle. However, unlike Park's prediction of demise in local attachment, residents in commodity neighborhoods feel very attached to their local area although not because of their relations with fellow neighbors. Instead, homeownership and pride to be living in a private condominium are the primary sources of neighborhood attachment (Pow and Kong, 2007; Zhu et al., 2012).

However, it is also important to note that not all residents living in private estates necessarily belong to the middle class. Another growing sub-category of privatized homes is relocation estates (*dongqian anzhi fang*), which are built to accommodate former residents of redeveloped areas. These neighborhoods are often situated in less favorable locations compared to the previous homes of the relocated residents but have considerably better housing quality and more living space although still below the quality of purchased commodity estates. Residents own the property and have to pay a service charge. With regards to neighborhood governance, relocation estates are governed by residential associations rather than *juweihui* (residential committees). However, residents tend to have a lower socioeconomic status and are also more engaged with their neighbors (Wang et al., 2017a), indicating that the urban lifestyle has less influence on them.

Informal settlements

These primarily consist of urban villages and have attracted by far the most attention from researchers (Song et al., 2008; Chung, 2010; Li and Wu, 2013; Wu et al., 2013). Given the large amount of literature on urban villages, we will not describe the development process of urban villages and instead elaborate on its residential composition and the interpersonal relationships of its residents. Urban villages can be considered the Chinese version of what Park refers to as foreign immigrant colonies and resemble them in terms of the high presence of rural migrants but also their difficulty to "assimilate" into the host society (Park, 1915: 597). Figures show that migrant residents can account for up to 80% of the urban village population in large cities including Shanghai, Guangzhou, and Shenzhen (Chung, 2010: 20; Wang et al., 2017b). Indigenous villagers who hold a local rural *hukou* (household registration) and are the landlords of urban villages make up the other major residential group. However, the relationship between migrants and indigenous villagers remains relatively superficial despite the fact that both groups often share a similar rural background (Chung, 2010; Liu et al., 2012). An often-cited reason for the paradoxical view of indigenous villagers toward migrants is because migrant tenants are considered by rural landlords as a vital source of income but also a source of unruly activities (Chung, 2010). As a consequence, migrants rely on social ties with fellow migrants who mostly live in the same urban village (Liu et al., 2012, 2015). Although migrant residents in urban villages resemble immigrant enclaves in terms of their inability to adopt similar values as the mainstream society, many migrant residents have found their own way to settle into such neighborhoods. Since urban villages are built on rural land, the governance of such neighborhoods is still within the jurisdiction of the village committee, which is unable to cope with the disproportionally large number of migrant tenants. The lack of a strong formal governance structure has therefore enabled migrant residents to create their own migrant community that not only provides support for everyday matters but in some cases also leads to the emergence of a migrant economy. Zhejiang village in Beijing (Ma and Xiang, 1998) and Xiaohubei in Guangzhou (Liu et al., 2015), for instance, both possess a vibrant migrant economy based on garment production and show that migrants can also participate actively in the city by relying on the migrant community.

This brief account of the various neighborhood types in Chinese cities reveals that the urban way of living characterized by anonymity, detachment from the neighborhood and secondary relationship does not apply to all segments of the Chinese urban society. Residents living in well-organized work-unit compounds but also informal urban villages still display a significant level of local interactions and high dependence on the neighborhood community. At the risk of overgeneralizing, in the next section we will use the social life of rural migrants at the local level as evidence to suggest that the traditional moral order continues to exist in the post-socialist Chinese city.

The migrant's way of life in Chinese cities

Studies often cite the marginalized life of rural migrants as evidence for the urban–rural dualism in Chinese urban society (Fan, 2002; Roberts, 2002; Jiang et al., 2012). As mentioned earlier, it was primarily the better-educated residents who were employed in favorable professions in the city that benefited from China's reforms. However, rural migrants have benefited little from the commodification of public services. Although rural migrants form an integral part of Chinese cities by supplying the world's factory with cheap labor, they are otherwise largely isolated from the city. The lack of mobility of migrants is caused by the privatization of public services such as schooling and medical care, which their income cannot cover. The social surplus generated by rural migrants mostly benefits their employers, while the local state does not act on behalf of migrants to negotiate with enterprises for a fairer distribution of such social surpluses. Instead, the local state often uses its regulatory power to improve the city's economic competitiveness by investing in infrastructure such as airports and deepwater ports but also by minimizing resistance stemming from workers' unions (Wu, 2010a). In this sense although rural migrants may share a similar social class and are employed in similar professions, they lack the ability to mobilize as a collective entity in order to negotiate for better conditions. Park's (1915) argument that the division of labor would result in different vocational groups which according to Wirth (1938: 14) would gain wider representation and more influence in the city based on their size is therefore effectively removed by the Chinese state. As a consequence, although migrants lack a sense of attachment and integration to the city (Wu, 2012; Yue et al., 2013). it is because of the fact that they cannot afford to participate in the city life rather than their increased mobility.

So instead of changing into urbanized residents who supposedly only have superficial personal interactions, what kind social life do rural migrants in Chinese cities actually experience and how does that shape their moral order? To shed light onto the localized social network of migrant residents, we draw on a household survey conducted in Shanghai in 2013 with 1,420 households, including both native and migrant residents. We argue that the moral order of rural migrants in Chinese cities does not underlie the trajectory of change articulated by the Chicago School. The survey was carried out in Shanghai at a citywide scale by a group of professional surveyors of which the team leader was a former staff member of the Shanghai Statistical Bureau. We adopted a two-stage random sampling strategy and interviewed 40 randomly selected households in 35 *juweihui* (residential committees). In total the survey yielded 1,420 valid samples including 1,046 Shanghai residents holding an urban *hukou*, 128 residents holding a local rural *hukou* as well as 86 migrants holding an urban *hukou* from another city than Shanghai and 158 migrants holding a rural *hukou*. Despite the lower number of migrant respondents, a comparison of our survey sample and official statistics show that our data is still representative and will not affect the analysis of this study. Further information about how we collected the survey data and the reliability of the survey can be found in Wang et al. (2017a).

Various studies have shown that the social network of migrants in Chinese cities consist largely of ties with fellow migrants (Li and Wu, 2010; Liu et al., 2012; Yue et al., 2013). Liu et al.'s (2012) study of the social network of migrants living in Guangzhou's urban villages show that more than 70% of migrant residents primarily rely on their kin ties. Furthermore, migrant respondents state that more than 60% of their social network consists of ties with migrants coming from the same region or hometown (*laoxiang*). With regard to neighborhood-based social relations, our household survey in Shanghai reveals that a significant share of both local and migrant residents still retain a very localized social network. Table 3.1 presents the frequency of three types of neighbor interactions including visiting each other's homes, helping each other, and greeting each other. It is important to note here that for Table 3.1 we asked respondents about how often they interacted with neighbors belonging to the same group as them. For example, migrants were asked how often they interacted with other migrant neighbors while local Shanghai residents were asked how often they interacted with other local Shanghai neighbors. The reason why we differentiated between interacting with fellow group members and members belonging to another social group is because our previous study has found that *hukou* status has an important impact on the neighborly behaviors of residents (Wang et al., 2016). Our survey results show that more than 53% of rural migrant residents visit their migrant neighbors on an occasional or frequent basis. In comparison, more than 44% of local Shanghai residents state that they sometimes or frequently visit the home of their local neighbors or vice versa. Furthermore, around 67% of migrant respondents report that they sometimes or frequently exchange help with other migrant neighbors while more than 70% of native Shanghai residents do the same with other native neighbors. Finally, nearly 80% of migrant residents exchange greetings with their migrant neighbors while more than 88% of native residents greet their native neighbors.

The evidence presented in Table 3.1 already indicates that a large share of rural migrants and native Shanghai residents are still very engaged with their neighbors. Our results here also confirm existing studies such as Wu and Logan (2016) who also found that a large share of migrants continue to have strong neighborly relations. In addition, our survey shows that migrants do not restrict their neighborly interactions to fellow migrants. Migrants also engage with their local Shanghai neighbors as a means to gain more support to integrate into the city (Wang et al., 2016). Table 3.2 presents the frequency of neighborly interactions between migrant and local residents reported by both native and migrant respondents. More than 28% of rural migrant respondents state that they sometimes or frequently visit the homes of their native neighbors or vice versa. Furthermore, more than half of migrant respondents report that they exchange support with native neighbors on a frequent or occasional basis while only a quarter of native residents exchange help with migrant residents. Finally, nearly 80% of migrant respondents state that they frequently or sometimes exchange greetings with their native neighbors.

Table 3.1: Frequency of in-group neighborly interactions (percentages)

Visiting each other (N = 1,414)	Locals	Rural migrants
Frequently	14.30	9.50
Sometimes	30.04	44.30
Seldom	35.99	25.95
Never	19.67	20.25
Helping each other (N = 1,200)		
Frequently	13.93	13.93
Sometimes	57.54	53.16
Seldom	25.17	29.11
Never	3.36	3.80
Greeting each other (N = 1,200)		
Frequently	43.52	43.04
Sometimes	44.67	36.71
Seldom	10.66	18.35
Never	1.15	1.90

Table 3.2: Frequency of neighborly interactions between migrants and locals (percentages)

Visiting each other (N=1,200)	Locals	Rural migrants
Frequently	1.15	3.80
Sometimes	9.80	24.68
Seldom	32.47	46.20
Never	56.58	25.32
Helping each other (N=1,200)		
Frequently	2.21	6.33
Sometimes	23.63	45.57
Seldom	48.61	39.87
Never	25.55	8.23
Greeting each other (N=1,200)		
Frequently	11.91	29.75
Sometimes	37.66	50.00
Seldom	36.50	17.09
Never	13.93	3.16

Frequent local interactions have also significantly affected the way rural migrants construct their sense of social solidarity and contradict Park's assertion that social solidarity in an urbanized world is based largely on common interest rather than sentiment and habit (1915: 587). A household survey conducted in Shanghai shows that rural migrants have stronger feelings of mutual care, trust, and amity toward those native residents with whom they also frequently exchange support and visits (Wang et al., 2017a). Furthermore, the survey also shows that rural migrants tend to be generally more trustful toward the native population (Wang et al., 2017b) indicating that good neighborly relations with their native neighbors may also affect their general sense of trust and sentiment toward the urban population.

Table 3.3: Social trust between migrants and locals in Shanghai by *hukou* status (percentages)

Hukou status	Most locals (asked of migrants) / migrants (asked of locals) living in Shanghai are trustworthy (1 = highly disagree, 5 = highly agree, in %)				
	1	2	3	4	5
Local urban	0.93	12.09	44.16	34.19	8.63
Rural migrants	0.39	2.13	29.15	56.28	12.06

Source: Adapted from Wang et al., 2017b: 9

Conclusion

Research on the political economic structure of China has matured along with the economy of the country and has arguably reached an important turning point. Social issues related to the integration of rural migrants, the decline of social cohesion, and overall concerns for the harmony of Chinese society require a more nuanced understanding of the consequences of urbanization (Wang et al., 2017c). Park's paper reminds us that simply understanding the political economic structure of the city is not enough and that a more human-centered focus is needed to really understand the nature of the city. The human ecology approach not only reveals insights into the city but also the essential nature or, as Park calls it, the *Gesetzmaessigkeit* of humans (1915: 581). Research on the mundane everyday life of urban residents helps us to unpack the somewhat abstract concepts of state entrepreneurialism or state retreat. It helps us understand how state and market processes can also have an impact on the moral order of societies. This in turn reveals that the commoditization of services and increasing reliance of money can also replace our primary relations with anonymity and utilitarian social behavior. Park's explanation of the industrial organization and increasing commoditization of urban processes resonate with the growing number of middle-class residents in the Chinese urban society. The privatization of housing provision coupled with the closure of most state-owned enterprises meant the demise of the socialist city based on the work-unit system. Urban residents employed in favorable professions thus gained the opportunity to escape from the state-controlled system and to retreat into gated private estates characterized by privacy and the supposed modern way of living. The social solidarity and attachment of residents in commodity estates (Wang et al., 2017a) is strong, but as asserted by Park (1915) and Wirth (1938), such sentiments are mainly built on their common interest. In China's case, residents often share the same interest to defend themselves against the exploitations of private developers and rogue estate management as well as their shared sense homeownership (Pow, 2007; Yip, 2012).

However, despite the relevance of the Chicago School's contribution to the understanding of Chinese cities, it is also important to consider the specific political economic context of China and the necessity to examine the role of the state in shaping and creating alternative pathways of urban life. In this sense, the Chinese case also contributes to the debate with some novel findings. China's government has played an undeniable role in the marginalization of certain urban population segments (Wu, 2010b). The greatly varying levels of neighborly relations and sentiments and different reasons for neighborhood attachment that can be found in China's urban neighborhoods indicate that more marginalized residents and those who are affiliated with the state lead a different life than Park predicted. Work-unit compounds, which are a living legacy of socialist China, continue to exert considerable influence on their residents through their well-organized neighborhood-governance structure. On the other hand, the lack of formal governance has led to the emergence of migrant economies and communities in informal settlements. Our brief analysis of the neighborhood types in China reveals that different segments of the population also experience Chinese urban life in variegated ways. Our study chose to focus on the social life of rural migrants and showed that the state's intervention has effectively excluded rural migrants from harvesting the benefits from participating in the market economy (Wu, 2010a). As a consequence, rural migrants tend to rely on what Park considers as the traditional moral order, which is based on neighborhood and primary relations. Our survey results show that migrants can improve their livelihood and chance of survival by depending on their kinfolk and fellow migrants but also neighborhood relationships with both fellow migrants and members of the host society. Our findings here also conform with existing studies on migrants in urban China (Wang et al., 2016; Wu and Logan, 2016). It is these primary relations and local sentiments that shape their sense of solidarity and trust toward other people (Wang et al., 2017a, 2017b), which is in stark contrast to the shared social solidarity based on common interest between middle-class residents.

The Chinese city therefore does not strictly follow Park's and the Chicago School's observations as the role of the state is much more accentuated in the Chinese case. Active state intervention in the various aspects of city life and its development processes has produced various forms of urban life. This study has tried to illustrate one of the presumably many ways of urban living by focusing on rural migrants. The social life and moral order of migrants was not a voluntary choice but rather a necessary means to respond the actions of the state. Similarly, China's urban poor, consisting of laid-off state workers, may also find themselves in the same situation where they have to rely on their informal social relations to get by in the city. One interesting question for future studies would be to investigate whether those marginalized residents who have managed to integrate into mainstream society would retain their traditional moral order or rather adopt similar preferences and interests as the new middle class. In this study we also consciously attempted to reconcile two seemingly contradictory approaches of research by first explaining how China's specific political economic context has shaped the opportunities of rural migrants, and how this in turn would affect their social life. The outcome has hopefully shown that the structural and the human ecology approach can be combined to produce an even more nuanced understanding of how political economic forces can also shape the nature of urban societies.

References

Chan, K. (2009) "The Chinese *hukou* system at 50," *Eurasian Geography and Economics*, 50(2): 197–221.

Chung, H. (2010) "Building an image of villages-in-the-city: A clarification of China's distinct urban spaces," *International Journal of Urban and Regional Research*, 34(2): 421–37.

Fan, C. C. (2002) "The elite, the natives, and the outsiders: Migration and labor market segmentation in urban China." *Annals of the Association of American Geographers*, 92(1): 103–24.

Forrest, R. and Yip, N.-M. (2007) "Neighbourhood and neighbouring in contemporary Guangzhou," *Journal of Contemporary China*, 16(50): 47–64.

Gaubatz, P. (1999) "China's urban transformation: Patterns and processes of morphological change in Beijing, Shanghai and Guangzhou," *Urban Studies*, 36(9): 1495–521.

Hazelzet, A. and Wissink, B. (2012) "Neighborhoods, social networks, and trust in post-reform China: The case of Guangzhou," *Urban Geography*, 33(2): 204–20.

Jiang, S., Lu, M., and Sato, H. (2012) "Identity, inequality, and happiness: Evidence from urban China," *World Development*, 40(6): 1190–200.

Li, S., Zhu, Y., and Li, L. (2012) "Neighborhood type, gatedness, and residential experiences in Chinese cities: A study of Guangzhou," *Urban Geography*, 33(2): 237–55.

Li, Z. and Wu, F. (2008) "Tenure-based residential segregation in post-reform Chinese cities: A case study of Shanghai," *Transactions of the Institute of British Geographers*, 33(3): 404–19.

Li, Z. and Wu, F. (2013) "Residential satisfaction in China's informal settlements: A case study of Beijing, Shanghai, and Guangzhou," *Urban Geography*, 34(7): 923–49.

Li, Y. and Wu, S. (2010) "Social networks and health among rural–urban migrants in China: a channel or a constraint?," *Health Promotion International*, 25(3): 371–80.

Liu, Y., Li, Z., and Breitung W. (2012) "The social networks of new-generation migrants in China's urbanized villages: A case study of Guangzhou," *Habitat International*, 36(1): 192–200.

Liu, Y., Li, Z., Liu, Y., and Chen, H. (2015) "Growth of rural migrant enclaves in Guangzhou, China: Agency, everyday practice and social mobility," *Urban Studies*, 52(16): 3086–105.

Liu, Z., Wang, Y., and Tao R. (2013) "Social capital and migrant housing experiences in urban China: A structural equation modeling analysis," *Housing Studies*, 28(8): 1155–74.

Ma, L. J. C. (2002) "Urban transformation in China, 1949–2000: A review and research agenda," *Environment and Planning A*, 34(9): 1545–69.

Ma, L. J. C. and Xiang, B. (1998) "Native place, migration and the emergence of peasant enclaves in Beijing," *The China Quarterly*, 155: 546–81.

Park, R. E. (1915) "The city: Suggestions for the investigation of human behavior in the city environment," *American Journal of Sociology*, 20(5): 577–612.

Pow, C. P. (2007) "Securing the 'civilised' enclaves: Gated communities and the moral geographies of exclusion in (post-)socialist Shanghai," *Urban Studies*, 44(8): 1539–58.

Pow, C. P. and Kong, L. (2007) "Marketing the Chinese dream home: Gated communities and representations of the good life in (post-) socialist Shanghai," *Urban Geography*, 28(2): 129–59.

Roberts, K. D. (2002) "Rural migrants in urban China: Willing workers, invisible residents," *Asia Pacific Business Review*, 8(4): 141–58.

Shen, J. and Wu, F. (2013) "Moving to the suburbs: Demand-side driving forces of suburban growth in China," *Environment and Planning A*, 45(8): 1823–44.

Song, Y., Zenou, Y., and Ding, C. (2008) "Let's not throw the baby out with the bath water: The role of urban villages in housing rural migrants in China," *Urban Studies*, 45(2): 313–30.

Wang, Z., Zhang, F., and Wu, F. (2016) "Intergroup neighbouring in urban China: Implications for the social integration of migrants," *Urban Studies*, 53(4): 651–68.

Wang, Z., Zhang, F., and Wu, F. (2017a) "Affective neighbourly relations between migrant and local residents in Shanghai," *Urban Geography*, 38(8): 1182–202.

Wang, Z., Zhang, F., and Wu, F. (2017b) "Social trust between rural migrants and urban locals in China: Exploring the effects of residential diversity and neighbourhood deprivation," *Population, Space and Place*, 23(1): e2008.

Wang, Z., Zhang, F., and Wu, F. (2017c) "Neighbourhood cohesion under the influx of migrants in Shanghai," *Environment and Planning A*, 49(2): 407–25.

Whyte, M. K. and Parish W. L. (1984) *Urban life in contemporary China*, Chicago: University of Chicago Press.

Wirth, L. (1938) "Urbanism as a way of life," *American Journal of Sociology*, 44(1): 1–24.

Wu, F. (2008) "China's great transformation: Neoliberalization as establishing a market society," *Geoforum*, 39(3): 1093–6.

Wu, F. (2010a) "Property rights, citizenship and the making of the new poor in urban China," in F. Wu and C. Webster (eds.) *Marginalization in Urban China*, Basingstoke: Palgrave Macmillan, pp. 72–89.

Wu, F. (2010b) "Retreat from a totalitarian society: China's urbanism in the making," in G. Bridge and S. Watson (eds.) *The new Blackwell companion to the city*, Malden, MA: Wiley-Blackwell, pp. 701–12.

Wu, F. (2010c) "Gated and packaged suburbia: Packaging and branding Chinese suburban residential development," *Cities*, 27(5): 385–96.

Wu, F. (2012) "Neighborhood attachment, social participation, and willingness to stay in China's low-income communities," *Urban Affairs Review*, 48(4): 547–70.

Wu, F. and He, S. (2005) "Changes in traditional urban areas and impacts of urban redevelopment: A case study of three neighbourhoods in Nanjing, China," *Tijdschrift voor economische en sociale geografie*, 96(1): 75–95.

Wu, F. and Logan, J. (2016) "Do rural migrants 'float' in urban China? Neighbouring and neighbourhood sentiment in Beijing," *Urban Studies*, 53(14): 2973–90.

Wu, F., Zhang, F., and Webster, C. (2013) "Informality and the development and demolition of urban villages in the Chinese peri-urban area," *Urban Studies*, 50(10): 1919–34.

Xiao, Y., Li, Z., and Webster, C. (2016) "Estimating the mediating effect of privately-supplied green space on the relationship between urban public green space and property value: Evidence from Shanghai, China," *Land Use Policy*, 54: 439–47.

Yip, N. M. (2012) "Walled without gates: Gated communities in Shanghai," *Urban Geography*, 33(2): 221–36.

Yue, Z., Li, S., Feldman, M. W., and Du, H. (2010) "Floating choices: A generational perspective on intentions of rural–urban migrants in China," *Environment and Planning A*, 42(3): 545–62.

Yue, Z., Li, S., Jin, X., and Feldman, M. W. (2013) "The role of social networks in the integration of Chinese rural–urban migrants: A migrant–resident tie perspective," *Urban Studies*, 50(9): 1704–23.

Zhu, Y., Breitung, W., and Li, S. (2012) "The changing meaning of neighbourhood attachment in Chinese commodity housing estates: Evidence from Guangzhou," *Urban Studies*, 49(11): 2439–57.

4

Learning from Chicago (and LA)?

The Contemporary Relevance of Western Urban Theory for China

Bart Wissink

Introduction

"What on earth is a Central Business District?" I can still clearly remember my confusion when, a long time ago, I was initiated into the basics of urban theory during an Introduction to Social Geography. My point of reference was Amsterdam, a Dutch city that doesn't really have a "business district," let alone at its center, where historic canals circle the most expensive residential real estate. It was an early reminder that cities can be radically different, and that the concepts through which we describe and understand them might not be universally applicable. Of course, since the early 2000s this has become something of a commonplace. On the back of a general critique of Western thought by postcolonial scholars, it is now well recognized that the inspiration for urban theory has mainly come from European and American cities, and that this translates into biases that at best prompt wrong interpretations, and at worst help reproduce existing forms of domination (for example, Robinson, 2006; McFarlane, 2011; Roy and Ong, 2011; Peck, 2015). As globalization has incited dramatic urban development beyond the traditional economic core of the "former West," researchers are encouraged to draw cities around the world into wider theoretical conversations, thus helping to produce "new geographies of theory" (Roy, 2009; Robinson, 2016).

The relevance of these observations for urban China cannot be overstated. It is well documented how global economic restructuring coincided with a "great urban transformation" (Hsing, 2010) by which Chinese cities have grown dramatically while their internal structure radically changed (Douglass et al., 2012. for example). In response, an often Western-trained group of mainly Chinese scholars has produced an impressive urban China literature. But while this literature borrows many concepts from the Western urban studies literature, comparisons with cities elsewhere are short-circuited with the argument that Chinese cities are unique. The limited contribution to "trans-China" conversations is mirrored in an underrepresentation of urban China scholars in the comparative urbanism discussion.

Against this background, this chapter strives to reach two related aims. First, it seeks to reflect on the relevance of Western urban theory for China. Taking inspiration from modes of theorizing that focus on the localization of global developments in specific cities, it questions the strong tendency toward universalism in urban theory; perhaps we should complement urban theory that is "true" everywhere with approaches that seek to describe and explain differences. Second, by reflecting on the characteristics of the urban China literature, this chapter aims to inspire a conversation of differences and similarities between Chinese urbanism and urbanism elsewhere, and to stimulate a more explicit engagement with the comparative urbanism literature. These aims translate into the following research questions:

- How should we understand the relevance of the Western urban theory for urban China research?
- And how can we stimulate a larger involvement of urban China research in the comparative urbanism literature?

I answer these questions in the following five sections. Using Park's human ecology approach and the LA School of urbanism as examples, I first illustrate that Western urban theory is universalist, implicitly assuming that cities around the world function according to singular urban logics and follow similar developmental trajectories. Next, I take inspiration from modes of theorizing that focus on the localization of global developments in specific cities to reflect on ways of theorizing differences. From this perspective I then turn to the urban China literature, suggesting that this literature employs Western concepts easily, but that it shies away from explicit comparisons with urbanisms elsewhere in view of China's "exceptionalism." I then illustrate this situation through the literature on "gated communities" in China. In the conclusion I argue that an explicit comparative approach would benefit both urban China research and the urban studies literature in general.

Chicago and LA as prototypes of universal transformations

The question of whether research should produce universal knowledge that is true for every city, or whether it should focus on understanding the uniqueness of place is a long-standing debate within urban studies; it for instance formed the core of the infamous debate between geographers Schaefer (1953) and Hartshorne (1955). However, when looking at the well-documented history of American urban theory (for example, Judd and Simpson, 2011), it is clear that it is the "universalist" attitude that has especially informed scholarship. Two schools of thought are indicative of this: the human ecology approach of the Chicago School and the LA School of urbanism. Robert Park's (1915) seminal essay "The city" is the foundation of the first of these. Responding to the dramatic transformation of early 20th-century Chicago under the influence of industrialization, migration, and technological innovation, Park criticized approaches of the time that merely focused on the artifacts that make up the city. Instead, he stressed that these artifacts have their basis in human nature: "As the whole the city is a growth. It is the undesigned product of the labors of successive generations of men" (Park, 1915: 578). With Ernest Burgess, Louis Wirth, Roderick McKenzie, and others, Park laid the groundwork for the application of biological metaphors to urbanization. The resulting human ecology approach would come to define urban research for decades.

The contributors to the human ecology approach certainly had their differences. Abu-Lughod (2011: 23), for instance, argues that Burgess had a distinct focus on the formation of urban patterns, which resulted in his well-known concentric circle model of urbanization. However, considerable similarities nonetheless justified the denomination of a Chicago "school." One of these is the aforementioned use of biological metaphors and the related functionalist persuasion that stressed structure over agency. A general concern that urbanization would result in a breakdown of social norms and increase in vice was another. And the assumption that developments observed in Chicago were representative for urban developments in general was a third.

Park presented Chicago as his laboratory of choice to study urbanization, but he assumed that the city's development reflects "human behavior and human nature generally" and that similar processes are taking place in "every city" (1915: 582). After all, his paper is not called "The city" for nothing. Elsewhere, when reflecting on a range of studies into "natural areas" in Chicago, Park was more explicit: "There is implicit in all these studies the notion that the city is a thing with a characteristic organization and a typical life history, and that individual cities are enough alike so that what one learns about one city may, within limits, be assumed to be true of others" (Park, 1929: 8). This universalist conviction was echoed on the back cover of Zorbaugh's (1929) *The Gold Coast and the slum*, where Christian Century argued that "[t]his is a book about Chicago. It is also, and for that very reason, a book about every other American city." Meanwhile, Jenny Robinson (2006: 43) suggests that Wirth (1938) framed his seminal *Urbanism as a way of life* "in a very general way—as if to explain cities everywhere." While researchers from the Chicago School thus studied Chicago, they had the ambition to talk about urbanism in general. Their theories were not only about Chicago; they presented Chicago as a prototype for a city of a certain period: the "modern" industrial city. Prioritizing variation over time over differences over space, their ambition was to present a universal theory about "the city" *tout court*.

We know that it took until the latter parts of the 20th century before the ecological view lost its dominance within urban studies. The approach was seriously discredited by the 1970s Marxist critique (Harvey, 1973; Castells, 1977, for example), but the definitive downfall came in the course of the 1980s, when academics in Los Angeles started to stress that cities had entered another *time*. At the core of this criticism was a group of loosely tied scholars including Soja, Davis, Scott, Storper, and Dear who argued that postindustrial capitalism, migration, and technological innovations had transformed concentrated concentric cities into endless, chaotic, fragmented, and uneven landscapes, that supported a radical, racial, and economic inequality. As spatial fragmentation went hand in hand with political fragmentation, any power base for adequate action was dissolved as well, and nothing much to be optimistic about remained. Chicago might have been the epitome of the "modern" industrial city, but Los Angeles was the prototype of a newly emerging bleak "postmodern" urbanism.

In the LA School we again find a diverse group of scholars that take reference from one city, but present it as a future for all. According to Jencks (1993: 7), "Los Angeles, like all cities, is unique, but in one way it may typify the world city of the future: there are only minorities." Dear and Flusty (2002: 14) stress that "[t]he luxury compound atop a matrix of impoverished misery, the self-contained secure community, and the fortified home can be found first in places such as Manila and São Paolo." Sorkin (1992: xv) asserts that the "sites discussed are representative; they do not simply typify the course of American urbanism but are likely to be models for urban development throughout the world." And Soja (1989: 191) wonders "[w]hat better place can there be to illustrate and synthesize the dynamics of capitalist spatialization? ... Being more inventive, one might call the sprawling urban region ... a *prototopos*, a paradigmatic place." Storper and Scott (2016: 1125) thus conclude recently "the LA School called attention at an early stage to a developmental pathway that many other cities all over the world have subsequently followed, and from this perspective it was most certainly exemplary."

The theory of the LA School was presented in direct and explicit opposition to the Chicago School. But notwithstanding this confrontational rhetoric, in style there are considerable similarities: both have a strong focus on urban form, both have a "noir" view on the consequences of urbanization (Pow, 2015), and while both start to write from one city, they each claim to generate knowledge about urbanism generally. The main difference is that they write about cities in different *periods* and that Chicago and Los Angeles are presented as the metaphor for the modern and postmodern city respectively. The explanatory models of the Chicago and LA Schools thus prioritize variations in time over spatial differences. They both start to write from one city, but they aim to produce universally applicable "theories from nowhere" (Shapin, 1998).

Of course, many scholars from the "former West" do not speak from one city alone. But theories on diverse topics like neoliberal urbanism, political economy, and agglomeration effects do have in common that they want to speak for urbanism in general as well (Leitner and Sheppard, 2016). Variations between cities are downplayed as just that: variations on a general rule, or "epiphenomena" in Marxist terminology. The pervasiveness of that view was highlighted in a recent discussion on difference and variation between cities, when Scott and Storper (2015: 12) stressed "there *are* systematic regularities in urban life that are susceptible to high levels of theoretical generalization" (see also Peck, 2015; Robinson and Roy, 2016; Storper and Scott, 2016). Urban theory, so they claim, has to focus on these regularities. From this universalist perspective, urban China research obviously could learn from Western urban studies. After all, it would locate Chinese urbanism on a timeline: as an instantiation of the postmodern urbanism of Los Angeles, or as an example of an urbanism that is "not yet" fully postmodern. Learning would then mean understanding what will come, or where Chinese cities will go. Or maybe, China would represent a new period with a new urbanism, for which a Chinese city could be the prototype?

Toward new geographies of theory

Of course, universal "Western" theory can provide inspiration for research into Chinese cities. While there is broad agreement that the human ecology approach is no longer sufficient to describe realities in Chicago, if it ever was (Judd, 2011; Scott and Storper, 2015), this approach could still stimulate research into Chinese cities that experience circumstances that compare remarkably to Chicago and Los Angeles. For example, are not the dramatic immigration of rural migrants combined with rapid industrial development and proletarianization, and the introduction of new technologies in the 1980s and 1990s, similar to the setting of Chicago in the early twentieth century? The Chicago School research can thus help inspire a conception that the city is not a physical artifact, and that there needs to be attention to differences between neighborhoods and to the habits and customs of their inhabitants. This could guide attention to life in "natural areas" to which Forrest's chapter, next in this book, alludes. Segregation research would certainly also be part of such a project.

Similarly, as the section on "gated communities" in China in the latter part of this chapter will show, the dramatic sprawl of Chinese cities since the 1990s and their internal fragmentation displays clear similarities to the urbanism of Los Angeles. LA School research into topics such as gated communities, the privatization of public space, creative clusters, and the consequences of private governance could certainly inform research into Chinese cities as well. But does this mean that the dynamics in Chinese cities are the same as developments in Chicago or Los Angeles? Do theories from the "former West" suffice to explain the developments in China? Are China's urban futures as "noir" as the scholars of American urbanism foresee? Do these theories provide a basis to prevent such forecasted negative outcomes? Are there no alternative ways in China to understand and judge these developments that could be equally informative, and that could inform the interpretation of urbanization elsewhere as well?

These and other questions put the discussion about the possibilities of universal urban theory firmly back on the agenda. Interestingly, there are several other occasions in recent decades when the universalist tendencies of urban theory were criticized as well. One example is the "locality debate" (Massey, 1994), which took place in the UK in response to a certain kind of "essentialist" Marxism (Graham, 1990) that came to dominate geography in the 1970s. According to Doreen Massey (1994: 117), structuralist Marxism makes the study of "the local" or "places" problematic as it locates causality solely in capital accumulation, which operates at "a somehow unlocatable level of 'the global.'" Stressing that the effects of capital accumulation on different cities differs, she arguing that "place matters" (Massey, 1984), and that theory should also focus on the sources of those differences, which often operate on other, more local, geographical scales. In some quarters, this attention to differences between places was fiercely contested; for instance by Neil Smith (1987) who criticized the attention to place for its empiricism. In response, Massey (1994: 129) stressed that Smith confused the locality with the concrete (an argument that, as we will, see Ananya Roy repeats): "Those who conflate the local with the concrete, therefore, are confusing geographical scale with processes of abstraction in thought" (Massey, 1994: 129). Explanations of developments in localities still necessitate theory, but a universal theory that is true everywhere is now complemented with a theory that explains differences.

Second, universalism has been criticized within American urban theory itself as well (Judd, 2011). In response to the universalism of the LA School, Halle (2003), for instance, argues that its assumptions do not make sense when studying New York. Studying the effects of globalization on *New York, Chicago, Los Angeles*, Janet Abu-Lughod concludes that it does not result in uniform cities, as there are "preexisting legacies of the built environment and the traditions of governance" (1999: 7). Judd (2011) shows that a similar theoretical approach to difference can be found in the writings of a new group of scholars from Chicago who argue "that politics, as an expression of human agency, is the primary shaper of the spatial and social dynamics of cities and metropolitan regions. The implication is that there is likely to be no singular urban form, but many, each reflecting the influence of local political culture and institutional dynamics" (Judd, 2011: 4). Again this research zeroes in on factors at the subnational scale, and theory is used to explain differences between cities by focusing on one factor in particular: the institutional configuration of the political system.

Third, criticism of the universal pretensions of "Western" urban theory has recently been especially pronounced within the postcolonial urban literature. This literature builds on the work of theorists like Edward Saïd, Achille Mbembe, and Dipesh Chakrabarty, who show that social theory in general and its concepts and categorizations are thoroughly Western. In Chakrabarty's (2000) well-known argument, it is therefore crucial to "provincialize Europe." This has resulted in projects that investigate global modernities (Featherstone et al., 1995), multiple modernities (Eisenstadt, 2000), or alternative modernities (Gaonkar, 2001) as alternatives to the idea that there is one modernity that originated in the "former West," and see modernity as a constellation with many sources, centers, and flows (Appadurai, 1996).

Robinson (2003, 2006), Roy (2009, 2016), and others have taken up these ideas in urban theory. Arguing that "[m]uch of the theoretical work on city-regions is firmly located in the urban experience of North America and Western Europe" (Roy, 2009: 820; also see Kanai et al., 2018), they stress that the concepts and categories on which urban theory is built reflect the urban realities in the "former West." For Robinson (2011: 10) this "restricts the variables or topics to be considered to those relevant to the privileged locations of theory production. Perhaps, other places would make one think of exploring different issues?" Chen (2010: 245) agrees that "[u]niversalist arrogance serves only to keep new possibilities from emerging, since it allows only one set of accepted analytic language to enter the dialogue and is itself a product of a specific set of historical experiences." In order to rectify this situation, postcolonial urban scholars suggest dislocating the center of urban theory with comparative research in cities beyond the "former West" (Robinson, 2011). This should not just show that cities in the global South and East are different, but take these differences seriously and "produce a new set of concepts in the crucible of a new repertoire of cities" (Roy, 2009: 820).

In view of the fierce response to earlier critiques of the universalist pretensions of urban theory it is probably not surprising that postcolonial urban theory has received scathing criticism. According to Peck (2015: 160) "in practice, the challenge of more worldly, comparative theorization has been unevenly met, often more through difference-finding and deconstructive manoeuvres than through projects of urban-theoretical renewal and reconstruction." Storper and Scott (2016: 1114) criticize "postcolonial urban theory for its particularism and its insistence on the provincialization of knowledge." Instead they propose "a foundational concept of urbanization and urban form as a way of identifying a common language for urban research." Open to broadening the locations of research beyond the "former West," the authors of both texts at the same time argue that in the end this should still result in universal theory that is applicable everywhere.

Roy (2016) has explicitly responded to these criticisms. Noting that Storper and Scott (2016) interpret differences between cities as variations of the same basic form, she argues that they confuse globalization with universalization: "While urbanization may indeed take a global form, while capitalism is undeniably global, the universality of such processes is another matter" (Roy, 2016: 203). Echoing Massey's (1994) criticism of the conflation of the "local" with the "concrete," she stresses that urbanization might be a global phenomenon, but that urban transformation should not be understood as the "universalization of a singular and basic urban form" (Roy, 2016: 204). After all, while some determinants of urbanization might be part of global systems, at the same time their specific localization comes about in interaction with a host of factors operating at other geographical scales. Urban research should theorize the many different urban forms that result from this process, and should be open to a variety of vocabularies to express this development. From this view learning is not the application of context-free knowledge onto specific cities; instead from a relational understanding, learning entails shifts in perception "from one way of seeing a problem, issue, relation or place, to another" (McFarlane, 2011: 15). McFarlane continues to note that learning thus "emerges through practical engagement in the world" (2011: 15); for instance while researching urban China.

Urban China as a new geography of theory

In view of these arguments for the decentering of Western urban theory, it becomes interesting to see how urban China scholars position themselves vis-à-vis the international urban studies literature and among other new geographies of theory. Those questions necessitate a closer look at the development of the field of urban China research. Since the late 1990s, this development has been as explosive as Chinese urbanization itself (Ren and Luger, 2015). New academic and institutional arrangements and extensive funding have supported a dramatic growth of Chinese urban scholars, who often had at least part of their training at a Western university. While many of these scholars found employment at universities in the "former West" or in former colonies like Singapore or Hong Kong, new joint ventures like the Xi'an Jiaotong-Liverpool University or branch universities like NYU Shanghai added to the opportunities to work in an "international" setting. This translated into a rapidly growing number of publications on China in urban studies journals, as well as the establishment of various professional organizations such as the China Planning Research Group. Meanwhile, there are now regular urban China conferences, and various urban studies conferences like the American Association of Geographers (AAG) have dedicated urban China sessions. Unfortunately, however, as Ren and Luger (2015: 150) argue, the isolation of urban China researchers in area-specific meetings "is reminiscent of a new form of parochialism."

In view of the emerging area-studies orientation, it is probably not surprising that the vast majority of the work on urban China has an exclusive focus on Chinese urbanism. Remarkably, various themes that dominated the research agenda in earlier decades actually had international resonance, as is illustrated by He and Qian's (2017: 827) listing of "four well-established themes: (1) globalisation and the making of global cities; (2) land and housing development; (3) urban poverty and socio-spatial inequality; (4) rural migrants and their urban experiences." But with explanatory models that give prime attention to specific Chinese institutions like the land lease system, the *hukou* (household registration) system, and (former) state-owned enterprises, the publications resulting from this research have an exclusive urban China outlook.

Maybe in the coming years, this exclusive focus on China will be traded for a broader perspective? After all, various scholars suggest that the research agenda will have to change considerably. In Chapter 3 in this book, Wu and Zheng for instance, observe that "[r]esearch on the political economic structure of China has matured," stressing that "[s]ocial issues related to the integration of rural migrants, the decline of social cohesion, and overall concerns for the harmony of Chinese society require a more nuanced understanding of the consequences of urbanization." He and Qian (2017: 827) meanwhile see "a transition from a focus on economic development and spatial changes, to diverse social groups and the multifaceted experiences of living in rapidly changing cities," resulting in three new research frontiers: urban fragmentation, enclaves, and public space; consumption, middle-class aestheticization, and urban culture; and the right to the city and urban activism.

Of course, it is hard to generalize about such a broad field, but for this new research agenda, Park's "The city" (1915), which similarly expresses the need for a shift of attention from artifacts to social relations certainly could be an inspiration. After all, the urban China research up till now has been no stranger to the borrowing of concepts of the international urban studies literature, and terms like "segregation," "social cohesion," "activity-space," and, as we will see, "gated communities" have easily found their way into the English-language urban China research papers.

However, despite the easy use of Western concepts, Zhou et al. (2017) observe that "there is a noticeable weak participation among Chinese geographers" in the comparative urbanism literature. This is confirmed by the observation that comparisons are actually actively evaded with reference to the uniqueness of China, because, as Pow (2012: 61) has argued, "exceptional countries can neither draw lessons from other countries nor can other countries draw lessons from them."

Initially, this seems rather strange. After all, "borrowed" terms seem to provide a great basis for comparative research. But on further reflection, it suggests that contradictions both between international urban studies and urban China studies, and within urban China studies itself, can help to explain the combined limited participation to the comparative urbanism discussion and easy use of "borrowed" concepts. Contradictions with the international urban studies literature dominated by the hegemonic discourse from the "former West" mainly relate to understandable postcolonial sensitivities, generating a reluctance to participate in explicit comparisons. Chinese intellectual Wang thus stresses in a discussion on the applicability of the term "new left" to his thinking that "[o]ur historical context is Chinese, not Western, and it is doubtful whether a category imported so explicitly from the West could be helpful in today's China" (2005: 62). Against the background of a history of orientalism, which, according to Saïd (1978: 7) "puts the westerner in a whole series of possible relationships with the Orient without ever losing him the relative upper hand," the exceptionalism argument creates a relatively free space for urban China scholars to develop their concepts and categories. In that sense, the critique of Chinese exceptionalism is as much a critique of Western urban studies as it is a critique of urban China research, and an urban studies that aims to cross the boundaries between China and elsewhere need efforts from China scholars as well as from scholars elsewhere.

On top of this, however, there are also contradictions within urban China research itself that prevent a more active contribution to the comparative urbanism discussion. Partly, these can be found in the participation in area-specific conferences and sessions, which contributes to the risk of "isolating Asian research into its own canon of parochial urban theory" (Ren and Luger, 2015: 145). Partly, as Logan and Fainstein (2008) stress, these relate to the fact that available theoretical frameworks within urban China research are inadequate for interpret comparative work (see also Ren and Luger, 2015). Partly, the a-critical use of Western concepts also might relate to the Western training of many scholars. But partly, the combined a-critical use of Western concepts and lack of comparative research also relates to the tensions under which scholars on urban China operate. For, as one of the participants to the workshop that resulted in this book explained, Chinese scholars need international publications for their career advancement, which is most easily achieved by using existing conceptual frameworks; but at the same time, they often also depend on state funding. As Zhu et al. (2014) explain, in view of sensitivities, state definitions dominate the Chinese urban research agenda, which in short means that there is little support for conceptual work. As a result of these contradictions, in the end there is limited space for a productive debate about the specific global urbanism of Chinese cities, nor for contributions to the comparative urbanism literature that build on this.

China's "gated communities": An example

The literature on "gated communities" in China can help to illustrate the unproductive dynamic resulting from these contradictions within the urban China research setting and within a universalist urban studies dominated by a Euro-American perspective. Attention to "gated communities" is firmly rooted in North American urban literature. While the Chicago School presented segregation as a prime topic for urban research, the LA School radicalized this by presenting inequality-driven urban fragmentation as a core characteristic of the sprawling centerless postmodern city. Or, as Judd (2011: 8) summarizes the argument: "What does Los Angeles reveal about the future? That the stark inequalities of the Third World are being exported, and that these are written on urban landscapes in a patchwork of prosperity and despair." Developing a range of new concepts like "privatopia" and "carceral archipelagos," LA School researchers have painted an especially grim picture of this "ecology of evil" (Davis, 1990: 3) to which politics can have no answer. Presenting Los Angeles as a "paradigmatic place," it is this rather dystopian view of the future, which has become the mold for interpreting urbanization worldwide (Hogan et al., 2012; Pow, 2015).

Remarkably, scholars like Dear and Flusty (2002) acknowledged that gating traveled from cities in the global South to the United States. However, the interpretation of this development that came to structure the interpretation of the causes and effects of gated communities worldwide, was firmly rooted in the urban realities of the "former West." Admittedly, some researchers have called for a decentering of this Euro-American discourse. While painting a bleak picture of the consequences of "splintering urbanism," Graham and Marvin (2001: 417) for instance stress the need "to undertake detailed and comparative empirical investigations into the ways in which physical and socio-technical shifts towards splintering urbanism, and unbundled networked infrastructures, are being politically and socially constructed in profoundly different political, cultural, economic and historical contexts." Responding to such calls, Sabatini and Salcedo (2011) argue that gated communities in Latin American cities have reduced large-scale patterns of segregation; Huang and Low (2008) argue that gating is not always exclusionary; and Hendrikx and Wissink (2017) suggest that government involvement might mediate the consequences of "gated communities" in urban China. However, in addition to these rare examples there has been a striking lack of multi-sited comparative work into "gated communities." Instead, researchers observe a "global spread of gated communities" (Webster et al., 2002) and interpret the consequences through the grim picture painted by the LA scholars.

In this constellation it has obviously been hard not to draw comparisons between Los Angeles' sprawling, fractured patchwork landscape and the enclave structure of China's rapidly expanding cities (Douglass et al., 2012; He, 2013). After all, walled and gated commodity housing estates or *xiaoqu* (小区; literally "small district") are an essential element of China's new urban landscapes (see also Wissink, 2019). The model for these estates was developed with support of the Ministry of Construction in the late 1980s, through trials in Wuxi, Jinan, and Tianjin with the design of communal spaces of compounds that could result in social cohesion (*ningjuli*), neighborliness (*linliguanxi*), and feelings of security and belonging (Bray, 2006). But while such terms have clear affinities with concerns regarding urban development in European and North American cities, they should be understood in the very different context of dramatic urbanization, Chinese sociality, and the ambition of the Chinese state to control social development. Eventually, successful trials were translated into national planning codes that require walls and gates as well as basic service provision for estate inhabitants and—in case services are not available—also for the wider neighborhood (Hendrikx and Wissink, 2017). As a consequence the majority of China's urban population now lives in gated commodity housing estates; something that in the meantime has resulted in a critical consideration by the Chinese government of the potential negative effects of gating for social harmony as well.

Against the background of the international literature on "gated communities" it is not surprising that China's commodity housing estates receive considerable scholarly attention (for example, Wu and Webber, 2004; Wu, 2005, 2010; Bray, 2006; Huang, 2006; Webster et al., 2006; Huang and Low, 2008; Xu, 2008; Pow, 2009; Xu and Yang, 2009). It is also not surprising that this literature generally interprets China's commodity housing estates as "gated communities," applying the "gated communities" literature to urban China. Webster et al. (2006), for instance, use club good theory to explain the emergence of commodity housing estates in China.

However, this interpretation of commodity housing estates as "gated communities" is also criticized (see, for example, Huang and Low, 2008; Pow, 2015). Many researchers point out that these estates differ from "gated communities" elsewhere. Employing exceptionalist arguments, they criticize explanations of Chinese commodity housing estates through the international literature. Critics also specify the nature of differences between commodity housing estates in China and "gated communities," for instance stressing that Chinese estates are larger, that gates are more permeable, that densities are higher, or that they contain mixed housing types. However, strikingly there is no systematic comparison with gated estates elsewhere, nor is there an attempt to explain both similarities and differences (for exceptions, see Low, 2005; Huang and Low, 2008). Meanwhile, explanations are rather parochial, stressing "typically Chinese" causes like collectivism (Huang, 2006) or characteristics of the local housing market and middle-class place-making (Pow, 2009). Meanwhile, explanations of differences with other housing enclaves in China like former work-unit estates or urbanized villages mainly focus on institutional explanations, while socio-spatial differences are under-researched.

With these characteristics, the literature on Chinese commodity housing estates seems remarkably in line with urban China research in general. The concepts and categories of the international urban studies literature are applied to the urban realities of Chinese cities with relative ease. However, with reference to the uniqueness of China's urban structure and the urban enclaves that are its building blocks, the inadequacy of those same concepts for the realities of urban China is highlighted at the same time. And while the literature makes general references to potential differences between commodity housing estates in China and "gated communities" in a mostly unspecified "elsewhere," precise research into differences and similarities is virtually nonexistent: notwithstanding some exceptions (Huang and Low, 2008, for example), there is hardly any serious comparative work between China's estates and gated developments elsewhere. As variations of the same basic type of the "gated community," precise research apparently is not warranted for the international urban studies literature, and the urban China researchers shy away from it for reasons discussed previously.

The limited trans-China discussion is regrettable for at least two reasons. On the one hand, by declining to engage explicitly with dominant interpretations of urban development from the "former West," urban China research does not contribute to a decentering of universal theories traveling the world. Would it not be important for the international urban studies literature to understand how the model of the "gated community" has been localized in Chinese and other cities; how this relates to specific socio-spatial practices; and how the consequences of these processes of localization differ? A comparative study of "gated communities" around the world that included China's commodity housing estates certainly would benefit the international urban studies literature (Wissink, 2019).

However, a comparative approach to China's commodity housing estates would not benefit international urban studies alone. A provincialization of the international literature creates space for a reflection on urban development from China, accommodating interpretations of urbanisms in categories and concepts that do not come from the "former West." Such an approach could, for instance, start from reflections on different perspectives on walls (Breitung, 2012), on the importance of borderlands (Iossifova, 2015), or on collective urbanism (Huang, 2008). It would not respond to theories from the "former West"; instead it could itself be a starting point for comparative work in other cities "from elsewhere," helping to prevent essentialist interpretations. Giving content and perspective to the claim of uniqueness, certainly, such an approach would benefit research into urban China itself as well.

Conclusion: Beyond Chinese exceptionalism

How should we understand the relevance of the Western urban theory for urban China research? And how can we stimulate a larger involvement of urban China research in the comparative urbanism literature? In response to these questions, this chapter resulted in a strong qualification to the suggestion that Western urban theory provides universal knowledge that is true for every city, and that learning means applying this "true" knowledge to cities elsewhere. Park (1929: 8) suggested that "within limits," knowledge from one city might be assumed to be true for other cities as well. Perhaps those limits have not received sufficient attention? In line with that suggestion, and building on the work of others, this chapter has argued that the evolution of specific cities results from various determinants, each operating with their own geographical reach. As some of these determinants do not have a global range, urban theory has to have the capacity to theorize differences as well. On the one hand, it should be capable of showing how specific models that travel the world are localized and molded to fit in specific cities; and on the other hand it should be open to multiple vocabularies to study and problematize that process. In this view, learning is engaging with the world and thereby opening new perspectives. Such a process would highly benefit from comparative research that should certainly also including urban China. The responsibility for such a multi-sited approach lies with both international urban studies scholars who should be more sensitive and open to other perspectives, and with urban China scholars who should explicitly engage in comparative urban research. Unfortunately, the polarized discussions about comparative urbanism, as well as the limiting institutional setting for urban China research, suggest that it might be difficult to meet those requirements.

References

Abu-Lughod, J. (1999) *New York, Chicago, Los Angeles: America's global cities*, Minneapolis: University of Minnesota Press.

Abu-Lughod, J. (2011) "Grounded theory: Not abstracted words but tools of analysis," in D. R. Judd and D. Simpson (eds.) *The city, revisited: Urban theory from Chicago, Los Angeles, and New York*, Minneapolis: University of Minnesota Press, pp. 21–50.

Appadurai, A. (1996) *Modernity at large: Cultural dimensions in globalization*, Minneapolis: University of Minnesota Press.

Bray, D. (2006) "Garden estates and social harmony: A study into the relationship between residential planning and urban governance in contemporary China," paper presented at the 1st International Conference of China Development and City Planning and the 3rd China Planning Network Annual Conference, June 14–16, Beijing.

Breitung, W. (2012) "Enclave urbanism in China: attitudes towards gated communities in Guangzhou," *Urban Geography*, 33(2): 278–94.

Castells, M. (1977) *The urban question*, Cambridge, MA: MIT Press.

Chakrabarty, D. (2000) *Provincializing Europe: Postcolonial thought and historical difference*, Princeton, NJ: Princeton University Press.

Chen, K.-H. (2010) *Asia as method: Towards deimperialization*, Durham, NC: Duke University Press.

Davis, M. (1990) *City of quartz: Excavating the future of Los Angeles*, New York: Verso.

Dear, M. J. and Flusty, S. (2002) "The resistible rise of the L.A. School," in M. J. Dear (ed.) *From Chicago to L.A.: Making sense of urban theory*, Thousand Oaks, CA: Sage, pp. 3–16.

Douglass, M., Wissink, B., and Van Kempen, R. (2012) "Enclave urbanism in China: Consequences and interpretations," *Urban Geography*, 33(2): 167–82.

Eisenstadt, S. N. (2000) "Multiple modernities," *Daedalus*, 129(1): 1–29.

Featherstone, M., Lash, S., and Robertson, R. (eds.) (1995) *Global modernities*, London: Sage.

Gaonkar, D. P. (ed.) (2001) *Alternative modernities*, Durham, NC: Duke University Press.

Graham, J. (1990) "Theory and essentialism in Marxist geography," *Antipode*, 22(1): 53–66.

Graham, S. and Marvin, S. (2001) *Splintering urbanism: Networked infrastructure, technological mobilities and the urban condition*, London: Routledge.

Halle, D. (ed.) (2003) *New York and Los Angeles: Politics, society, and culture, a comparative view*, Chicago: University of Chicago Press.

Hartshorne, R. (1955) "'Exceptionalism in geography' re-examined," *Annals of the Association of American Geographers*, 55(3): 205–44.

Harvey, D. (1973) *Social justice and the city*, Baltimore, MD: Johns Hopkins University Press.

He, S. (2013) "Evolving enclave urbanism in China and its socio-spatial implications: The case of Guangzhou," *Social & Cultural Geography*, 14(3): 243–75.

He, S. and Qian, J. (2017) "From an emerging market to a multifaceted urban society: Urban China studies," *Urban Studies*, 54(4): 827–46.

Hendrikx, M. and Wissink, B. (2017) "Welcome to the club! An exploratory study of service accessibility in commodity housing estates in Guangzhou, China," *Social & Cultural Geography*, 18(3): 371–94.

Hogan, T., Bunnell, T., Pow, C.-P., Permanasari, E., and Morshidi, S. (2012) "Asian urbanisms and the privatization of cities," *Cities*, 29(1): 59–63.

Hsing, Y.-T. (2010) *The great urban transformation: Politics of land and property in China*, Oxford: Oxford University Press.

Huang, Y. (2006) "Collectivism, political control, and gating in Chinese cities," *Urban Geography*, 27(6): 507–25.

Huang, Y. and Low, S. M. (2008) "Is gating always exclusionary? A comparative analysis of gated communities in American and Chinese cities," in J. R. Logan (ed.) *Urban China in transition*, Malden, MA: Blackwell, pp. 182–202.

Iossifova, D. (2015) "Borderland urbanism: Seeing between enclaves," *Urban Geography*, 36(1): 90–108.

Jencks, C. (1993) *Heteropolis: Los Angeles, the riots and the strange beauty of hetero-architecture*, New York: St. Martin's Press.

Judd, D. R. (2011) "Theorizing the city," in D. R. Judd and D. Simpson (eds.) *The city, revisited: Urban theory from Chicago, Los Angeles, and New York*, Minneapolis: University of Minnesota Press, pp. 3–20.

Judd, D. R. and Simpson, D. (eds.) (2011) *The city, revisited: Urban theory from Chicago, Los Angeles, and New York*, Minneapolis: University of Minnesota Press.

Kanai, J. M., Grant, R., and Jianu, R. (2018) "Cities on and off the map: A bibliometric assessment of urban globalisation research," *Urban Studies*, 55(12): 2569–85.

Leitner, H. and Sheppard, E. (2016) "Provincializing critical urban theory: Extending the ecosystem of possibilities," *International Journal of Urban and Regional Research*, 40(1): 228–35.

Logan, J. R. and Fainstein, S. S. (2008) "Introduction: Urban China in comparative perspective," in J. Logan (ed.) *Urban China in transition*, Oxford: Blackwell, pp. 1–23.

Low, S. (2005) "Towards a theory of urban fragmentation: A cross-cultural analysis of fear, privatization and the state," *Cybergeo*, art. 349. Available at: www.cybergeo.eu/index3207.html.

Massey, D. (1984) "Introduction: Geography matters," in D. Massey and J. Allen (eds.) *Geography matters*, Cambridge: Cambridge University Press, pp. 9–11.

Massey, D. (1994) *Space, place and gender*, Minneapolis: Minnesota University Press.

McFarlane, C. (2011) *Learning the city*, Oxford: Wiley-Blackwell.

Park, R. E. (1915) "The city: Suggestions for the investigation of human behavior in the city environment," *The American Journal of Sociology*, 20(5): 577–612.

Park, R. E. (1929) "The city as a social laboratory," in T. V. Smith and L. D. White (eds.) *Chicago: An experiment in social science research*, Chicago: University of Chicago Press, pp. 1–19.

Peck, J. (2015) "Cities beyond compare?" *Regional Studies*, 49(1): 160–82.

Pow, C. P. (2009) *Gated communities in China: Class, privilege and the moral politics of the good life*, Abingdon: Routledge.

Pow, C. P. (2012) "China exceptionalism: Unbound narratives on urban China," in T. Edensor and M. Jayne (eds.) *Urban theory beyond the West: A world of cities*, Abingdon: Routledge, pp. 47–64.

Pow, C. P. (2015) "Urban dystopia and epistemologies of hope," *Progress in Human Geography*, 39(4): 464–85.

Ren, J. and Luger, J. (2015) "Comparative urbanism and the 'Asian City': Implications for research and theory," *International Journal of Urban and Regional Research*, 39(1): 145–56.

Robinson, J. (2003) "Postcolonial geography: Tactics and pitfalls," *Singapore Journal of Tropical Geography*, 24(3): 273–98.

Robinson, J. (2006) *Ordinary cities: Between modernity and development*, Abingdon: Routledge.

Robinson, J. (2011) "Cities in a world of cities: The comparative gesture," *International Journal of Urban and Regional Research*, 35(1): 1–23.

Robinson, J. (2016) "Comparative urbanism: New geographies and cultures of theorizing the urban," *International Journal of Urban and Regional Research*, 40(1): 187–99.

Robinson, J. and Roy, A. (2016) "Global urbanisms and the nature of urban theory," *International Journal of Urban and Regional Research*, 40(1): 181–6.

Roy, A. (2009) "The 21st-century metropolis: New geographies of theory," *Regional Studies*, 43(6): 819–30.

Roy, A. (2016) "Who is afraid of postcolonial theory?" *International Journal of Urban and Regional Research*, 40(1): 200–9.

Roy, A. and Ong, A. (eds.) (2011) *Worlding cities*, Oxford: Wiley-Blackwell.

Sabatini, F. and Salcedo, R. (2011) "Understanding deep urban change: Patterns of residential segregation in Latin American cities," in D. R. Judd and D. Simpson (eds.) *The city, revisited: Urban theory from Chicago, Los Angeles, and New York*, Minneapolis: University of Minnesota Press, pp. 332–56.

Saïd, E. (1978) *Orientalism*, New York: Pantheon Books.

Schaefer, F. K. (1953) "Exceptionalism in geography: A methodological examination," *Annals of the Association of American Geographers*, 43(3): 226–49.

Scott, A. J. and Storper, M. (2015) "The nature of cities: The scope and limits of urban theory," *International Journal of Urban and Regional Research*, 39(1): 1–15.

Shapin, S. (1998) "Placing the view from nowhere: Historical and sociological problems in the location of science," *Transactions of the Institute of British Geographers*, 23(1): 5–12.

Smith, N. (1987) "Dangers of the empirical turn: Some comments on the CURS initiative," *Antipode*, 19(1): 59–68.

Soja, E. W. (1989) *Postmodern geographies: The reassertion of space in critical social theory*, New York: Verso.

Sorkin, M. (ed.) (1992) *Variations on a theme park: The new American city and the end of public space*, New York: Hill and Wang.

Storper, M. and Scott, A. J. (2016) "Current debates in urban theory: A critical assessment," *Urban Studies*, 53(6): 1114–36.

Wang, H. (2005) "The new criticism," in C. Wang (ed.) *One China, many paths*, London: Verso, pp. 55–86.

Webster, C., Glasze, G., and Frantz, K. (2002) "The global spread of gated communities," *Environment and Planning B*, 29(3): 315–20.

Webster, C., Wu, F., and Zhao, Y. (2006) "China's modern gated cities," in G. Glasze, C. Webster, and K. Frantz (eds.) *Private cities: Global and local perspectives*, Abingdon: Routledge, pp. 153–69.

Wirth, L. (1938) "Urbanism as a way of life," *The American Journal of Sociology*, XLIV(1): 1–24.

Wissink, B. (2019) "Enclave urbanism in China: A relational comparative view," in R. Yep, J. Wang, and T. R. Johnson (eds.) *Handbook on urban development in China*, Cheltenham: Edward Elgar, pp. 171–86.

Wu, F. (2005) "Rediscovering the 'gate' under market transition: From work-unit compounds to commodity housing enclaves," *Housing Studies*, 20(2): 235–54.

Wu, F. (2010) "Gated and packaged suburbia: Packaging and branding Chinese suburban residential development," *Cities*, 27(5): 385–96.

Wu, F. and Webber, K. (2004) "The rise of 'foreign gated communities' in Beijing: Between economic globalization and local institutions," *Cities*, 21(3): 203–13.

Xu, F. (2008) "Gated communities and migrant enclaves: The conundrum for building harmonious community/*shequ*," *Journal of Contemporary China*, 17(57): 633–51.

Xu, M. and Yang, Z. (2009) "Design history of China's gated cities and neighbourhoods: prototype and evolution," *Urban Design International*, 14(2): 99–117.

Zhou, Y., Zhang, J., and Lin, G. (2017) "Uncomfortable theoretical fit? China in the lens of neoliberalism and post-colonialism," call for papers, AAG Annual Meeting, Boston, MA, April 5–7.

Zhu, H., Chen, X., and Qian, J. (2014) "Charting the development of social and cultural geography in Mainland China: Voices from the inside," *Social & Cultural Geography*, 15(3): 255–83.

Zorbaugh, H. W. (1929) *The Gold Coast and the slum: A sociological study of Chicago's near North Side*, Chicago: University of Chicago Press.

5

From Chicago to Shenzhen, via Birmingham

Zones of Transition and Dreams of Homeownership

Ray Forrest

Introduction

Are the processes of urban change, urban conflict, and the competition for housing very different in Chinese cities when compared to the experiences of their Western counterparts or are we mesmerized by the scale and pace of change in China so that the quantitatively different is sometimes mistaken for the qualitatively different? Every city, every nation-state, every culture will mediate common processes, common developments to produce distinct configurations and outcomes. Equally, apparently similar outcomes and patterns may be produced by quite different forces and relationships. In exploring these and related questions with regard to the competition for housing in cities, the narrative will traverse almost a century and progress from Park's Chicago, via Birmingham in England, to the contemporary Chinese city.

Park's Chicago was a city represented as having a hierarchy of housing circumstances with a distinct spatial pattern. Rex and Moore's research on Birmingham in the 1960s refined this conception in their work on racial tensions in the UK with their Weberian conception of housing classes and their greater attention to institutional gatekeepers. Their idea of competition for housing being related to, but distinct from, processes of social stratification and class structuring in the workplace was highly influential as well as widely critiqued at the time (see, for example, discussion in Thorns, 1989). But it may be that their ideas find new resonance with regard to the impact of housing commodification on wealth accumulation and social stratification in the contemporary Chinese city.

It is appropriate to comment initially on the nature and understanding of competition for housing and how that varies across the narrative. In Park's 1936 essay in the *American Journal of Sociology*, the Darwinian influence on his view of competition is explicit. Among other things he observed "Human ecology, in so far as it is concerned with a social order that is based on competition rather than consensus, is identical, in principle at least, with plant and animal ecology. The problems with which plant and animal ecology have been traditionally concerned are fundamentally population problems" (Park, 1936: 14–15).

For Park, it was human culture in its various forms which made societies work in the face of potentially unrestrained competition. When the institutions and norms that mediated between processes of competition and populations broke down, the equilibrium was disturbed and a rearrangement of these fundamental relationships was required. In the residential sphere, this process of competition for space could be seen in the shifting morphologies of neighborhoods. "As the CBD expands, the housing stock is reduced and the population is forced outwards, invading the other residential areas and eventually succeeding the previous population" (Bassett and Short, 1980: 11).

The mediation of competition over access to adequate housing finds its strongest institutional form as decommodified living space represented, for example, by the council housing of British cities which expanded particularly in the post–Second World War period. This produced two parallel but interconnected spheres of competition—the market for owned and rented housing and the bureaucratically rule-based competition for public rental housing. The essence of this competition in both spheres, however, revolved primarily around use value and social status as evidenced by tenure, location, and housing size. Birmingham in the 1960s (as was Britain as a whole at the time) was still some way from housing booms, privatization, and monetization. In contrast, the fevered competition for housing in the major Chinese cities of today is situated in a very different global context, in which real estate has become deeply and extensively commodified and associated with financial gain—and most notably in the high-growth, lead cities of the eastern coastal region.

More generally, with regard to the dominant idea that competition is (and should be) central to the economic and governance processes that shape cities, neoliberal thought is at least as influential today as was the work of Darwin in the early 20th century. In this ideological context, the tension between housing as home and housing as real estate is evident and explicit (Forrest and Hirayama, 2015). The asset form of the commodity becomes more important in the shaping of social structures—a commodity form in which "the exchange is motivated primarily by the possibility of re-selling the object for a profit at some point in the (more or less distant) future" (Boltanski and Esquerre, 2017: 70). Urban populations are habituated into the norms of self-regulation and individual responsibility of neoliberal governmentality (Dardot and Laval, 2014). They become sellers as well as buyers, landlords as well as owner-occupiers. It is the capitalization of property assets that is also the key means by which some, but not others, are enabled to afford and access the privileged routes and resources of more comprehensively, commodified economies. Thus, in the contemporary Chinese city, multiple property ownership grows among the most affluent and household wealth, primarily associated with real estate, is becoming an increasingly important factor in social stratification (for a detailed analysis, see Xie and Jin, 2015).

Residential property ownership as the social glue

Park's description of "vast, casual and mobile aggregations which constitute our urban population" (1925: 22) seems very apposite for China, given its urbanized, floating populations of millions, and there are obvious parallels to be drawn with the momentous social changes to which Park was referring and the experience of Chinese cities over recent decades—rapid urbanization, proletarianization, and mass migration. Moreover, the ways in which new migrants adapt to, and cope with, their new urban lives have not fundamentally changed. Aspirations which may be spontaneous, culturally embedded, or social constructed via policy and related instruments also have a strong element of continuity in their basic features. Rapid urbanization is associated with wider social ruptures, which erode the traditions, and institutions that have helped to maintain social stability and social integration. In Chinese cities, in the Communist era, the *danwei* system involved a strong and direct socio-spatial relationship between work and residence, a wide-ranging and intensive regime encompassing almost every aspect of social life to replace the traditional village and kin-based social structure that had preceded it (Chai, 2014). With its gradual but accelerating disappearance in the reform era, new institutional forms and social norms have had to evolve to replace that system. The new forms of social cement to maintain social harmony and social cohesion in Chinese cities have focused on the residential neighborhood and particularly the defense of space, property rights, and property values by a new breed of urban homeowners.

In the Chinese Dream, just as in the American Dream or, indeed in any other version, the role of residential property as a stabilizing force for the unruly city shows remarkable consistency regardless of historical or geographical context. Park's 1925 essay anticipated the emergence of new forms and norms that would potentially substitute for the crumbling US traditions and institutions of the past, which were rooted in smaller scale rurality, revolving around family and village networks. In the US, homeownership would become a key element of the policy prescription to counter a nomadic urbanism which was perceived as problematic by policy makers (Rossi and Shlay, 1982). Renters moved and did not put down roots. Owners were assumed to be, or to become, more stable, settled citizens. It was not, however, till after the Second World War that the necessary economic and political conditions for the organized expansion of homeownership emerged—occasioning the development of the iconic suburban dream of a new American middle class. As will emerge later, the dream may be articulated in the same way, but the relationship between ownership, renting, and social stability takes a rather different form in today's Chinese cities.

There are, of course, major differences with regard to the role of central and local governments, policy histories, culture, ideology, and the sheer scale of the changes impacting on Chinese cities when compared to the US at the beginning of the 19th century or the UK in the mid-20th century. But, for the ordinary citizen, the exploding cities of Chicago or Shenzhen present the same basic challenges of everyday life with regard to space and opportunity, adaptation and assimilation. Many of the major moments of political unrest in cities have been provoked by, or revolved around, the struggle to secure decent housing. If the urban masses become agitated (Park, 1925: 22), then that agitation is often associated with shelter and the processes by which some succeed and some fail to gain access to adequate accommodation—issues of segregation, displacement, eviction, gentrification, and so on. As Madden and Marcuse observe in their provocative analysis of the contemporary urban world, conflicts around housing are more acute than ever and more global. "London, Shanghai, Sao Paulo, Mumbai, Lagos, indeed nearly every major city faces its own residential struggles. Land grabs, forced evictions, expulsions, and displacement are rampant" (2016: 3). A recent review of China urban studies identified "the profound consequences of the commodification of housing" as a complex, evolving, and continuing key area for research (He and Qian, 2017: 832–3). And one of the most evident consequences of commodification has been the dramatic growth of private residential property ownership in China and the growing displacement and marginalization of the low-income and unofficial population in the urban villages and informal areas in the major cities (Wu and Webster, 2010; Wang and Lo, 2015; Wu, 2016). These enclaves of communal rural landownership engulfed by rapid urbanization, have become dormitories, the contemporary Chinese "zones of transition," for a mainly floating population of low-income service and manual workers.

Migration, urban expansion, and the home

There is a unifying thread that links Park's Chicago, Rex and Moore's Birmingham, and cities such as Shenzhen. The movement of people to the city—from rural hinterlands, more distant rural locations or provincial cities, or from overseas—intensifies the competition for residential space. Other housing problems arise with changing demographics or economic decline but they are of a different complexion. The exploding city, unlike the shrinking city, is a place of both new opportunities and new social divisions. For some newcomers it can be a place far from the comforting norms of friends and families, and from the familiarities and regularities of home towns or villages. For others, it can be a place where these close relationships are recreated in a new setting, as neighborhoods of intimacy in a wider context of unsettling strangeness. With regard to housing, it is also a circumstance in which the family home may become a rented, overcrowded, and precarious perch in a new and unstable urban world. Renting has been typically the dominant tenure in urbanizing societies in which rural populations have been transformed into urban proletariats. Hence, in the initial stages of fast urban growth, homeownership levels tend to fall as societies become increasingly dominated by large cities. Residential property ownership in this context takes on new meanings and new roles. The social and economic construction of the house or apartment as both a symbol of social status and as a vehicle for financial security has acted as a powerful wedge between groups. There are the evident and explicit conflicts around the demand for shelter but there is an equally if less overt tension around the achievement of residential property ownership as consequence of, and indicator of, wider social advantage and status. The way in which the competition for housing and homeownership is playing out in contemporary China is different from the European or North American context with regard to urban form, state involvement, and policy development because the residential structures of today's cities are always built on the past, literally and metaphorically. And this is particularly true of Chinese cities, given the critical role that marketization has played in relation to the reshaping of previously collective forms of housing provision and the profound impact of the *danwei* system on their socio-spatial structure. As Chai observes, "Socialist development shaped the collectivized landscapes to structure daily life and social interactions in particular ways. The influence of this period continues to affect urban China in many ways and will do so for many years to come" (2014: 184).

Residential differentiation and conflict in Chicago

It is a well-rehearsed critique of the Chicago School that its explanatory power was limited by its methodological individualism. This perspective and approach, which dominated urban studies well into the 1960s, explained urban processes and patterns mainly through the "individual subjectivities of urbanites" (Dear, 2002: ix). The collective impact of their individual choices produced the evident tapestry of neighborhoods and differentiated living conditions. The pioneering work of the Chicago School produced rich accounts about which groups lived where and what conditions were like but we learn rather little about the power imbalances which structured these outcomes. As Bassett and Short put it,

> The ecological approach, by considering the nature of housing supply and allocation in early twentieth century North America as a constant, given and often 'natural' variable, is unable to say anything meaningful about the structure of the housing market and consequently has little explanation to offer for the patterns of residential differentiation which it describes. (1980: 24)

There was also scant evidence of conflict or resistance to the hierarchy of locations and conditions which Burgess topologized (Burgess, 1925). Although the early Chicago School sociologists produced rich ethnographies of those on the margins of Chicago's rapidly growing metropolis, the experiences of real people, of the daily lives of the masses, is rather absent from the more influential and better-known work on residential patterns.

More recent work on early 20th-century Chicago adds a more conflictual picture of the housing situation. In particular, the struggle over homeownership and its attributes figure prominently. Garb's (2005) exploration of the emergent American Dream, in which the ownership of residential property is shown to be of primary importance, is focused on the period between the growing resistance to new regulations and zoning introduced following a major fire in Chicago in 1871 and a race riot in 1919—only a few years before the publication of Park's revised essay on "The city" (Park, 1925). During this period, according to Garb, there was a struggle over the meaning and role of homeownership and the development of the class-segregated housing market described by the Chicago School sociologists. As in other urbanizing societies at the time, a tradition of working-class homeownership embraced residential property in an instrumental way—as an asset that could supplement income from other sources. This was especially important to immigrants to a city in which cheap rooming houses offered low-rent accommodation to newcomers. New waves of immigrants provided the demand for rental housing from an earlier cohort of migrant households that had managed to buy housing in the lower-value parts of the city—the zones of transition, the places of assimilation, referred to by Burgess (1925). Garb offers a historian's perspective on the interconnected events and processes in which homeownership was transformed into an asset in which the preservation of property values became paramount, and location and housing tenure began to be a mark of social status (although see Bigott, 2006).

More critically, the social composition of neighborhoods, dwelling types, and levels of ownership gained greater importance in the determination and maintenance of property values. Stricter building regulations and greater attention to public health increased the costs of homeownership and were intimately linked to the growth of the suburban, middle-class lifestyle. In parallel, other neighborhoods deteriorated and racial divisions in terms of housing quality, location, and tenure became sharper. Those in the poorer, inner-city, mainly Black areas were progressively left behind, facing declining property values and highly restricted access to loan finance.

Interestingly, Garb (2005) connects the plight of lower-income homeowners in the contemporary postindustrial US of the 21st century to the shifts in the role and meaning of property ownership a century earlier—and by implication links these developments to China's economic ascendancy and rising living standards. She suggests that as the new middle class of Chinese cities competed for their stake in the homeownership society, and others are relegated to the margins, residential property ownership in the US was reassuming its role as a means to boost income and survive in a more hostile economic environment. Garb argues that via secondary mortgages "home ownership was once again used to buttress households of falling or stagnant income, blue and white-collar workers whose jobs were exported to lower-wage societies or eliminated in corporate mergers and cutbacks" (2005: 206).

Zones of transition: From Chicago to Birmingham

Leaving early 20th-century Chicago but taking forward the idea of homeownership as a generator of income and as signifier of social status, we can advance half a century to Birmingham, UK, in the mid-1960s. This is not an arbitrary leap. A notable advance, theoretically and empirically, in the study of urban conflict and competition, and particularly over housing, was represented by the work of Rex and Moore (1967). Most pertinently they drew explicitly on the earlier Chicago studies. Rex and Moore's research is less widely known in the US or, indeed, outside the European context, but it was an explicit and novel fusion of Weberian conceptions of social stratification with the ecological model of the Chicago School. In broad terms, it progressed debates in urban studies from conceiving of the competition for scarce urban resources in individualistic terms—as atomized households competing with one another—to one in which the institutional constraints were recognized explicitly as a critical factor. Individuals competed and made choices about where they moved in the city, and what they moved to, but under conditions which were not of their own choosing. The varied mobility patterns of different groups were constrained in different ways through the operation of key urban gatekeepers such as housing managers or those responsible for arranging loan finance. They also conceived of a hierarchy of desirability for housing with outright and mortgaged ownership at the top and lodging houses at the bottom. Rex and Moore associated these different housing types with the zonal geography of the city—with clear echoes of Chicago.

The most direct connection, however, with the earlier Chicago research is their description of "zones of transition"—the areas of relatively cheap housing which offered a source of income to an earlier wave of immigrants and cheap rental accommodation to those who had more recently arrived in the city. With explicit reference to the work of Park and Burgess, the concluding Chapter 12 (Rex and Moore, 1967: 272–85) is titled, "The sociology of the zone of transition." Having emphasized that Birmingham of the 1960s could not be assumed to replicate the processes of urban change of Chicago of the 1920s, they nevertheless argued that "we recognize the importance of their emphasis upon competitive processes and upon a 'zone of transition' as recurrent urban phenomena" (1967: 273). One critic of their work (Haddon, 1970) observed that their assumption about a hierarchy of desirability, a unitary value system with homeownership at the top, misunderstood the role of lodging houses, of residential landlordism, as a key element of the income-earning strategies of the different waves of immigrants that had arrived in the city. In the housing status hierarchy of the immigrant population, in the zones of transition, resident landlordism rather than owner-occupation was a more valued housing circumstance.

Rex and Moore's explanation of why a zone of transition was a significant part of the city's urban morphology, and how it evolved and operated in the context of competitive urban processes, is very clearly expressed—and rather instructively so for contemporary standards of urban theorizing. They offered a specific, nuanced, and detailed account of a more general phenomenon in a form and manner that would sit well with current debates around comparative urbanism and the appropriateness or otherwise of imported concepts (see, for example, Robinson, 2016). In broad terms, the zone of transition as conceived by Rex and Moore was the product of a more complex process than the rather unidimensional struggle around land use posited in the original Chicago model. There was not only a continuing competition around what to build on available sites but also competition for the use of existing buildings where the patterns of demand had shifted and the original users had moved elsewhere—or more correctly, where the types of households for whom such dwellings were originally built now preferred to live elsewhere in the city. This point was essentially the same as the process identified in the Chicago model, which involved moves from the inner city to the suburbs. Rex and Moore refer to dwellings being "abandoned" by their original users but it would be more appropriate to conceive of this process as a more gradual change in residential patterns. Shifting norms and preferences, partly but critically shaped by the impact of immigration on the social composition of neighborhoods, combined with changes in employment and incomes, to provoke and enable a move to more attractive residential locations for some sections of the majority White population. Their third point was the most context specific, namely that pure economic competition for material resources had produced outcomes that had necessitated some element of state intervention in property rights. Here, they were referring to the British city of the 1960s in which local government was a significant stakeholder in the form of council housing. Thus, there was not only market competition for resources but also competition around how state resources were allocated. In this particular context, the question was about who got the housing owned and managed by local government.

Without going into unnecessary detail, Rex and Moore's study was concerned with the ways in which immigrants were priced out of homeownership and excluded from council housing because of eligibility requirements. They were thus squeezed into these "illegitimate" housing areas, these twilight zones, which were neither "legitimated in terms of the ideal of 'property owning democracy'" or "in terms of the values of 'the welfare state'" (1967: 275–6). These areas of primarily immigrant housing (landlords and tenants) were heavily policed by public health and other regulatory bodies but represented a necessary, if illegitimate, housing function. They argued that without these lodging-house areas, essentially confined to certain inner areas of the city, the pressures on public housing authorities would have been much greater and the housing shortage more acute. As Rex and Moore observe, "Yet someone has to be found to do this job [providing housing for immigrants], for neither the free market nor the welfare state provides adequately for the whole population." They continue, "So the city, having failed to deal with its own housing problem turns on those upon whom it relies to make alternative provision, and punishes them for its own failure" (1967: 40–1).

Thus, in the Birmingham of the 1960s, the competition for scarce housing resources operated in two interconnected domains—a domain in which the logic of the market prevailed in terms of eligibility for loan finance and the other in which the logic of bureaucratic allocation determined access primarily in terms of what we would now call citizenship rights. We might contrast this with early 20th century Chicago where the logic of the market dominated, aided by collusive, regulatory forces, and the competitive logic of the contemporary Chinese city in which a speculative housing market is circumscribed by pervasive Chinese state policy and ideology, and shaped by the legacy of collective property ownership.

Achieving homeownership in the contemporary Chinese city

Homeownership is as central to the Chinese Dream as to the earlier American or British version. Wu and Gaubatz (2013: 211) observe that "For millions of urban Chinese, home ownership is part of the new, middle-class dream. The building and inhabitation of new, commercial housing have created new forms of identity for residents, as well as new forms of governance for communities" (and see Lui and Liu, Chapter 11 in this volume). The delinking of housing rights and housing access from place of employment, the shift from collective to private ownership status and the creation of quasi-commercial housing sectors have been among the most visible elements of the economic reforms, particularly after 1990, when residential property rights were extended. In post-reform China, much of the early increase in homeownership derived from the transfer of (mainly) sitting tenants from tenancy to ownership status and the high homeownership rates would never have been reached without collective housing to commodify. Fu (2016) shows that it was housing privatization rather than commodification that was initially responsible for the dramatic shift in tenure change (and see Shi et al., 2016). As early as 2002, some 80% of the previously collectively owned housing was already held privately (Davis, 2006) and more recent estimates suggest that 95% of the housing stock is now privately owned (Piketty et al., 2017). These Chinese cities of private property have emerged within a very compressed timescale and mass homeownership in China has been achieved to an extent that far outstrips past and current rates in Western societies. It is now, it seems, an ultra-homeownership society.

There are numerous references to the overall homeownership rate for China having reached 90% (for example, Wu et al., 2018; Trading Economics, 2018; Ieconomics, 2018). Here, however, we encounter the need for some qualification of the statistics on homeownership in China and issues of social construction and conceptual translation (Kemeny, 1984). Closer scrutiny indicates a gap between the homeownership rate for urban residents with and without *hukou* (official record specifying whether someone is a legal resident of a particular area). Moreover, in line with trends in other societies, homeownership levels may have actually fallen in some cities. Taking Shenzhen as an example, in 2005 some 90% of residents with *hukou* were homeowners. However, only 27% of those without *hukou* were owners and the overall rate of homeownership was only 41%. In 2010, with a further expansion of the non-*hukou* population, the overall figure had dropped to 27%: 76% for those with *hukou* and 11% for those without (Urban Planning, Land, and Resources Commission, 2016; GF Securities, 2018). And recent data from a survey of the inner core districts in the city, records an overall home ownership level in 2018 of 43% (Forrest et al., forthcoming).

There are various explanations for the disconnect between references to very high homeownership rates nationally and the apparently lower levels of homeownership in Chinese cities such as Shenzhen. It may well be that almost all the housing stock in China is privately owned. But this is not inconsistent with lower levels of *owner-occupation* in the major Chinese cities if many households or individuals renting properties own a property somewhere else. The transfer of residential properties from collective to private ownership has produced a mass of owners. But many of the owners of private housing are renting elsewhere—in the major cities. Moreover, serious affordability problems in cities such Shenzhen have pushed younger households to look elsewhere for cheaper properties to buy. Households in this situation would be better classified as *renter-owners* to differentiate them from tenants without any property assets and from owner-occupiers. There is a further issue concerning what constitutes a household. Again, statistics are not readily available but in China it is not uncommon for parents to transfer ownership of their home to their (one) child. Are the parents in this situation owners or tenants and who is included in the household?

The important point is that in other cultural contexts, in the Chicago of the 1920s and the Birmingham of the 1960s, and in most contemporary Western narratives, homeownership is used interchangeably with owner-occupation. It is a term, a concept, laden with meaning in relation to social identity, social status, and ontological security—you own the home you live in without fear of eviction or interference, your "haven in a heartless world" (Lasch, 1995). The ownership of private property and owner-occupation may be less coincident in Chinese than in Western cities. The dream of owning private residential property is common, the achievement of homeownership is probably less so. This signals important differences in the relationship between ownership and urban social cohesion and the notion of homeownership giving people a "stake in the system."

Those without a stake in this new homeownership society are most likely to be found in these migrant zones of transition. However, some of the renter-owners referred to above, may well be tenants of the resident landlords in the urban villages, as these and similar such enclaves also serve many poorer, younger college graduates seeking better jobs in the big cities. Timberlake et al. refer to one such area, Tangjialing in the outer suburbs of Beijing, in which college graduate and others had "average living space of less than 10 square meters and the average monthly rent was less than 400 yuan" (2014: 166). They also give the example of Shipai in Guangzhou in which 100,000 people occupy 0.28 square kilometers. A newspaper article referred recently to the hundreds of thousands of residents facing displacement in Shenzhen as the urban villages there are being progressively upgraded and revalorized for more affluent urbanites (Haack, 2018; and see O'Donnell, Chapter 7 in this volume).

Thus, the urban villages of Shenzhen or Guangzhou can be easily described in the same terms as were the lodging-house areas of Birmingham—areas of "overcrowding, high density and low quality accommodation, poor infrastructure provision social and environmental problems and high crime rates" (Wang et al., 2009: 970)—reception areas for migrants where homeownership provides a local landlord class with an essential source of income and employment by providing housing for low-income newcomers without citizenship rights (*hukou*) to qualify them for the various forms of housing subsidy. And Wang et al. (2009) emphasize the multiple role of these urban villages, these particular zones of transition or "transitional neighborhoods" (Liu et al., 2010), as examples of informal, creative, and spontaneous adaptations in terms of housing and employment amid rapid and socially destabilizing urbanization. Moreover, just as in Chicago and Birmingham, public health and public safety measures are used to sanitize these undesirable but functionally necessary enclaves of immigrant housing.

Homeownership, tenancy, and the unequal Chinese city

The post-reform Chinese city has been fundamentally reshaped in less than three decades. The close relationship between work and residence has all but disappeared, cars and congestion have replaced bicycles, and the residential social structure reflects price and status rather than land use. Private residential property dominates and there is an emergent new middle-class, consumption-based culture (Davis, 2006; Lui and Liu, Chapter 11 in this volume). Old spatial patterns associated with pre-1949 China are argued to be re-emerging with references (again with explicit tones of Chicago theorizing), to "rings of differentiated urban space; pre-1949 historic areas, a socialist planned work unit ring (1949–1985), and the new estates ring (built during the property boom years since 1985)" (Wu and Gaubatz, 2013: 155). These transformations have also seen a sharp rise in urban inequalities and new patterns of residential segregation (see. for example, Feng et al., 2008; Li and Wu, 2008; He, 2013). Li and Wu (2008: 404) suggest that Chinese cities that were once characterized by low-income egalitarianism are now among some of the most unequal cities in the world.

The shift from state socialism to state capitalism has involved a major transformation of housing-tenure situations. As in post-Soviet Eastern Europe, and most notably in Russia, the privatization and monetization of state rental housing have been at the forefront of wider economic changes and with profound distributional consequences (Wang and Murie, 1996). Much has depended on being in the right place at the right time—and also having been in the right place in a previous time. In housing terms, those who had fared best through how they were ranked and where they worked, supplemented by social connection and luck in the socialist era, were also among those who were best placed to gain advantage in the new market era. When housing was distributed as part of the social wage, "Senior government officials had more generous housing than lower-level residents, official professionals more generous than non-official professionals, and employees of large state enterprises more generous than those in small state enterprises and non-state sectors" (Wu and Gaubatz, 2013: 198). Similarly, research on housing histories across generations in Shanghai has shown that, "Multiple allocations via the work unit translate into monetary advantage and offer opportunity for a rapid climb up the housing asset ladder" (Forrest and Izuhara, 2012: 42). The more privileged workers of the Chinese state-socialist city became the new asset-rich of the Chinese state-capitalist city as they were advantageously placed to "capitalize properties that were not distributed equally during the socialist period" (Wu, 2002: 1591; Huang and Jiang, 2009). The housing stock may have been comprehensively privatized, or monetized, but the properties acquired vary substantially in value and quality. This is a further important dimension of private property ownership in China. Tenants in Shenzhen, for example, may own properties elsewhere but some may be low value and in poor condition.

The rapidity and unprecedented scale of urban development in China have also placed some homeowners at the center of conflicts around the "modernization" of the Chinese city and the rights of individual owners versus the rights of developers and government. Urban renewal typically involves the displacement of older and settled communities and is inherently conflictual. In European or US cities the people being displaced have generally been poorer renters and ethnic minorities with limited property rights. In the Chinese city, however, urban transformation has often involved the destruction of properties with long-standing homeownership lineage (albeit modified during the Communist collectivization of residential space) stretching across generations and has been on such a scale that this process of demolition and renewal (chaiqian) has been particularly visible. It has also at times been overtly brutal, what Zhang (2010: 138) refers to as "'postsocialist primitive accumulation' propelled by the newly formed pro-growth coalitions of between local governments and developers." This is often a collision, again with echoes of earlier accounts of Chicago, between traditional working-class homeownership and its replacement by homes for the new breed of middle-class owners—the gentrification of homeownership.

In the creation of this new, homeowning society, tenancy has become associated with lower status—a remarkable and rapid turnaround for a society in which work-unit housing had been the norm of the socialist period. As Fu suggests, the function of workplace tenancy as a key element of social security in the socialist era has been supplanted by homeownership as "a source of security, prestige and marketable assets by urban residents" (2016: 1230). Tomba, in an earlier exploration of China's emerging middle class, makes a similar point about the importance of residential property ownership in China's new urban order when he states that "early access to the privatization of housing has become a major determinant between social actors … and it often determines social status more than income does" (2004: 6). However, as has been argued, many households or individuals in China may wear multiple hats—homeowners in one context, tenants in another. The least secure and lowest status are low-income tenants without property elsewhere.

Chinese cities in which, until fairly recently, most residents were equally poor are now sharply segregated by wealth and income (Yi, 2017; and see Gu, 2013). And an expanding middle class and inward migration from poorer cities and provinces has fueled house-price inflation. This has taken homeownership beyond the reach of many in the younger, professional classes with price–income ratios in the major cities now among the highest in the world. This is a key part of the explanation of the disconnect between ownership and occupation discussed previously. Timberlake et al. (2014: 166) report that in these cities the "average house price–income ratio was 11.4 in 2000 but increased to 21.4 in 2009, and the situation is much worse for the bottom 20% for whom the house price–income ratio increased from 19.1 to 44." Only Hong Kong, itself a special administrative region of China, has higher ratios—currently at 24:1 (Demographia, 2018). However, at the other end of the property ownership spectrum are those households which were best placed with regard to the path-dependent advantages referred to earlier. Data from the China Housing Finance Survey show that almost of fifth of urban families own at least two homes. Some 3.6% own three or more (Yi, 2017). These homes may be rented out or simply left empty. And they may be in different towns and none occupied by the owners.

Concluding observations

In all three urban contexts that feature in this narrative, housing tenure acts as a significant factor in social and spatial divisions. However, in the era of neoliberal globalization, residential location has become pervasively monetized and exchange value has come to dominate use value as real estate has become the primary vehicle for wealth accumulation among the middle masses. This is the capitalism into which China re-emerged in the 1980s and which has shaped its cities and the nature of its homeownership. The dwelling as a generator of income now encompasses the elite, the middle mass as well as the resident landlords in the zones of transition. The conflict between the different meanings and functions of homeownership described by Garb's account of early 20th-century Chicago—as an income booster in hard times for the poorer or a store of value and status for the middle classes—has taken on much wider ramifications. The shared dream of an owned home has been superseded by a purer form of housing commodity in which apartments are valued as much, if not more, for their investment value and wealth-generating potential as for their comforts and amenities. In this context, the competition for housing centers on the value of the housing investment, the maintenance of that value and much of the residential mobility is fueled by the fear of losing momentum in a booming market.

This transformation of housing from use value to a deposit box for savings is perhaps most visible in China with its so-called "ghost cities." According to Shepard (2015), the housing market operates much the same way as the stock market: "Just as one doesn't need to mould a piece of gold into something usable, like a piece of jewellery, for it to have value and an economic function, an apartment in China doesn't need to have people living in it for it to be economically viable."

This stark view of the new role for residential property is a far cry from the housing conditions and housing conflicts in earlier periods in Chicago or Birmingham. In these contexts, overcrowding and dereliction were prevalent and there was an absolute housing shortage. The competition for housing certainly pivoted around the security and status of homeownership but also for simply a decent place to live, regardless of tenure. Now it is a competition for asset value, for asset-based welfare, rooted in private residential property. This fits the new mood of China described by Yu (2018) as one in which "money or material interest, has become the main motivating force." This mood is by no means confined to China, it pervasive, but it is there that the ethos of the investor-subject (Watson, 2010), what Dardot and Laval (2014: 156) refer to as the "capitalization of existence," seems to have taken hold most dramatically—a particular conjuncture of social, economic, and cultural change. The significant dislocation between private ownership and occupancy points to this distinctive and intense competition for owner-occupation but not necessarily property ownership among Chinese urban residents. The coalescence of financialized real estate and the Chinese state capitalism form (as opposed to the early and welfare capitalisms we would associate respectively with Chicago and Birmingham) is shaping urban social divisions in distinct ways—dualisms not only of local/non-locals but also formal/informal, official/unofficial, and, also, gender. Fincher (2016) has argued that in terms of wealth accumulation through residential property, the Chinese city remains very much the domain of men through the omission of the majority of women from title certificates. Moreover, the sharp tenure differences in Chinese cities and the lack of the settled stability of owner-occupation for large sections of urban populations points to a potential future, restlessness among its urban populations. It may appear that while the American Dream is fading (Temin, 2018), the Chinese Dream is reaching out to an ever-greater proportion of its population. But the already evident and growing divisions around property ownership and the current overreliance on residential real estate as a source and store of wealth suggests that housing is likely to be a growing source of conflict and discontent, of agitation as Park would have put it, in the Chinese city—rather than necessarily a force for stability and harmony.

Acknowledgment

This chapter forms part of a research project supported by the Hong Kong Research Grants Council, *Frontier City: Place, belonging and community in contemporary Shenzhen* (Grant No. 11608115).

References

Bassett, K. and Short, J. R. (1980) *Housing and residential structure: Alternative approaches*, London: Routledge and Kegan Paul.

Bigott, J. (2006) *Review of Garb, City of American Dreams: A History of Home Ownership and Housing Reform in Chicago, 1871-1919*, H-Urban, H-Net Reviews. Available at: http://www.h-net.org/reviews/showrev.php?id=11760.

Boltanski, L. and Esquerre, A. (2017) "Enrichment, profit, critique: A rejoinder to Nancy Fraser," *New Left Review*, 106: 67–76.

Burgess, E.W. (1925) "The growth of the city: an introduction to a research project," in R.E. Park, E.W. Burgess and R. McKenzie (eds.) *The city*, Chicago: University of Chicago Press.

Chai, Y. C. (2014) "From socialist *danwei* to new *danwei*: A daily-life-based framework for sustainable development in urban China," *Asian Geographer*, 31(2): 183–90.

Dardot, P. and Laval, C. (2014) *The new way of the world: On neoliberal society*, London: Verso Books.

Davis, D. (2006) "Urban Chinese homeowners as consumer-citizens," in S. Garon and P. (eds.) *The ambivalent consumer: Questioning consumption in East Asia and the West*, Ithaca, NY: Cornell University Press.

Dear, M. (ed.) (2002) *From Chicago to L.A.: Making sense of urban theory*, London: Sage.

Demographia (2018) *14th Annual Demographia International Housing Affordability Survey: 2018*, St. Louis, MI: Demographia. Available at: www.demographia.com/db-dhi-index.htm.

Feng, J., Wu, F., and Logan, J. (2008) "From homogenous to heterogeneous: The transformation of Beijing's socio-spatial structure," *Built Environment*, 34(4): 482–98.

Fincher, L. H. (2016) *Leftover women: The resurgence of gender inequality in China*, London: Zed Books.

Forrest, R. and Hirayama, Y. (2015) "The financialisation of the social project: Embedded liberalism, neoliberalism and home ownership," *Urban Studies*, 52(2): 233–44.

Forrest, R. and Hirayama, Y. (2018) "Late home ownership and social re-stratification," *Economy and Society*, 47(2): 257–79.

Forrest, R. and Izuhara, M. (2012) "The shaping of housing histories in Shanghai," *Housing Studies*, 27(1): 27–44.

Forrest, R., Tong, K.-S., and Wang, W. (forthcoming) *The residential neighbourhood in the city of the future*.

Fu, Q. (2016) "The persistence of power despite the changing meaning of homeownership: An age–period–cohort analysis of urban housing tenure in China, 1989–2011," *Urban Studies*, 53(6): 1225–43.

Garb, M. (2005) *City of American dreams: A history of home ownership and housing reform in Chicago, 1871–1919*, Chicago: University of Chicago Press.

GF Securities (2018) *Industry report: An analysis of Shenzhen's housing stock*, Guangzhou: GF Securities.

Gu, W. (2013) "What percent are you in China?" *The Wall Street Journal*, September 23. Available at: https://blogs.wsj.com/chinarealtime/2013/09/23/what-percent-are-you-in-china/.

Haack, M. (2018) "Hundreds of thousands displaced as Shenzhen 'upgrades' its urban villages," *The Guardian*, August 23. Available at: www.theguardian.com/cities/2018/aug/23/hundreds-of-thousands-displaced-as-shenzhen-upgrades-its-urban-villages.

Haddon, R. F. (1970) "A minority in a welfare state society: The location of West Indians in the London housing market", *New Atlantis*, 2, 80–133.

He, S. (2013) "Evolving enclave urbanism in China and its socio-spatial implications: The case of Guangzhou," *Social & Cultural Geography*, 14(3): 243–75.

He, S. and Qian, J. (2017) "From an emerging market to a multifaceted urban society: Urban China studies," *Urban Studies*, 54(4): 827–46.

Huang, Y. and Jiang, L. (2009) "Housing inequality in transitional Beijing," *International Journal of Urban and Regional Research*, 33(4): 936–56.

Ieconomics (2018) "China home ownership rate." Available at: https://ieconomics.com/china-home-ownership-rate.

Kemeny, J. (1984) "The social construction of housing facts," *Scandinavian Housing and Planning Research*, 1(3): 149–64.

Lasch, C. (1995) *Haven in a heartless world: The family besieged*, New York: W. W. Norton.

Li, Z. and Wu, F. (2008) "Tenure-based residential segregation in post-reform Chinese cities: A case study of Shanghai," *Transactions of the Institute of British Geographers*, 33(3): 404–19.

Liu, Y., He, S., Wu, F., and Webster, C. (2010) "Urban villages under China's rapid urbanization: Unregulated assets and transitional neighbourhoods," *Habitat International*, 34(2): 135–44.

Madden, D. and Marcuse, P. (2016) *In defense of housing: The politics of crisis*, London: Verso Books.

Park, R. E. (1925) "The city: Suggestions for the investigation of human behavior in the urban environment," in R. E. Park, E. W. Burgess, and R. McKenzie (eds.) *The city*, Chicago: University of Chicago Press.

Park, R. E. (1936) "Human ecology," *The American Journal of Sociology*, 42(1): 1–15.

Piketty, T., Yang, L., and Zucman, G. (2017) *Capital accumulation, private property and rising inequality in China, 1978–2015*, National Bureau of Economic Research working paper No. w23368, Cambridge, MA: NBER. Available at: www.nber.org/papers/w23368.

Rex, J. and Moore, R. (1967) *Race, community and conflict*, Oxford: Oxford University Press.

Robinson, J. (2016) "Comparative urbanism: New geographies and cultures of theorizing the urban," *International Journal of Urban and Regional Research*, 40(1): 187–99.

Rossi, P. H. and Shlay, A. B. (1982) "Residential mobility and public policy issues: 'Why families move' revisited," *Journal of Social Issues*, 38(3): 21–34.

Shepard, W. (2015) "Do China's ghost cities offer a solution to Europe's migrant crisis?" *Reuters*, September 18. Available at: www.reuters.com/article/idIN414456248720150918.

Shi, W., Chen, J., and Wang, H. (2016) "Affordable housing policy in China: New developments and new challenges," *Habitat International*, 54: 224–33.

Temin, P. (2018) *The Vanishing Middle Class: Prejudice and power in a dual economy*, Cambridge, MA: MIT Press.

Thorns, D. C. (1989) "The impact of homeownership and capital gains upon class and consumption sectors," *Environment and Planning D: Society and Space*, 7(3): 293–312.

Timberlake, M., Wei, Y. D., Ma, X., and Hao, J. (2014) "Global cities with Chinese characteristics," *Cities*, 41(B): 162–70.

Tomba, L. (2014) "Creating an urban middle class: Social engineering in Beijing." *The China Journal*, 51: 1–26.

Trading Economics (2018) "Home ownership rates." Available at: https://tradingeconomics.com/country-list/home-ownership-rate.

Urban Planning, Land, and Resources Commission of Shenzhen Municipality (2016) *The Planning for Housing Construction in Shenzhen (2016–2020)*, Shenzhen Municipality.

Wang, M. and Lo, K. (2015) "Displacement and resettlement with Chinese characteristics: An editorial introduction," *Geography Research Forum*, 35: 1–9.

Wang, Y. P. and Murie, A. (1996) "The process of commercialisation of urban housing in China," *Urban Studies*, 33(6): 971–89.

Wang, Y. P., Wang, Y., and Wu, J. (2009) "Urbanization and informal development in China: Urban villages in Shenzhen," *International Journal of Urban and Regional Research*, 33(4): 957–73.

Watson, M. (2010) "House price Keynesianism and the contradictions of the modern investor subject," *Housing Studies*, 25(3): 413–26.

Wu, F. (2002) "Sociospatial differentiation in urban China: Evidence from Shanghai's real estate markets," *Environment and Planning A*, 34(9): 1591–615.

Wu, F. (2016) "State dominance in urban redevelopment: Beyond gentrification in urban China," *Urban Affairs Review*, 52(5), 631–58.

Wu, F. and Webster, C. (eds.) (2010) *Marginalization in urban China: Comparative perspectives*, Basingstoke: Palgrave Macmillan.

Wu, L., Bian, Y., and Zhang, W. (2018) "Housing ownership and housing wealth: New evidence in transitional China," *Housing Studies*, ahead of print, DOI: 10.1080/02673037.2018.1458291.

Wu, W. and Gaubatz, P. R. (2013) *The Chinese City*, Abingdon: Routledge.

Xie, Y. and Jin, Y. (2015) "Household wealth in China," *Chinese Sociological Review*, 47(3): 203–29.

Yi, C. D. (2017) "Housing equity and inequity in China," paper presented at ASPA Conference, Tsinghua University, October 12–14.

Yu, H. (2018) "'Human impulses run riot': China's shocking pace of change," *The Guardian*, September 6. Available at: www.theguardian.com/news/2018/sep/06/human-impulses-run-riot-chinas-shocking-pace-of-change.

Zhang, L. (2012) *In search of paradise: Middle-class living in a Chinese metropolis*, Ithaca, NY: Cornell University Press.

6

Urbanization and Economic Development

Comparing the Trajectories of China and the United States

Jan Nijman

Introduction

"The city" by Robert Park (1915) was a seminal piece of writing because it provided a new way of looking at society, at social structures and processes, and at human agency, in light of the transformational effects of the urban environment. It directed attention to the nature of human ecology (even if that term is not employed in "The city"), socio-spatial organization, individual identities, belonging, the definition and development of neighborhoods, social networks, mobility, residential segregation, and other questions that still occupy us today in urban studies and other branches of the social sciences. Park's perspective occasionally reflects the mechanistic or deterministic tendencies of the epistemologies of the time, especially in his use of metaphors (humans as ants, neighborhoods as ant nests, and the like). Nonetheless, original and wide-ranging, it set the stage for an enormous literature containing many other landmark pieces, such as Wirth's "Urbanism as a way of life."

It should perhaps be emphasized that "The city" is not so much about the city itself as an entity or unit of analysis but, rather, about human behavior or social life in urban context. Park's proposed inquiries are of a sociological nature; the city is context. Even if the theoretical contours of Park's agenda were impressively broad from a sociological point of view, the geographic (and historical) perspective is narrowly fixed: human individuals, groups, neighborhoods, suburbs, *within* the city. The article offers little, then, in terms of a contextual understanding of the city itself or of processes of urbanization: where did this growth come from? There is mention of various cities in the US (Chicago, New York, San Francisco, Boston) and of London but comparative questions are not raised. Historical context is equally absent. The world was at war in 1915 but one would never know it from reading "The city."

In this chapter, it will be argued that present-day Chinese urbanization bears some fundamental similarities to US urbanization at the time of Robert Park. Indeed, in a different academic culture, China today might have had its "Chicago School" in Shanghai, Shenzhen, or Nanjing. Hence, "The city" can be read as a stimulus to investigate present-day Chinese urbanization from a comparative angle. As such, this chapter counters the peripheral treatment of Chinese cities in current comparative urban debates and the inward-looking and exceptionalist tendencies of Chinese writings.[1] The focus is not so much on the "urban social ecology" that characterized the Chicago School but rather on the process of urbanization in a broader sense, and mainly in relation to equally broad macroeconomic and demographic trends.

Recent debates on comparative urbanism (see, for example, Nijman, 2007, 2015b; McFarlane and Robinson, 2012; Ward, 2012; Peck, 2015) are fueled by the acceleration of globalization trends, the growing interconnectedness of cities, and emerging questions about urban convergence or differentiation. Thinking about comparative urbanism is deeply influenced by political economy perspectives and considerations of city-state relations. In a Western context, urbanization is generally understood in relation to markets and economic development, which are in turn shaped in political context.

Most comparative urban approaches are focused on cities or urbanization in the "north" (North America, West Europe) and the more theoretical debates have increasingly focused on the portability of "northern" theory vis-à-vis the "global South." China is rarely considered integral to the "global South" and its political economy, and role of the state, seems to preclude comparison altogether. Put differently, if the applicability of northern theory to the global South is a matter of intense debate, its non-applicability to China often appears a foregone conclusion.[2]

The particularities of Chinese cities today are obvious in terms of, for example, the role of the state and the Communist Party or the nature of the newly emerged land market (Hsing, 2010). While the question of the relative importance of structural economic trends versus policies, especially in the Chinese context, is difficult to answer, this chapter focuses on the fundamentals of the process of urban agglomeration and especially the relationship between economy and urbanization. What economic and demographic developments are driving Chinese urbanization and what are its likely future directions? How can a comparison with the US be helpful in furthering our understanding of developments in China?

To set the stage for this discussion, Figure 6.1 overlays the historical periods during which the US and China experienced their most rapid (relative) increases in urbanization: for the US from 1860 to 1920 and for China from 1960 to 2020—exactly one century apart. They are comparable trajectories, even if the pace of China's urbanization has been faster that than of the US. As will be argued, in both the US and China, urbanization and industrialization were closely entwined. More generally, this chapter is premised on the basic interrelationships between urbanization, evolving modes of economic production, and demography.

Figure 6.1: US and Chinese urban population growth, 1860–1920 (for the US) and 1960–2020 (for China)

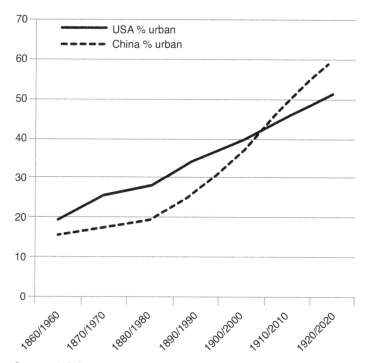

Sources: US Census; World Bank.

To be clear, the comparison with the United States is not normative in any way, nor is there a suggestion of exceptionalism on part of the US (or China). On the contrary, this chapter underscores the importance of exploring common (if variegated) logics in the process of urbanization across time and space, while acknowledging notable particularities. Cognizant of the need to avoid "errors of developmentalism," the comparison serves mainly as a heuristic device, particularly in thinking about the direction of China's cities in the near future, which is discussed later. The nature of a useful comparison is that it can shed light on key commonalities *and* critical differences.[3]

Urbanization and industrialization in the United States

In hindsight, it is not difficult to ascertain the broader societal and historical context that was missing from Park's writings in the early 20th century. Chicago and other big cities in the US were rapidly industrializing. The US, around the turn of the century, had become the industrial powerhouse of the world, surpassing England and Germany, and well ahead of France, Russia, or Japan. The industrial rise of the US in the second half of the 19th century coincided with the "first wave of globalization," an era of rapid international integration of commodity and capital markets (Bordo et al., 2003; WTO, 2008) that was conducive to the growth of overseas markets for US manufacturers.

US cities had become sites of industrial production and attracted unprecedented numbers of migrants, growing bigger and more dynamic than ever before. Chicago in 1850 counted barely 30,000 people; by 1870, its size had increased tenfold and tripled again within the next two decades (Badger, 2017). By 1920, when the urban share of the US population for the first time exceeded 50%, roughly a third of the total workforce was employed in manufacturing (Leon, 2016).

Figure 6.2 shows the rapid increase in the US share of global GDP (gross domestic product) from the middle of the 19th century to about 1960, alongside the growth of the US urban population. Clearly, urbanization and economic growth (that is to say, industrialization) were closely correlated: gathering momentum in the 1820s, accelerating in the mid-19th century, and continuing in a steep upward trajectory into the 1950s.[4] Park wrote "The city" just about halfway this century-long, steady, development of urbanization and industrialization. Urban and industrial growth must have seemed the norm and it may have been hard to imagine an end to this era.

Figure 6.2: US share of global GDP (smoothed curve) and the share of the US population living in urban areas, 1800–1960

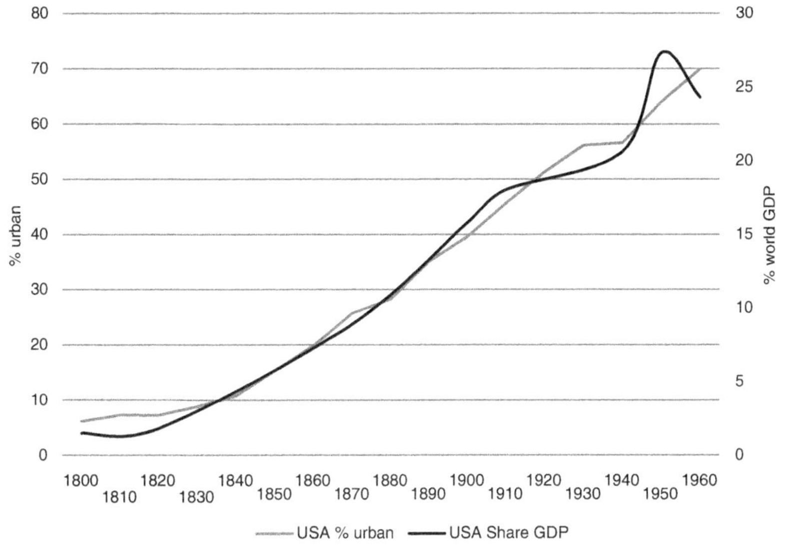

Sources: Maddison, 2007; US Census.

Industrialization and urbanization moved in tandem because the former involved labor-intensive production, accommodated by the latter through forces of agglomeration and economies of scale (for example, Scott, 2017). Cities became sites of production, in addition to already existing (preindustrial) functions of exchange and services. This social transformation, through the second half of the 19th century and the first half of the 20th century, was integral to the evolving mode of capitalist production often denoted as Fordism: spatially concentrated and vertically integrated mass manufacturing, named for the company that seemed to have perfected the business model. The revolutionary Ford Model T had been rolling off the Detroit assembly lines since 1908.

Cities were growing in size as never before. New major manufacturing centers such as Pittsburgh, Detroit, and Chicago expanded at a fast pace, and the US urban system dispersed across the Northeast, into the Midwest, and reached the California coast. Densities increased, as did congestion. Pollution was common, especially near the urban centers. The first half of the 20th century witnessed major social change and gradual betterment of the lives of the urban working class. Fordist conditions were conducive to the organization of labor (such as the United Auto Workers, in 1935), working conditions improved, and the middle class expanded.

Urban growth in the US, throughout this long urban century, was also sustained by steady natural population growth and through immigration, together meeting the demands for labor in the industrializing cities. About halfway along the US upward urban trajectory, in 1920, the total decadal growth rate of the population was a robust 15% and the annual birth rate was "healthy" 2.5. It was still a relatively young population, with a median age of 25 years and plenty of growth ahead (US Census; see also Table 6.1).

Urbanization and industrialization in China

There is a structural similarity between the United States in 1915, when "The city" was published, and China one hundred years later.[5] Between 1980 and 2010, in a mere 30 years, the urban share of China's population jumped from 20% to 50%. It is expected to reach 60% by 2020.[6] In the ten years leading up to 2015, it is estimated that China added 194 million people to its urban population. In the same year, there were at least six cities with a population over 10 million and a hundred cities with more than 1 million.

China's urban transformation began with the declaration of the so-called Special Economic Zones in the late 1970s and early 1980s (Friedmann, 2005). There, in coastal urban areas, the government allowed foreign investment (in production) and stimulated trade. In subsequent years, these conditions of economic and urban growth were further relaxed and extended to other areas.[7] As was the case in the US in earlier times, the Chinese urban system has rapidly dispersed and has expanded westward. The interior regions that were considered remote rural backwaters not long ago, now harbor major cities such as Chengdu and Lanzhou. Through deliberate policies, the country's coastal cities assumed key roles as centers of agglomeration, sites of production, theaters of capital accumulation, and employment centers. China's extremely fast urbanization could not have materialized if it were not for equally impressive industrialization—and vice versa.

Figure 6.3 reflects the close correlation between urbanization and industrialization, the latter measured indirectly in terms of China's share of global GDP. The approximate share of manufacturing in China's labor force roughly doubled from 13% in 1980 to 25% in 2010 (Lu et al., 2002; Majid, 2015). China is now the industrial powerhouse of the world. By way of illustration, it is estimated to produce 80% of the world's air-conditioners, 70% of its mobile phones, and 60% of its shoes. China's share of the global economy has quadrupled since 1980. In the process, its cities became centers of industrial production, attracting enormous numbers of

Figure 6.3: China's share of global GDP and the share of the Chinese population living in urban areas, 1960–2020

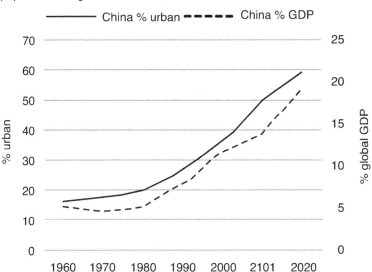

Sources: Maddison, 2007; UN Population Division.

migrants and growing into megacities or, rather, megacity regions. The polycentric urban regions in the Pearl River Delta, around Beijing, and around Shanghai, each comprise more than 100 million people. The Pearl River Delta alone is said to house more manufacturing laborers than the entire United States. The immense Foxconn factories are emblematic: they manufacture and assemble a range of electronics and computer goods and employ more than 1 million people. With their largest plant located in Shenzhen, Foxconn is in some ways the 21st-century avatar of the Ford Motor Company in Detroit a hundred years earlier.

As noted in the previous section, US industrialization can be understood in part in the context of the "first wave of globalization" that gathered momentum in the second half of the 19th century. The "second wave of globalization" (Bordo, 2003; WTO, 2008), that gathered speed since the 1970s, has been equally (or even more) important to China's industrialization. From foreign investment in China's manufacturing sector to Chinese access to overseas consumer markets, China's industrialization has depended significantly on open global markets.

China's rapid urban growth has thus far been fueled by massive rural–urban migration[8] and substantial natural population growth. At the start of the China's urbanization drive, in 1980, the birth rate stood at 2.6, the median age was 22 years, and overall population growth rate was about 15% over the previous decade. On these counts, China's demographic state was comparable to that of the United States in 1920. However, China's population growth was about to come down in dramatic fashion, in no small part due to the one-child policy that was introduced in 1979 and that was particularly consequential in China's cities. This demographic shift, as will be elaborated below, is a critically important factor in China's postindustrial urban future.

Deindustrialization and urban America

The industrial era in the US lasted about a century and its ending proved painful. Deindustrialization represented a shock in terms of job losses and social dislocation. The growth of major cities came to a sudden halt and turned negative. The largest cities, that had thrived during industrialization, experienced a major decrease in employment and population, for the first time in four generations.

The reasons for deindustrialization are well known: automation facilitated by new technologies and relocation to other parts of the world as capital became more mobile. Across the US, especially in the Northeast, urban areas declined and many central cities witnessed decay. Labor unions lost much of their power in the transition to a post-Fordist mode of production. Production dispersed globally and many manufacturers closed down or threatened to leave. Cities' tax bases shrank and services were reduced. Crime increased. New York City's bankruptcy in 1975 was a dramatic marker of decline. It was not just about declining urban population growth. As Wilson (1999) has argued compellingly, the long-term disappearance of work had deep consequences for the social fabric of urban societies—particularly when economic inequalities and deprivation is compounded by deep racial divisions.

Figure 6.4 shows the declining population at this time of New York City and the City of Detroit. New York's population first stagnated around mid-century and began to decline around 1960. The decade of the 1970s was the most severe, witnessing a population decline of more than 10%. The decline continued until the mid-1980s. Detroit's rise and decline was more extreme: the very fast growth of "motor city" in the first half of the 20th century came to an abrupt halt by 1960. In 1980, the population had dropped to the level of 1930. And, unlike for New York, there was not to be a revival. Detroit had no real prehistory as a center of exchange and was very much itself a product of the industrial era. The city has now experienced a half-century of deindustrialization and decline. Detroit may be extreme but it is certainly not alone in its persistent troubles: the rustbelt in the Northeastern US contains more cities like it, from Cleveland to

Pittsburgh, from Syracuse to St. Louis. For New York and other more fortunate cities, the deindustrialization downturn of the US economy lasted about 20 to 25 years, roughly from 1960 to 1985.

Figure 6.4: The population of New York City (left) and the City of Detroit (right), 1860–2020

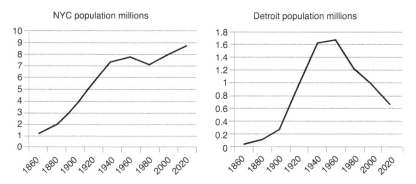

Source: U.S. Census, various tables on largest city populations in the U.S., 1860 through 2010; estimates, for 2020.

Note: the vertical axes are scaled differently.

Urban revival and the new economy in the United States

The share of the US workforce in manufacturing dropped steadily from 24% in 1960 to 8% in 2016. It never returned to previous levels. The recovery of urban growth since around 1990 was in essence based on the emergence of the information economy; a new mode of production that involved different means of production but that was, perhaps even more than during the industrial age, emphatically situated in urban areas. Instead of manufactured goods, this new economy revolved around information products and was propelled by the digital revolution. The new economy involves mainly finance and professional and business services (accounting, insurance, advertising, consulting, marketing), cultural industries (Scott, 2004), and, in some urban areas, high-tech industries (such as Silicon Valley in California; Austin, Texas; Raleigh-Cary, North Carolina).

New York's population growth turned positive again in the late 1980s and has been on an upward trajectory since (Figure 6.4). New corporate and job growth was accompanied with population increases, an expanding tax base, and increased infrastructure spending, construction, and so on. A look at the biggest companies based in New York is illustrative.

According to the *New York Business Journal* (2017), the ten biggest (publicly traded) companies in terms of revenues headquartered in New York are Verizon, JPMorgan Chase, Citigroup, MetLife, Pfizer, AIG, New York Life Insurance, Morgan Stanley, Goldman Sachs, and TIAA. Half of them are in finance, three in insurance, and the other two in information technology and pharmacology. Even in cities where more traditional companies dominate (such as manufacturing and foods, as in Chicago or Pittsburgh), most jobs in these companies in the city are filled with what Robert Reich (1991) calls "symbolic analysts," highly educated and highly paid white-collar workers.

However, if cities such as New York and others revived against the backdrop of this dynamic new economy, and even if overall wealth in cities increased significantly, the benefits did not accrue equally across the urban population. In fact, the new economy has only deepened the inequality that crystallized during the period of deindustrialization and urban decline. Deindustrialization resulted in the loss of many typical middle-class manufacturing jobs. Subsequently, the labor market and income distribution of the new economy did anything but restore the middle class. Professional workers in the new economy tend to be highly educated, highly skilled, and highly paid. The service workers in that same economy, from retail personnel to clerical staff to hospitality workers, tend to be low-skilled and low-paid. The new urban economy is characterized by a bimodal income distribution, a bifurcated workforce, and a polarized social structure (for example, Sassen, 2012). To stay with the example of New York: in 2016, the top 1% of income earners took 40% of all income while the bottom half had to make do with 6% (NYIBO, 2017). In terms of wealth (of greater significance than income to the truly advantaged), in 2014 the top 0.1% of the US population had more than doubled its wealth since 1980 and controlled as much as the bottom 90% (Saez and Zucman, 2014).

Related to the shifting mode of production, and important for the revival of cities in the US and elsewhere in the "north," has been the rise of cities as sites of *consumption* (Jayne, 2005). The sharp decline in manufacturing employment and, eventually, its replacement with new employment in high-tech and/or information activities, resulted in growing inequality and the formation of a class of high earners who either work and live in the city or who work further out but choose to *live* in the city for its amenities. This is what Ehrenhalt (2012) termed "the great inversion": corporate activity, retail, restaurants, entertainment, people, the young especially, choosing to move back into the city, drawn to "urban chic" and amenities. These revitalized urban environments also have become places of consumption for lower-income classes living away from the central city. More than ever, "going to the city" is not about going to work, but about leisure and consumption. This means that cities and city centers in this latest stage have become the preeminent sites of an industry that revolves around consumption, consumer services, and amenities. As Glaeser et al. (2000) had already observed at an early stage: "the future of cities depends on the ability of particular urban areas to provide attractive places for increasingly rich workers."

This situation has resulted in the growing incidence of reverse commuting, where high-income earners work in edge cities or elsewhere in the urban periphery but live in city centers. In the Bay Area, for example, the flow of commuters leaving the city of San Francisco every morning going south (to Silicon Valley) exceeds the opposite flow (Walker and Schafran, 2019). Mere urban growth figures tend to mask intra-metropolitan shifts, population turnover, displacement, and replacement. Many have had to leave central cities to find more affordable housing in the suburbs (Nijman and Clery, 2015; Nijman, 2019). Gentrification has been a prominent feature of the emerging consumption city. The consumption/information city is by definition a highly unequal place and it serves as an important backdrop to recent writings about the continually widening gap between rich and poor.

Still, the case of Detroit reminds us that not all cities in the US followed this path. For those that did not, deindustrialization had lasting and deeply erosive effects; the transition to an urban information economy, high-tech production, and, especially, consumption never quite arrived and the return to growth never happened. In 2017, one in ten US cities had shrinking populations. This experience is not unique to the United States: for example, a third of Germany's cities are losing population; the same in happening in varying degrees across Europe, and, notably, so too in Japan and South Korea. Unlike the situation in the US, in these countries the problem is compounded by low birth rates and slow or even negative overall population growth.

Chinese urbanization beyond the industrial era

One might be tempted to raise the question whether China's urban future will be more like New York or like Detroit. It is, however, the wrong question because presently Chinese cities are the scene of a conjunction of manufacturing, deindustrialization, and the new economy all at once. One could say that successive developments that shaped US cities over three or four decades are compressed in time and space across Chinese cities today. For our purposes, speculation about China's urban future over the next 20 years or so should consider trends in manufacturing, the emergent new economy, demographics, and possibilities of emergent consumer cities.

First, we can be quite certain that China has already experienced some deindustrialization and there will be more to come—but deindustrialization will not be as massive or disruptive as in the US. Presently, manufacturing constitutes about 20% of all employment and has been steady over the last decade or so (Levinson, 2017). Productivity continues on an upward trajectory: the increase in value added through manufacturing from 2008 to 2015 was 80% (adjusted for inflation), compared to only 2% for the US (Levinson, 2017). Nonetheless, China is (and has been) subject to selective deindustrialization.

It is important to differentiate between various manufacturing sectors, of various ages and efficiency. China's traditional coal, steel, and oil industries, concentrated in the Northeast, had already stagnated in the 1980s. These industries, it should be noted, predated the major post-Mao reforms and were not central to the industrial/urban take-off since the 1980s. Between 1995 and 2003, the government closed down operations in many of these old industries, resulting in major layoffs: during these years, the manufacturing share of all employment dropped from 20% to 17% nationwide. Subsequently, new investment in modern manufacturing sectors resulted in a return to about 20% of manufacturing employment by 2015 (see, for example, Lardy, 2015; Majid, 2015). Most of these new investments bypassed the Northeast. The scarce data available suggests that the major cities of the Northeast, Harbin and Dalian, have witnessed very slow or even negative population growth.

There are also signs of selective deindustrialization in the cities and manufacturing zones that have emerged since the 1980s, in provinces such as Guangdong and Jiangsu, or toward the interior, as in Sichuan. Reports of labor unrest have surged in recent years, often related to layoffs, pay cuts, or demands for higher wages (*The Economist*, 2012; Beech, 2016). According to one count, there were 2,700 worker protests and strikes across China in 2015, twice as many as in 2014 (Hernandez, 2016). Most took place not in the Northeast but in the Pearl River Delta. The problems in these particular industries, that involve much low-skilled labor, are apparently caused by overcapacity and/or large-scale automation. Wages are now relatively high in China compared to places such as Vietnam or Nigeria (Sun, 2017). The same kind of relocation of manufacturing that eroded the industrial base of cities in the US since the late 1960s, is now affecting some Chinese manufacturing (Sun, 2017).

Events in Beijing in 2017 seemed to underscore this selective deindustrialization and economic transition. The authorities demolished large, dense residential areas in Beijing that were populated by rural migrants without *hukou* (official residency permit). The government cited safety hazards and a recent deadly fire in one neighborhood. But observers pointed to a declining need for low-skilled employment in the major cities and an aggressive government policy to make room for more highly educated workers in the new economy (Buckley, 2017).

Hence, notwithstanding the relative overall stability of manufacturing, it is clear that China's economy is in transition and that the new economy has been growing in importance. According to a recent OECD report, between 2006 and 2016 the contribution of manufacturing to GDP decreased steadily from 48% to 40% and dropped below the contribution of services for the first time in 2012 (OECD, 2017). To be sure, the urban information economy and its high-tech accompaniments are already there. The economy in the last two decades has been diversifying and investments in IT and high-tech sectors are substantial and growing. Alongside manufacturing giant Foxconn, there are companies like Alibaba and Baidu. The total valuation of China's "unicorns" (startup companies valued at $1 billion or more) in 2016 was roughly on a par with that of the US, a powerful indicator of the presence of a mature and dynamic new economy—and one that does not seem constrained by China's political system (McKinsey Global Institute, 2017a). In e-commerce and mobile payments, China is well ahead of the US (McKinsey Global Institute, 2017a).

The rapid emergence of the new urban economy, where incomes tend to be higher, often much higher, than in manufacturing or low-skilled services, has contributed to growing inequality and this will likely increase further in the years to come (particularly in a generational sense). It is a different inequality, however, from that which characterized US cities in recent decades: if in the US the middle class dwindled due to deindustrialization, in China it did not. Rather, the growing inequality in Chinese cities is related to the introduction of a new class of (very) high-income earners in the new economy. Inequality in Chinese cities is also different, and perhaps less intractable, due the absence of the deep-seated racial divisions that characterize urban America.

The third factor pertains to demography. When the US became 50% urban in 1920, its demographic profile and openness to immigration would ensure continued urban growth in subsequent years. China faces an entirely different situation. Table 6.1 and Figure 6.5 compare the demographic profiles of China and the US *at the moment their urban population share reached 50%*, for the US in 1920 and for China in 2010. US overall population growth was nearly three times that of China and the average person was nearly ten years younger.

The population pyramid for China illustrates the impact of the one-child policy and signals the ramifications. During the year 2017, China's working-age population declined by about 5 million, setting a trend that will continue at least for a generation. China today boasts roughly five workers for every retiree. By 2040, this ratio will have collapsed to about 1.3. By 2050, the median age will be about 46 and China will be among the most aged societies in the world (French, 2016).

Table 6.1: Demographic comparison of China in 2010 and the US in 1920, when their respective populations were 50% urban

	United States 1920	**China 2010**
Urban share of population	50%	50%
Birth rate, annual	2.5	1.5
Median age	25 years	35 years
Population growth, decadal	15%	5.8%

Sources: US Census, 1920; World Bank.

Figure 6.5: Population pyramids for the US in 1920 (left) and China in 2010 (right), the respective years that their urban populations reached the 50% mark. The graphs display age cohorts in percentage shares for males and females.

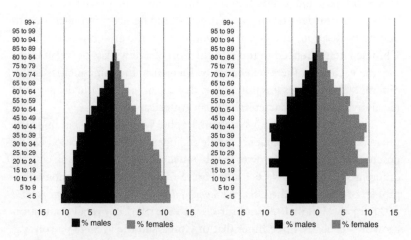

Data sources: US Census, 1920 (see table 6.1); for China, National Bureau of Statistics, 2012.

As a consequence, China's postindustrial urban labor problem—a labor shortage—is rather the opposite of the structural unemployment that plagued US cities in the wake of deindustrialization.[9] The shortage in China's cities could fuel further relocation of low-skilled manufacturing to other parts of the world (Sun, 2017), thereby hastening the transition from manufacturing to an economy dominated by information, finance, professional services, and high-tech.

The fourth and final issue in China's postindustrial urban development is the possible transition of cities as sites of production to sites of consumption. To be sure, the overall consumption of goods and services in China has increased rapidly in recent years and will probably continue in the foreseeable future (see, for example, McKinsey Global Institute, 2016). But buying refrigerators, jewelry, smart phones, cars, or clothes is not the same as consumption *of* the city, where urban space itself becomes an essential part of evolving consumer lifestyles.[10]

The transition toward cities as sites of consumption requires appeal of the urban environment and its amenities to high-income consumers, to work there, perhaps, but even more so to *live* there. In the US experience, it is emphatically not about large-scale shopping malls or other forms of mass consumption but rather about distinguished consumption patterns that are intrinsically tied to an exclusive urban environment: high-end real estate, upscale restaurants, eateries, clubs, private schools, gyms, parks, concert halls, boutiques, bars, theaters, and so on (Bridge, 2001). In these cities, the remnants of the industrial past are often carefully maintained, as in loft apartments or trendy restaurants in former factories. It is a form of romanticism, because in reality these comfortable, trendy, sanitized, places are a long way from the gritty industrial past.

The dearth of studies on the *social* restructuring of China's cities (He et al., 2017) impedes a firm assessment but this may not be a very likely scenario for most Chinese cities. Like Detroit, many of the newer Chinese cities have little preindustrial history to romanticize; most seem to lack the typical late 19th or early 20th century industrial sites with historical cachet that have been such popular targets of urban refurbishing in Western cities (loft apartments, restaurants, performance spaces, and so on). There have been some early signs of central city gentrification, actively supported by local governments, but it appears to concern mainly residential renewal (less so commercial) in older metropolises such as Shanghai and Beijing (Zhang et al., 2014; Shin, 2016).

Conclusion

This chapter considers the long-term trajectory of Chinese urbanization in relation to macroeconomic and demographic developments. It does so against the backdrop of the US historical and contemporary experience which, in some respects but not in others, has been ahead of that of China. The discussion gives way to eight observations that are more or less conclusive or speculative.[11]

First, it is clear that China's rapid urbanization in recent decades has moved in tandem with fast-paced industrialization and as such closely resembles developments in the US about a century earlier. China's urban and economic growth rates are higher than was the case in the US but are driven by the same logic of agglomeration, with labor-intensive manufacturing fueling urban population growth. China's age of urbanization and industrialization will have been faster and shorter than that of the US. The year 2016 recorded the slowest economic growth in China in nearly two decades and may prove a turning point already. According to World Bank data, the urban growth rate has already steadily dropped over the last decade, from nearly 4% in 2005 to 2.7% in 2017 (World Bank, 2018).

Second, the size of China's urban-based labor-intensive manufacturing sector is bound to decline substantially in the 2020s and after, both in relative and absolute terms. It will decline as a result of automation, relocation to lower-cost regions outside China (mainly Africa and Southeast Asia), and a sectoral shift from manufacturing to less labor-intensive high-tech and information-based economic sectors. The US is not the only precursor in this regard: closer to home and more contemporary to the Chinese experience, South Korean manufacturing employment decreased 14% from 1990 to 2015 (Levinson, 2017). As with South Korea, China's transition is emphatically *not* a case of "premature deindustrialization" (Rodrik, 2015) but rather a natural shift toward more highly productive and value added economic activities.

Third, deindustrialization in China will not be accompanied by the kind of economic disruption and social dislocation that scarred US cities for several decades. In the US, an entire generation lapsed between the onset of deindustrialization and the emergence of the new economy; in China, the new economy is already well under way even while manufacturing is still strong. This means that there will not be a temporary dip in urban population growth of Chinese cities as witnessed in New York in the wake of deindustrialization, nor a steep structural decline as in the case of Detroit.

Fourth, and somewhat more speculative, China's economic transition will probably imply a decreasing overall demand for labor and a shift toward higher-educated and highly skilled workers. This means that overall urban growth rates will come down and that China's urban labor markets would become increasingly bifurcated and polarized. Apparently, these trends are also already under way. Between 2010 and 2016, overall urban employment in China dropped from 4.1% to 2.5% (OECD, 2017). The government-stimulated shift to high-tech is evident in aggressive investment in bio-pharmacy, mobile communications, electric cars, aircraft, robots, artificial intelligence, and more (Bradsher and Mozur, 2017).

Fifth, the expected overall decline in the demand for labor would coincide with reduced labor supply due to demographic change: there is no doubt that the share and absolute number of working-age Chinese is going to come down considerably over the next 25 years or so, as discussed in the previous section. As a consequence, and contrary to the Western experience at the time of deindustrialization, China would not face persistent unemployment but rather worker *shortages*, which in turn may accelerate relocation of investments.

Sixth, China's major cities are already witnessing declining population growth rates as a result of decreasing overall labor needs, demographic change, and government policies aimed at containing the size of the largest cities. Government policies have for some time stimulated dispersed, integrated, regional urban growth, especially around Beijing and Shanghai, and in the Pearl River Delta. Other regions may soon experience shrinkage, following the examples of the US, West Europe, Japan, South Korea, and China's own early experience in the Northeast. Due to the country's extreme demographic shift, urban shrinkage in China may well be more severe than anything seen before in other countries and urban areas.

Seventh, it is not so clear if Chinese central cities could follow in the footsteps of now-vibrant central cities in the US that have themselves become consumptive spaces for gentrifying classes of high-income young urbanites. There cannot be a "great inversion" where there has not first been central city decline. And, while individual consumption in urban China is undoubtedly increasing at a fast pace, many Chinese cities do not appear to be suited to this kind of place-based reinvention of urban living space. Perhaps more likely, Chinese cities will witness the proliferation of more "manufactured" suburban consumption and amenity-oriented living for the affluent.

Finally, China's cities will most likely experience growing economic and social inequality. This is due to the transition toward high-tech and producer services combined with the growth of low-skilled services in hospitality and health care—the latter related to increased consumption and an aging population (McKinsey Global Institute, 2017b; OECD,

2017). Generational inequality is likely to become more pronounced as well. Government will face a major challenge in containing these growing disparities and in reconciling these emergent social realities with communist principles. Apparently, this trend, too, is already under way: Chinese workers have become increasingly vocal in their demands (see, for example, Beech, 2016; Hernandez, 2016) and growing inequality may be accompanied with rising social and political tension. The old German notion that "Stadtluft macht frei" (city air liberates), invoked by Park in 1915 in regards to early 20th century social change in US cities, may well apply to urban China.

If Park's early 20th century writings on the American city were decidedly inward-looking, so is much of the work on Chinese cities a century later. Comparison (in a non-normative fashion), over time and across space, can be instructive if we want to discern the general logic of urbanization and possible future directions. Indeed, if we are interested in the development of urban theory itself, comparison is all but unavoidable. China's urbanization makes for a special case, to be sure. But it is not *that* special.

Notes

[1] For example, a recent article by Wang et al. begins with the unsubstantiated claim that "China has followed a unique path to urbanization" (2015: 279).

[2] A small and growing number of specialist urban China scholars views the role of the Chinese state in urbanization more dynamically and in more nuanced ways (see, for instance, Lin, 2007; Wu et al., 2007; Hsing, 2010; He and Lin, 2015; Zhang and Peck, 2016; Wu, 2016; He et al., 2017).

[3] In addition, there is no suggestion here that comparison with the US is the only or best way to understand urbanization in China. Comparisons of urban-economic-demographic dynamics with, for example, South Korea, Japan, or India, could be equally instructive.

[4] Toward the end of the period, the graph shows a slowdown in the 1930s due to the Great Depression (both in GDP share and urban growth) and then a very steep rise of GDP share due to the devastations of the Second World War elsewhere in the world. It also shows a notable downturn in GDP share in 1960. This was in part a reaction to the abnormal and temporary increase of the US share due to the war but it also signaled a structural shift, that of deindustrialization in the US and economic recovery elsewhere in the world, especially Germany and Japan.

[5] It is not self-evident that the model of industrialization and urbanization should apply outside the experience of North America and West Europe—in India and much of Africa, for example, it appears that it does not. See, for example, Nijman, 2015a; Turok and McGranahan, 2013.

6   China's "urban" definitions are complex and have changed over time. The accuracy of Chinese statistics (that find their way into the data sets of the World Bank and other international agencies) is debatable (see, for instance, Chan, 2007). The same can be said about Chinese economic data, including labor statistics, which tend to be incomplete. In regards to the manufacturing sector, for many years the official data were biased to older, state-owned industries (see, for example, Banister, 2005). For our purposes, it is assumed that the data are sufficiently reliable and consistent to allow a general analysis.

7   It was a dramatic reversal from the very particular policies of earlier times, when migration and urbanization were repressed and foreign investment was deterred. In that sense, China's urbanization "burst" and the explosion of industrial activity also reflected this suddenly (partially) freed movement of capital and people (Friedmann, 2005).

8   By 2015, the total number of "permanent" rural–urban migrants exceeded 300 million people, nearly as many as the total US population (Majid, 2015).

9   There appears a contradiction in reporting from China about labor shortages on the one hand, and labor unrest due to wage disputes or layoffs (which might suggest a labor surplus) on the other hand. Layoffs seem mostly confined to old manufacturing sectors only. The wage disputes reflect rising expectations among China's workers and can also be attributed to increasing demand for labor relative to supply.

10   The number of shopping malls in Chinese cities has proliferated at a dizzying pace in recent years, to the point where there is now a glut and where many are thought to be unsustainable. This is compounded by the fast growth of e-commerce in China, which threatens conventional retail (Fong, 2017).

11   In the short run, the Chinese economy is subject to volatility, with possible implications for the pace and direction of urbanization. Particularly, at the time of writing at the end of 2017, China's debt levels and highly speculative urban real estate markets were said to pose substantial stability risks (see, for example, Sharma, 2016; Elliott, 2017). These are important matters, to be sure, but they are outside the scope of this essay.

Acknowledgment

The author is grateful to Julie Ren, Fulong Wu, and Fei Li, for their helpful comments on earlier drafts. The usual disclaimer applies.

References

Badger, E. (2017) "What happened to the America boomtown?" *The New York Times*, December 6. Available at: www.nytimes.com/2017/12/06/upshot/what-happened-to-the-american-boomtown.html.

Banister, J. (2005) "Manufacturing employment in China," *Monthly Labor Review*, July 2005. Washington, DC: U.S. Bureau of Labor Statistics.

Beech, H. (2016) "Labor unrest grows in China, even in the historic heartlands of the revolution," *Time Magazine*, April 11. Available at: http://time.com/4286397/china-labor-social-unrest-strikes-pingxiang-coal/.

Bordo, M. D., Taylor, A. M., and Williamson, J. G. (eds) (2003) *Globalization in historical perspective*, Chicago: University of Chicago Press.

Bradsher, K. and Mozur, P. (2017) "China's plan to build its own high-tech industries worries Western businesses," *The New York Times*, March 7. Available at: www.nytimes.com/2017/03/07/business/china-trade-manufacturing-europe.html.

Bridge, G. (2001) "Bourdieu, rational action and the time-space strategy of gentrification," *Transactions of the Institute of British Geographers*, 26(2): 205–16.

Buckley, C. (2017) "Why parts of Beijing look like a devastated war zone," *The New York Times*, November 30. Available at: www.nytimes.com/2017/11/30/world/asia/china-beijing-migrants.html.

Chan, K. W. (2007) "Misconceptions and complexities in the study of China's cities: Definitions, statistics, and implications," *Eurasian Geography and Economics*, 48(4): 383–412.

The Economist (2012), "A dangerous year: Unrest in China".

Ehrenhalt, A. (2012) *The great inversion and the future of the American city*, New York: Vintage.

Elliott, L. (2017) "China's debt levels pose stability risk, says IMF," *The Guardian*, December 6. Available at: www.theguardian.com/world/2017/dec/07/china-debt-levels-stability-risk-imf.

Fong, D. (2017) "China has too many shopping malls," *Wall Street Journal*, January 3. Available at: www.wsj.com/articles/china-suffers-from-glut-of-shopping-malls-1483458666.

French, H. (2016) "China's twilight years," *The Atlantic Monthly*, June. Available at: www.theatlantic.com/magazine/archive/2016/06/chinas-twilight-years/480768/.

Friedmann, J. (2005) *China's Urban Transition*, Minneapolis: University of Minnesota Press.

Glaeser, E., Kolko, J., and Saiz, A. (2000) "Consumer city," *Harvard Institute for Economic Research*, Discussion Paper 1901 (June), Cambridge, MA: Harvard University. Available at: https://econpapers.repec.org/paper/fthharver/1901.htm.

He, S. and Lin, G. C. S. (2015) "Producing and consuming China's new urban space: State, market, and society," *Urban Studies*, 52(15): 2757–73.

He, S., Kong, L., and Lin, G. C. S. (2017) "Interpreting China's new urban spaces: State, market, and society in action," *Urban Geography*, 38(5): 635–42.

Hernandez, J. C. (2016) "Labor protests multiply in China as economy slows, worrying leaders," *The New York Times*, March 14, 2016.

Hsing, Y. (2010) *The great urban transformation: Politics of land and property in China*, Oxford: Oxford University Press.

Jayne, M. (2005) *Cities and consumption*, London: Routledge.

Lardy, N. R. (2015) "Manufacturing employment in China," *Real Time Economic Issues Watch*, Peterson Institute for International Economics, December 21. Available at: https://piie.com/blogs/china-economic-watch/manufacturing-employment-china.

Leon, C. B. (2016) "The life of American workers in 1915," *Monthly Labor Review*, February, Washington, DC: U.S. Bureau of Labor Statistics.

Levinson, M. (2017) "U.S. manufacturing in international perspective," *Congressional Research Service*, January 18, R42135. Washington, DC. Available at: https://fas.org/sgp/crs/misc/R42135.pdf.

Lin, G. C. S. (2007) "Chinese urbanization in question: State, society, and the reproduction of urban spaces," *Urban Geography*, 28(1): 7–29.

Lu, M., Fan, J., Liu, S., and Yan, Y. (2002) "Employment restructuring during China's economic transition," *Monthly Labor Review*, August: 25–31. Available at: www.bls.gov/opub/mlr/2002/08/art3full.pdf.

Maddison, A. (2007) *Contours of the world economy, 1–2030 AD*, Oxford: Oxford University Press.

Majid, N. (2015) "The great employment transformation of China," *Employment Working Paper 195*. Geneva: ILO Employment Policy Department. Available at: https://www.ilo.org/wcmsp5/groups/public/---ed_emp/documents/publication/wcms_423613.pdf.

McFarlane, C. and Robinson, J. (2012) "Introduction: Experiments in comparative urbanism," *Urban Geography*, 33(6): 765–73.

McKinsey Global Institute (2016) *Urban world: The global consumers to watch*, April. Available at: www.mckinsey.com/featured-insights/urbanization/urban-world-the-global-consumers-to-watch.

McKinsey Global Institute (2017a) *China's digital economy: A leading global force*, Discussion Paper, August. Available at: www.mckinsey.com/featured-insights/china/chinas-digital-economy-a-leading-global-force.

McKinsey Global Institute (2017b) *Jobs lost, jobs gained: Workforce transitions in a time of automation*, discussion paper, December. Available at: www.mckinsey.com/mgi/overview/2017-in-review/ automation-and-the-future-of-work/jobs-lost-jobs-gained- workforce-transitions-in-a-time-of-automation.

National Bureau of Statistics (2012) *Women and men in China: Facts and figures 2012*, Government of the People's Republic of China. Available at: www.unicef.cn/en/uploadfile/2014/0109/20140109030938887. pdf.

New York Business Journal (2017), "JP Morgan leads the list of 45 New York companies on the new Fortune 500 ranking".

Nijman, J. (2007) "Introduction: Comparative urbanism," *Urban Geography*, 28(1): 1–6.

Nijman, J. (2015a) "India's urban future: Views from the slum," *American Behavioral Scientist*, 59(3): 406–23.

Nijman, J. (2015b) "The theoretical imperative of comparative urbanism: A commentary on 'Cities beyond compare?' by Jamie Peck," *Regional Studies*, 49(1): 183–6.

Nijman, J. (ed.) (2019) *The life of North American suburbs*, Toronto: University of Toronto Press.

Nijman, J. and Clery, T. (2015) "The United States: Suburban imaginaries and metropolitan realities," in P. Hamel and R. Keil (eds.) *Suburban governance: A global view*, Toronto: University of Toronto Press, pp. 57–79.

NYIBO (New York City Independent Budget Office) (2017) "How has the distribution of income in New York City changed since 2006?" April 19. Available at: www.ibo.nyc.ny.us/iboreports/ printnycbtn72.pdf.

OECD (Organisation for Economic Co-operation and Development) (2017) *OECD economic surveys: China 2017*, Paris: OECD. Available at: www.oecd.org/eco/surveys/economic-survey-china.htm.

Park, R. E. (1915) "The city: Suggestions for the investigation of human behavior in the city environment," *The American Journal of Sociology*, 20(5): 577–612.

Peck, J. (2015) "Cities beyond compare?" *Regional Studies*, 49(1): 160–82.

Reich, R. (1991) *The work of nations: Preparing ourselves for 21st-century capitalism*, New York: Vintage.

Rodrik, D. (2015) "Premature deindustrialization," *IAS School of Social Science, Economics Working Papers, No. 107*, January. Available at: www.sss.ias.edu/files/pdfs/Rodrik/Research/premature- deindustrialization.pdf.

Saez, E. and Zucman, G. (2014) "Wealth inequality in the United States since 1913: Evidence from capitalized income tax data," *NBER Working Paper Series, No. 20625*, Cambridge, MA: National Bureau of Economic Research. Available at: www.nber.org/papers/w20625.

Sassen, S. (2012) *Cities in a world economy* (4th edn.), Los Angeles, CA: Pine Forge Press.

Scott, A. J. (2004) "Cultural-products industries and urban economic development," *Urban Affairs Review*, 39(4): 461–90.

Scott, A. J. (2017) *The constitution of the city: Economy, society, and urbanization in the capitalist era*, Cham: Palgrave Macmillan.

Sharma, R. (2016) "How China fell off the miracle path," *The New York Times*, June 3. Available at: www.nytimes.com/2016/06/05/opinion/sunday/how-china-fell-off-the-miracle-path.html.

Shin, H. B. (2016) "Economic transition and speculative urbanisation in China: Gentrification versus dispossession," *Urban Studies*, 53(3): 471–89.

Sun, I. Y. (2017) "The world's next great manufacturing center," *Harvard Business Review*, May–June. Available at: https://hbr.org/2017/05/the-worlds-next-great-manufacturing-center.

Turok, I. and McGranahan, G. (2013) "Urbanization and economic growth: The arguments and evidence for Africa and Asia," *Environment and Urbanization*, 25(2): 465–82.

UN Population Division, World Urbanization Prospects. Available at: https://data.worldbank.org/indicator/SP.URB.TOTL.IN.ZS?end=2017&start=1960.

US Census (1920). Available at: https://www2.census.gov/library/publications/decennial/1920/volume-3/41084484v3ch01.pdf.

US Census, Table 4. Population 1790 to 1990. Available at: https://www.census.gov/population/censusdata/table-4.pdf.

Walker, R. and Schafran, A. (2019), "The strange case of the Bay Area," in: J. Nijman (ed.) *The Life of North American Suburbs*, Toronto: University of Toronto Press.

Wang, X.-R., Hui, E. C.-M., Choguill, C., and Jia, S.-H. (2015) "The new urbanization policy in China: Which way forward?" *Habitat International*, 47: 279–84.

Ward, K. (2012) "Toward a comparative (re)turn in urban studies? Some reflections," *Urban Geography*, 29(5): 405–10.

Wilson, W. J. (1999) "When work disappears: New implications for race and urban poverty in the global economy," *Ethnic and Racial Studies*, 22(3): 479–99.

Wirth, L. (1938) "Urbanism as a way of life," *The American Journal of Sociology*, 44(1): 1–24.

World Bank (2018) *Urban Population Growth, 2005-2017.* Available at: https://data.worldbank.org/indicator/SP.URB. GROW?end=2017&start=2005&year_low_desc=false.

WTO (World Trade Organization) (2008) *World trade report 2008: Trade in a globalizing world,* Geneva: WTO. Available at: www.wto. org/english/res_e/booksp_e/anrep_e/world_trade_report08_e.pdf.

Wu, F. (2016) "Emerging Chinese cities: Implications for global urban studies," *The Professional Geographer,* 68(2): 338–48.

Wu, F., Xu, J., and Yeh, A. G.-O. (2007) *Urban development in post-reform China: State, market, and space,* Abingdon: Routledge.

Zhang, J. and Peck, J. (2016) "Variegated capitalism, Chinese style: Regional models, multi-scalar constructions," *Regional Studies,* 50(1): 52–78.

Zhang, X., Hu, J., Skitmore, M., and Leung, B. Y. P. (2014) "Inner-city urban redevelopment in China metropolises and the emergence of gentrification: Case of Yuexiu, Guangzhou," *Journal of Urban Planning and Development,* 140(4): 1–8.

7

The Handshake 302 Village Hack Residency

Chicago, Shenzhen, and the Experience of Assimilation

Mary Ann O'Donnell

Chicago: Assimilation

European immigrants and southern-born African-American migrants were not only the focus of Robert E. Park's work in Chicago, but also laid the foundation for sociological research in the US (Pedraza-Bailey, 1990). Like his European contemporaries, Max Weber, Emile Durkheim, and Ferdinand Tönnies, Park investigated the demise of traditional collectivities, the emergence of individuality, and the increasing valorization of civility between strangers as the basis of urban society. Indeed, sociology came of age as industrialization expanded and populations became increasingly mobile in the US and Europe. Migration to industrial centers such as East London and Chicago created "cities within cities" that were "composed of persons of the same race, or of persons of different races but the same social class" (Park, 1915: 582–3). However unlike his European contemporaries, whose work focused on how migration transformed extant cities—London and Paris, for example—Park and his students grappled to understand the social consequences of im/migration in Chicago, where genocide, settler expansion, European immigration, and African-American migration played roles not only in the construction of the city, but also dominated the city's self-understanding. In contrast to the European experience, the Chicago experience comprised forms of mobility—settlement and violent deterritorialization, as well as contemporary im/migration—that throughout Park's entire lifetime (1864–1944) relentlessly brought together diverse peoples and forced new social patterns and moralities to emerge among and between strangers.

The idea of the city as ongoing process grounded Park's sociology, especially his understanding of assimilation, which included both the gritty reality and utopian potential of modernization. Edward Shils suggests that, for Park, assimilation was "the formation of collective self-consciousness" (1996: 94). Shils further argues that Park considered assimilation an open-ended but necessary condition for collective living because the majority of Chicago's population came from elsewhere. Moreover, urban planners could neither anticipate nor control how new residents inhabited the city. Consequently, Park understood assimilation to be as important for urban morphology as geography, buildings, and transportation, arguing that:

> In the course of time every section and quarter of the city takes on something of the character and qualities of its inhabitants … The effect of this is to convert what was at first a mere geographical expression into a neighborhood, that is to say, a locality with sentiments, traditions, and a history of its own. (1915: 579)

In other words, there was no overreaching self-conscious identification with Chicago. Instead, assimilation was a situated praxis that constantly reproduced semi-autonomous neighborhoods with various degrees of internal organization. Simultaneously a spatial and cultural social form, the neighborhood mediated how ethnic and racial groups came to understand themselves as having a recognizable and shared identity within and against their host city. By implication, how neighborhood boundaries were policed and maintained (the Chicago "black line," for example) would have important consequences for how completely an individual or group could "assimilate" to Chicago, rather than the neighborhood. In this context, Park mentioned that throughout contemporary American cities, philanthropic groups worked to "renovate evil neighborhoods" and to "elevate the moral tone of the segregated sections of great cities" (1915: 582) to bring localized forms of assimilation (the neighborhood) to a generalized form of assimilation (the city).

With the publication of "The city: Suggestions for the investigation of human behavior in the city environment," Park framed sociological research with respect to the simultaneous construction of urban space and identities. "The city" was published 20 years after the last federally approved land rush allowed white settlers (both American- and European-born) to homestead the so-called "surplus lands" of the Kickapoo in the Oklahoma Territory. When Park turned his gaze to Chicago, the former meeting grounds of the Potawatomi, Miami, and Illinois nations was already the largest Norwegian city in the world besides Oslo, had a Polish population of 400,000, and about three fourths of its population was either a first- or second-generation immigrant (Cressey, 1938). Concurrently, "the Great Migration" of African Americans from the rural South to cities in the northern and western United States was underway (Tolnay, 2003). This larger background of crisscrossing and often incommensurable mobilities that abruptly came together contextualizes Park's emphasis on assimilation as the process through which modern society emerged. Not even four years after the publication of "The city," the 1919 Chicago Riots between European immigrants and African-American migrants broke out, a "display of uncontained rage by put-upon people directed toward the scapegoats of their condition" (Wilkerson, 2010: 273), tragically exemplifying how "incomplete assimilation" characterized Chicago's emergent urban form and ethos. Thus, when Park sent his students into immigrant and Black neighborhoods, he did so not only in order to theorize "human behavior in the city environment," but also with an understanding that ultimately "assimilation" produced the city as a spatial pattern and a moral order.

Park conceived modern civilization as an ever-widening circle that assimilated less developed peoples into itself and thereby fundamentally transformed them. Assimilation was universal, transcending national and regional borders, and although he did not use the expression "globalization," nevertheless Park seems to have understood incorporation into modern civilization as a planetary process, stating "the civilizational character of this modern form of assimilation would have to overcome both the aspiring nationalisms of racial and ethnic minorities as well as the racially biased ethnocentrism of such already established state societies as the United States" (Lyman, 1991: 291). Implicit in Park's understanding of complete assimilation was the concomitant transformation of the ruling class as a more just society emerged. In fact, by the end of his career, Park was comparing the rhetoric of the Ku Klux Klan and the Third Reich, predicting that "If conflicts arise as a result of the efforts [of Blacks] to get their place it will be because white people started them" (Lyman, 1991: 297). Aware of the relationship between settler colonialism and genocide, Park did not even predict that all groups would survive the fallout of "assimilation." Instead, he seemed increasingly resigned to what has become a familiar trope in genres as diverse as academic cultural studies and popular science fiction—immigrants and migrants, original peoples, and colonial decedents—all were ultimately assimilated or destroyed by the expanding city.

Shenzhen: Arrival

Like Chicago, Shenzhen self-identifies as a destination city that owes its morphology and ethos to *yimin*, which means both immigrants and migrants. In 1980, when Guangdong Province elevated Bao'an County to Shenzhen Municipality, the local population was roughly 300,000 people. Thirty-five years later, the population had reached 20 million with 3.67 million *hukou* or official residents, 10.77 million had long-term residence in the city, and approximately 6 million quasi-legal members of the city's administrative population (*Southern Daily*, 2016).

From 1980 through 2005, Shenzhen attempted to govern its non-resident population according to extant *hukou* policy. Rural migrants were denied social services and their children prevented from attending school, even though they were allowed to leave their hometowns (where services were provided) to work for wages in the Special Zone. However, beginning in 2003 Shenzhen loosened restrictions on travel and work permits, and in 2006 made a virtue of necessity, promoting the concept "Come and you are a Shenzhener." Shenzhen has also taken the lead nationally in adjusting the household residency system to not only accommodate its migrant population and maintain its workforce, but also to incorporate the children of migrants, including access to high school and the chance to sit the college entrance exam in Shenzhen. In 2012, the government released its anthem, "Come and you are a Shenzhener [*Laile, Jiushi Shenzhenren*]."

Park's work on Chicago emphasized that im/migrants were actively building the city and its ethos. Similarly, Shenzhen complicates accepted models of migration in China in three ways. First, the origin stories of both Chicago and Shenzhen begin with the deterritorialization of the original inhabitants. The early history of Chicago was coded in the American myth of manifest destiny, while early discourse about migration to Shenzhen functioned within the discourse of "rustification" (O'Donnell, 1999). Moreover, Native Americans in Chicago and Bao'an locals in Shenzhen have been deliberately excluded from their city's hegemonic self-consciousness because belonging in both cities has been imagined through arrival from elsewhere. Second, both cities have benefited not only from rural to urban migration, but also from urban to urban migration. In addition to unskilled workers, Chicago attracted businessmen and professionals from eastern cities, such as New York, Philadelphia, and Boston as well as from northern Europe. Similarly, Shenzhen has depended on urban migrants from both first- and second-tier cities such as Wuhan, Changsha, and Xiamen in addition Guangdong cities, including Shaoguan, Meizhou, and Chaozhou to provide administrative, technical, and design employees. Third, the emergence of Chicago and Shenzhen must be understood in relationship to their environmental and economic hinterlands. In Chicago, this region was the Great West, which extended from the Great Lakes to the Rocky Mountains. For Shenzhen, this region has been called "the interior (*neidi*)." Both cities expanded exponentially through privileged access to resources that was authorized by a distant, yet hegemonic, national government. The scale and speed of development in Chicago and Shenzhen has meant that informal development and institutions have crucially shaped the terms of assimilation. What is more, the cities' success not only legitimated informal institutions, but also made "informality" an important local value and resource.

Shenzhen's urban villages (*chengzhongcun*) have functioned as gateways to the city and all that it offers (O'Donnell et al., 2017). In contrast to discussions of rural migration to Beijing, Shanghai, and Guangzhou, Shenzhen urban villages are not tightly packed extensions of hometown societies that function to exclude rural migrants from forms of urban citizenship and belonging (Solinger, 1999; Zhang, 2001; Lin, 2013). Rather, more like the ethnic and racial neighborhoods that Park's students investigated, Shenzhen urban villages emerged informally within and against the planned city and its built form; to use Park's terminology, urban villages are the products and crucibles of assimilation. Not only young, single, rural migrants and factory workers have lived and live in the city's urbanized villages, but also college graduates and families comprising three generations. However, by 2005, Shenzhen began upgrading its economic structure from manufacturing to the creative economy, radically changed the working-class landscape that had been documented by Pun (2005), O'Donnell (1999), and Lee (1998). Concomitantly, as the city has demolished urban villages to build residential estates, Shenzheners have become increasingly aware of the importance of urban villages to the city as a whole. Key moments in the current appropriation of urban villages to Shenzhen identity include: efforts to preserve historic (but not classic examples) of traditional architecture throughout the city, including Hubei Village, Futian District's efforts to selectively integrate its 15 villages into tourist itineraries, the Gangxia Village *Roshamon* project, and the Handshake 302 Art Space, which is located in Baishizhou, the most comprehensive urban village remaining in downtown Shenzhen.

Handshake 302

Handshake members Zhang Kaiqin, Lei Sheng, Wu Dan, Liu He, and I came together in 2012 and in 2013 opened Handshake 302, hoping that through simple, everyday acts of inhabitation, artists, architecture students, and journalists would see the city's vernacular geography with fresh eyes. We believe that bringing refreshed eyes to the question of demolishing and redeveloping Baishizhou would provide insight into Shenzhen's vernacular geography and its emergent "collective self-consciousness." The Handshake 302 collective asserts that in contrast to the city's skyscrapers and shopping malls, urban villages are the vernacular form of Shenzhen's urban modernity. In turn, how the municipality defines, rezones, and rebuilds these neighborhoods simultaneously evaluates that history and posits the city's future. Previous Handshake 302 projects such as "Accounting," "Baishizhou Superhero," and "Paper Crane Tea" exploited the semiotic discrepancies between art space programs and low-cost housing to provide an accessible sociology of Baishizhou (O'Donnell, n.d.). With the Handshake 302 Village Hack Residency program, the Handshake collective wanted to engage the living history of Baishizhou specifically, and Shenzhen's migrant history more generally.

In the rest of this chapter, I offer an interpretation of the Handshake 302 Village Hack Residency with an eye to the experience and structure of assimilation in Shenzhen.

Baishizhou: Migrant spaces

Fully integrated into Shenzhen's transportation infrastructure, but not fully integrated into its regulatory apparatus, Baishizhou is easy to get to, but hard to pin down; the neighborhood's eponymous village-collective, Baishizhou is located south of Shennan Road. However, in Shenzhen, "Baishizhou" primarily refers to the villages and housing estates located north of Shennan Road, where most of Baishizhou's gray economy, including repurposed factories, large and small markets, and "Mom and Pop" shops are located. Consequently, the questions that Park asked about Chicago's ethnic and Black neighborhoods resonate with research on Shenzhen's urban villages: What part of the population is floating? How many people live in hotels, apartments, and tenements? How many people own their own homes?

As Park noted about Chicago neighborhoods, Baishizhou operates at two levels—spatial and social. First, Baishizhou is an important hub in Shenzhen's extensive transportation network. It is a stop on two subway lines and is a transfer hub for municipal buses that connect western Shenzhen to the city's downtown and is also a terminus for long-distance buses and mini-buses to other cities in the Pearl River Delta and cities in neighboring provinces. Second, Baishizhou refers to two neighborhoods. The northern neighborhood comprises informal buildings and factories owned by four former villages—Upper Baishi, Lower Baishi, Tangtou, and Xintang—as well as planned housing estates, such as Qiaoyuan Apartments and Xiangqi Estates. The southern neighborhood comprises Baishizhou proper. Together, the five villages and their partners own or manage 2,340 buildings and oversee the neighborhood's access to the municipal grid and security forces. Although property ownership in the villages is highly unequal, nevertheless, Baishizhou teems with people and low-capital enterprises, recently arrived migrants and the children of migrant who sit their high school and college entrances exams with an eye to securing a Shenzhen *hukou*, providing cheap, downtown housing for young white-collar workers and hi-tech park and migrant families.

It is difficult to know what Baishizhou's population or population density might be. Official figures claim 83,000 people, including 1,800 people who belong to one of the original five villages and another 5,500 who have Shenzhen *hukou*. The official Baishizhou footprint covers 0.73 square kilometers and, assuming a population of 83,000, has a population density that breaches 113,000 people per square kilometer. The ratio of non-resident to household residents in Baishizhou is at least 11:1 and most likely higher (Wan, 2014) and newspaper reports estimate the population of "Baishizhou" to be 140,000 people. Baishizhou's non-resident to official resident ratio seems representative of settlement patterns in Shenzhen, where non-residents and lower-income residents live in the villages while *hukou* holders and higher income residents live in the city's planned housing estates. In suburban Shenzhen, for example, anecdotal accounts claim that the local to migrant ratio can be as high as 1:40. The estimated population density of Baishizhou also seems representative of living conditions in Shenzhen, where roughly 50% of the city's population lives in the urban villages, which comprise 5% of the city's total area (Hao et al., 2011).

Handshake 302's name alludes to the dominant architectural typology in Shenzhen urban villages—the "handshake building (*woshoulou*)," so called because is possible to reach out one's window and shake hands with a neighbor. The space is located at Building 49, Block 2, Shangbaishi Road. Exiting Building 49 and heading east, one passes a wet market and small stores that sell Styrofoam lunchboxes, plastic utensils, disposable chopsticks, and produce. Fresh market and open stall venders sell commodities and fresh produce at rates that are cheaper than similar goods sold in the department store. There are side-alleys into other sections of the neighborhood, but Shangbaishi Road itself dead-ends at a section of the wall that isolates Baishizhou from Overseas Chinese Town (the OCT), Shenzhen's flagship neighborhood of residential estates, theme parks, and museums.

Across the street from Building 49 is the side entrance to Jiangnan department store; the front entrance is located on Shahe Street with access to the subway and bus stations on Shennan Road, a ten-minute walk south. The front of the department store is an exercise area that children and their caretakers have repurposed as a playground. Also on Shahe Street Two are gated communities and the residences of Xiasha New Village. These architecture typologies conform to mid-1990s standards for work-unit and commercial housing, giving the area the feel of a small and prosperous market town. Handshake storefronts on Shahe Street are noticeably cleaner and better constructed than alley shops. Shahe shops have tiled floors, glass windows, and neon and LED signs, as well as starchitecture facades, which are continuously upgraded out of readily available construction materials and worker know-how. In the narrow spaces between shops and restaurants, hawkers set up kiosks and pushcarts that sell roasted chestnuts, corn on the cob, boiled tea eggs, and sweet tofu, hair ribbons and barrettes, blue jeans, and batteries and small appliances.

North of the Jiangnan department store is an office building. A nondescript, repurposed factory building, the building houses representatives of Baishizhou's two main constituencies—the Five Villages Limited Company on the second floor and the Nanshan District Baishizhou Community Office on the third floor. There are separate entrances to the second- and third-floor offices, and there is little interaction between the employees on the two floors. Comprising representatives from the five villages, the Company manages collectively held property and represents villagers in ongoing negotiations with Lugem Developers to raze and redevelop Baishizhou. The community center organizes day programs for elders and after-school programs for elementary students, as well as provides a reading room and counseling services. Behind the office building is a cultural plaza that was built on the footprint of a demolished factory, and which includes a well-equipped outdoor stage, benches, and picnic tables. The Lugem redevelopment office is located in a repurposed factory adjacent to the plaza.

In March 2014, the Shenzhen government announced that the northern and most socially vibrant section of Baishizhou had been designated for demolition and redevelopment, while the southern and almost exclusively residential section would remain untouched. This large-scale gentrification of Baishizhou is part of the city's current vision of itself as a creative, global hub. At this writing there is no plan to relocate the tens of thousands of people who will be displaced by the project (SZ News, 2014).

Situated engagement: The Handshake 302 Village Hack Residency

During the Village Hack Residency, participants generated art and discussion through simple ethnographic explorations of Baishizhou. These explorations departed from questions that ranged from "How long does it take to set up an apartment in Baishizhou?" through "What is the sensory experience of Baishizhou?" to "What do people know about Baishizhou?" Participants pursued the answer to their question(s) through a range of interventions. Liu He provisioned the space, Zhang Kaiqin taught our young neighbors to paint with watercolors, Tadeus Rotzil pursued sensory exploration, Huang Huihui and Fang Qiangqiang used simple objects to decorate the apartment, Yin Xiaolong photographed the Baishizhou night markets, Xu Binlan wrote a comparative essay on Beijing urban villages, Zhou Ximin manipulated digital recording of local sounds, and Xu Tan wandered the Baishizhou. On the last day of their residency, each hacker held an open house where they shared their experience with a wide range of guests. These conversations were broadcast to members of the Handshake 302 WeChat group.

Three common experiences illustrate the potential and challenges of hacking Baishizhou and by extension how individual migrants have "assimilated" to Shenzhen.

First, all participants commented on the wary, but polite helpfulness of strangers in Baishizhou. Huihui and Qiangqiang had come to Shenzhen from Sanming City, Fujian in the 2014 fall semester to attend Shenzhen University's undergraduate architecture program and emphasized that the residency was their first urban village experience. They had thought that living in a small room would be unpleasant and that living in Baishizhou would be dangerous. They discovered that it was possible to make a small room comfortable and also safe to explore Baishizhou night markets. Liu He mentioned that when shopping or asking directions, shopkeepers and pedestrians answered questions and offered advice. However, they rarely pursued conversation. Instead, questions and answers were direct and unambiguous, with the simple phrase, "I don't know" ending further conversation. Consequently, all participants relied on social networks that predated their arrival in Baishizhou order to complete various tasks.

Second, most participants used Handshake 302 as a bedroom. Liu He had purchased a tea table, tea set, and water heater to prepare drinks for guests, and no one added to the furniture collection. Participants quickly realized that their partial inhabitation resembled the "full time" occupation of migrants to the extent that few people invested time or money into their rental property. One neighbor, for example, asked us why 302 had been recently painted and the lighting fixtures neatly installed. When we explained that we had painted and rewired the room ourselves, she seemed confused. We further explained that our actions constituted a social–artistic intervention and invited her to join the salon. She smiled and moved away from the doorframe. Participants also noted that neighbors furnished their apartments only with needed objects, and they outsourced as many costs as possible. Thus, singletons tended to eat at workplace cafeterias or fast food restaurants, sometimes returning home with take-out or instant noodles. As far as we could tell, in Building 49, only rooms with children were equipped for cooking. Moreover, cooking tools were limited to electric hot pots and rice cookers, while special condiments had been brought from hometowns.

Third, all participants mentioned the three sisters who lived with their parents next door in room 301. The sisters also brought friends to Handshake 302 to participate in different activities. Zhang Kaiqin, for example, had asked the question, "Would children be interested in art?" The first night that she opened the door and provided paper and watercolors, one sister came. By the end of the week, however, eight girls had come to paint. These eight girls would continue to participate in Handshake 302 events, including playing Chinese checkers with Tadeus and making interior design crafts with Huang Huihui and Qiangqiang. The girls also started attending the Friday evening salon, serving tea and snacks to visitors. The girls' participation suggested that although the door to Handshake 302 functioned as an intimacy threshold for adults, nevertheless children easily came and went between rooms. Moreover, it was easier to strike up conversations with parents after their children had participated in a 302 event, especially as parents were eager for their children to have more contact with better-educated and higher-status participants.

Shenzhen residents came to the project through WeChat. Handshake 302 has an open WeChat account and creates "cards" that can be easily circulated. Current and former Baishizhou residents also came to the project via WeChat (rather than through our posters), suggesting that although new people came to participate in the project, they did so via third-party introductions. Moreover, class status also informed self-selection to participate in the project. Both residency and salon participants were all white-collar workers engaged in design, architecture, or administration jobs. Consequently, some journalists, visitors, and current Baishizhou residents remarked that participants were not "true" Baishizhou residents and therefore "could not understand" everyday life in an urban village. The question of an "authentic" migratory experience haunted the project because it showed up the class stratification that enabled the residency. We discovered that the "real Baishizhou" was defined by working-class status, rather than actual residency in the neighborhood. Critics assumed that even when white-collar workers lived in Baishizhou, they would eventually leave the neighborhood for a higher-status residence because white-collar migrants could depend on family savings to make a down payment on a house, and also held jobs that could be used on a bank mortgage application. In contrast, although laborers and working-class families aspired to leave Baishizhou for a higher-class neighborhood in Shenzhen, experience had shown that the most reliable way of securing home ownership was to purchase or build a house in one's hometown or village.

The Village Hack Residency generated several conclusions about how Baishizhou mediated migrants' ongoing assimilation from hometown to Shenzhen lives.

First, Baishizhou has provided inexpensive, conveniently located bedrooms for service, administrative, and creative workers. Inexpensive housing has become increasingly important in Shenzhen because (1) the city phased out subsidized housing for state workers in the 1990s and (2) few companies still provide dormitory housing to workers, forcing migrants to turn to the market to find a place to live. In fact, many of the companies that do provide workers' housing prefer to rent rooms in a nearby urban village, rather than investing in dormitories.

Second, Baishizhou has operated as an economic launch pad for a variety of businesses, ranging from simple hawking through setting up a storefront to repurposing extant factory stock. Baishizhou is also an important transit center for inter-city express mail shipping. The variety of businesses beyond the immediate neighborhood of Building 49 include an alley of used furniture and appliance shops, thriving night markets, hair salons, hardware stores, bottled water delivery, garbage collection and sorting, and skilled labor, including plumbers, electricians, and Internet installers.

Third, despite Baishizhou's economic importance for low-income families and businesses, the area has not evoked emotional attachment as a "home." Instead, Baishizhou residents, visitors, and Village Hack participants considered the urban village to be a place of transition regardless of how long one had lived in the village. Children were the notable exceptions to the lack of neighborly feelings. Their friends brought them into other buildings and into contact with people outside their families' hometown networks. They also traversed imaginary boundaries between different sections of Baishizhou and, as at the exercise plaza, easily repurposed space. Moreover, children served as intermediaries between parents, their friendships enabling previously unconnected adults to make acquaintances.

Fourth, class stratification informs (assumed) life trajectories. Blue-collar workers and their families expected and are expected to remain in Baishizhou (or move to another urban village) in order to save money to purchase a house back in rural hometowns. In contrast, white-collar workers expect and are expected to move out of Baishizhou into a gated development. Participants mentioned that class stratification in Baishizhou revealed the ideological work of Shenzhen motto, "Arrive and you are a Shenzhener." The transition from outsider to Shenzhener seemed more accessible to white-collar migrants, begging the question of where Baishizhou's children belong in the city's vernacular geography.

The experience of assimilation

From the perspective of Shenzhen, where the majority of residents are first- and second-generation migrants, Park's theory of assimilation provides a structure for narrating experiences of Shenzhen's form and spatialized antagonisms. On the ground, Park's theory of assimilation not only rings true, but also has compelling parallels within both popular and academic discourse about how the city has been concurrently inhabited and built—one arrives in Shenzhen, struggles, and in doing so transforms oneself and the city (O'Donnell, 2006). Assimilation frequently appears in moral discourse about becoming a Shenzhener. "*Shiying*," for example, is the ability of individuals to adapt to the new environment of the Special Zone, while "*hexie*"—literally "harmony"—refers to the state's call for residents to transcend the antagonisms that have accompanied the consolidation of Shenzhen's class structure, another similarity that the Shenzhen shares with Chicago. Moreover, as with "assimilation" in Chicago, "*hexie*" has been a spatial and moral project. First, urban redevelopment in Shenzhen has meant demolishing extant urban villages and replacing them with housing estates and commercial property more in "harmony" with the city's changing vision of itself. Second, Shenzhen residents have visceral understanding of how the utopian potential of "harmony" can be appropriated for other purposes, as when dissenting voices are "harmonized (*bei hexie*)" into agreeing with prevailing ideologies.

These resonances between Chicago 1915 and Shenzhen 2015 help clarify the insights and blind spots of "The city." Insights include Park's attention to the urbanizing effects of large-scale mobility as both an effect and condition of industrial urbanization and the emergence of a modern society. Chicago and Shenzhen lurched into new states of being and only ethnographic attention to "neighborhoods" and "urban villages" have provided accounts of this transformation and resulting urban morphologies and cultures. Park's work on assimilation also implied that the political and economic work of managing differences between and within neighborhoods and urban villages would, over time, give each of the cities their distinct ethos; Chicago neighborhoods and Shenzhen urban villages embody the histories of their respective cities in ways that Chicago's Miracle Mile and Shenzhen's Citizen's Center cannot. Moreover, Park was acutely aware that assimilation was, in practice, often incomplete, creating and enforcing hierarchies between different groups. The physical borders between neighborhoods and "Chicago" and urban villages and "Shenzhen," for example, have had material consequences for the well-being of many who remain in, but not of, the city.

Theoretical blind spots in "The city," of course, derive from three main differences between Chicago 1915 and Shenzhen 2015. First, when Park was writing, relatively few cities had been decisively informed by the necessity of assimilation to the same extent as Chicago 1915. Today, cities expect and compete for certain kinds of migrants, while actively excluding others. Second, Chicago had at least a century of ongoing migration that shaped its neighborhoods. In contrast, the state had began restructuring Shenzhen's informal neighborhoods well before several generations of migrants could live and work there. Third, Park ignored the importance of children in transforming informal settlements into neighborhoods. In Baishizhou, adult migrants relied on preexisting relationships to navigate the city. In contrast, young migrants made Baishizhou their home through friendships that repurposed space.

I would like to end this chapter by suggesting that the Handshake 302 Village Hack Residency highlighted both the banal violence of incomplete assimilation and the attendant yearnings it inspires for more generalized, more equitable, forms of assimilation. Participants—even those who had never lived in an urban village—identified with the experience of residents in Baishizhou. They saw class and regional differences. They agreed that everyday life in Baishizhou could be uncomfortable and distressing. Moreover, most were happy to return to their homes in planned housing estates. Nevertheless, in the markets and shops and steady stream of workers in and out of Baishizhou, participants also saw the processes that had transformed (or would transform) migrants into

Shenzheners. Indeed, when participants held open houses, examples of quotidian assimilation, which ranged from housework to setting up a shop assumed existential meaning. Moreover, assimilation was practical; when Baishizhou no longer served its purpose, residents moved on even as they recognized the need for such transitional spaces if Shenzhen was to remain "Shenzhen." This too seems to me characteristic of the Chicago experience that Park invoked in "The city." Assimilation forces on im/migrants and their children the awareness that there are multiple, often incommensurable, ways of being human and urban life entails figuring out how to recognize, navigate, and use that knowledge of difference to construct the city. Indeed, as Park recognized in Chicago, assimilation in Shenzhen also lends itself to bittersweet utopianism (quoted in Lyman, 1991: 297): "The races and peoples which fate has brought together ... within the limits of the larger world economy will continue, in the emerging world society, their struggle for a political and a racial equality that was denied them in the world that is passing."

References

Cressey, P. F. (1938) "Population succession in Chicago: 1898–1930," *American Journal of Sociology*, 44(1): 59–69.

Hao, P., Sliuzas, R., and Geertman, S. (2011) "The development and redevelopment of urban villages in Shenzhen," *Habitat International*, 35(2): 214–24.

Lee, C. K. (1998) *Gender and the South China miracle: Two worlds of factory women*, Berkeley: University of California Press.

Lin, X. (2013) *Gender, modernity, and male migrant workers in China: Becoming a 'modern' man*, New York: Routledge.

Lyman, S. M. (1991) "Civilization, culture, and color: Changing foundations of Robert E. Park's sociology of race relations," *The International Journal of Politics, Culture, and Society*, 4(3): 285–300.

O'Donnell, M. A. (1999) "Path breaking: Constructing gendered nationalism in the Shenzhen Special Economic Zone," *Positions: East Asia Cultures Critique*, 7(2): 343–75.

O'Donnell, M. A. (2006) "What the fox might have said about inhabiting Shenzhen: The ambiguous possibilities of social- and self-transformation in late socialist worlds," *TDR: The Drama Review*, 50(4): 96–119.

O'Donnell, M. A. (n.d.) "Handshake 302," *Shenzhen Noted*. Available at: https://shenzhennoted.com/czc-special-forces/.

O'Donnell, M. A., Wong, W., and Bach, J. (2017) "Introduction: Experiments, exceptions, and extensions," in M. A. O'Donnell, W. Wong, and J. Bach (eds.) *Learning from Shenzhen: China's post-Mao experiment from special zone to model city*, Chicago: University of Chicago Press, pp. 1–19.

Park, R. E. (1915) "The city: Suggestions for the investigation of human behavior in the city environment," *The American Journal of Sociology*, 20(5): 577–612.

Pedraza-Bailey, S. (1990) "Immigration research: A conceptual map," *Social Science History*, 14(1): 43–67.

Pun, N. (2005) *Made in China: Women factory workers in a global workplace*, Durham, NC: Duke University Press.

Shils, E. (1996) "The sociology of Robert E. Park," *The American Sociologist*, 27(4): 88–106.

Solinger, D. J. (1999) *Contesting citizenship in urban China: Peasant migrants, the state, and the logic of the market*, Berkeley: University of California Press.

Southern Daily (2016) "General Secretary Ma Xingrui: This year Shenzhen has to increase the number of documented residents" ["Ma Xingrui: Jinnian Shenzhen Yao Dafu Tuijin Huji Renkou"], *Southern Daily* [*Nanfang Ribao*], January 30. Available at: http://epaper.oeeee. com/epaper/H/html/2016-01/30/content_9105.htm.

SZ News (2014) "Baishizhou renovation is placed on the 2014 list of urban renovation projects" ["Baishizhou Jiugai Lieru 2014 Nian Shenzhen Chengshi Gengxin Jihua Mingdan"], *Southern Net* [*Nanfang Wang*], March 5. Available at: www.sznews.com/news/content/2014-03/05/content_9180624_2.htm.

Tolnay, S. E. (2003) "The African American 'Great Migration' and beyond," *Annual Review of Sociology*, 29: 209–32.

Wan, Y. (2014) "The transformation of urban space in Chinese culture: A case study of Baishizhou" ["Zhongguo Shehui Wenmaixia de Chengshi Jiancheng Kongjian Bianqian"], Master's thesis, School of Architecture, Shenzhen University.

Wilkerson, I. (2010) *The warmth of other suns: The epic story of America's Great Migration*, New York: Random House.

Zhang, L. (2001) *Strangers in the city: Reconfigurations of space, power, and social networks among China's floating population*, Stanford, CA: Stanford University Press.

8

Beijing Ring Roads and the Poetics of Excess and Ordinariness

Jeroen de Kloet

Night rides

When I was doing fieldwork on rock music in Beijing in 1997, I lived at the campus of Beijing University. The concerts often took place in either the center of the city, or in the eastern part. Aside from my vivid memories of these concerts, Beijing in those days was also marked by the night rides on the ring roads in the little yellow vans, or bread taxis as they were called, back from the rock venue to the campus. Not hindered by traffic, the city would pass by in a flash, a miracle of lights, big buildings, and some remaining signs of the old Beijing, such as the Lama temple located on the north side of the second ring road. This spectacle of driving full speed through a city continues to mesmerize me to today; how I love these nightly taxi rides over the ring roads of Beijing. Used as I am to the highways in Europe, that are almost always located outside of the city, the ring roads turn the city into a graspable entity, a backdrop that provides security about one's location—"Ah, we are now at the Bird's Nest," "Ah, this is Beijing University," "Now we are at the CCTV building," and so on (see Figure 8.1). The rides sparked off an interest in the meaning of these ring roads, an interest that increased together with the number of ring roads over the past years—up to seven, if we wish to include the ship-shaped seventh ring of 940 kilometers (of which only 38 kilometers passes through Beijing).

Figure 8.1: The fourth ring road

Photograph © Jeroen de Kloet.

The ring roads serve as an important marker of identity in Beijing—they not only have come to signify one's class background, they also help people to easily locate others. Living around the third and fourth East ring road counts as a sign of luxury and inclusion, unlike the poor people and migrants who are located mostly beyond the fifth ring road. The ring roads are crucial for the cognitive mapping of the city; for example, when one asks someone where she lives, the answer is likely to be "between the third and fourth ring road in the East."

This gestures toward a more general concern regarding megacities: how to keep them livable, how to grasp them mentally, and how to avoid people feeling lost and alienated? With life becoming increasingly urbanized, these questions also gain importance. In his famous 1903 essay "The metropolis and mental life," Simmel (2002) refers to the blasé outlook, which is what individuals wear to protect themselves from the sensuous overdoses and money-driven experiences of the metropolitan city. But it may well be in, first, the mapping of the city, and, second, the mediations of the city through art and popular culture that we manage to regain control over the city. The ring roads of Beijing and their mediations in art and popular culture serve as a case in point, as I will show in this chapter.

142

Simmel's contemporary, Robert Park, also observes the sensuous overdose of the city, but argues more as an outsider rather than insider. "The city," he argues, "shows the good and evil in human nature in excess" (Park, 1915: 612) which inspires him to read the city as a laboratory to study human behavior. Following both Simmel and Park, we may thus conceive the city in terms of excess, of overdose, of too much to humanly handle. But if we move a hundred years forward, we face quite different theorizations. Jennifer Robinson's idea of cities as being ordinary, rather than global or exceptional, serves as a productive counterbalance to the narratives of excess and abundance. According to her, "[a]ll cities are best understood as 'ordinary'. Rather than categorizing and labeling cities as, for example, Western, Third World, developed, developing, world or global, I propose that we think about a world of ordinary cities, which are all dynamic and diverse, if conflicted, arenas for social and economic life" (Robinson, 2006: 1).

How are we to connect these two terms? After all, is excess not something extraordinary, rather than ordinary? For Park, transportation and communication (that in the context of this chapter are translated into the ring roads and their mediation in art and popular culture) "have multiplied the opportunities of the individual man for contact and for association with his fellows, but they have made these contacts and associations more transitory and less stable" (1915: 607). For Park, the city is above all a human product, and individualized, lived experiences are crucial if we are to understand life in the city.

The ring roads help to connect the excessive with the ordinary, and the collective with the individual. They give access to the excessive city, and as such turn it into a more humane and more ordinary city, in spite of the spectacular extravaganza of the night rides. This, say, pacification of the excessiveness of the city strikes me as all the more urgent in a city like Beijing, an excessive city *par excellence*: too big, too polluted, too crowded, too ugly, too controlled, with roads that are too wide, and a cityscape that is changing too fast, making one lose one's way time and again. Green parks are turned into neighborhoods, neighborhoods are turned into roads, and roads are turned into skyscrapers. The ring roads function as a symbolic device to keep a sense of control over this excess; they help to locate people and places, they function as the highway in the center, and they create the mental map of the city. But at the same time, they also serve as metaphors for the governmental control over the city, as such they are both, to use Lefebvre's terms, representations of space—referring to the hegemonic representations associated with the space that is being produced; as well as representational spaces, directly lived and transformed by the use of them (Lefebvre, 1991; Schmidt, 2012).

In what follows I will probe into the meaning and significance of the ring roads in Beijing, connecting them to this schism between hegemonic narrations and lived narrations of space, arguing that they serve as crucial cognitive markers that help to both control and gain a sense of control over the city, turning Beijing into something more ordinary than may be expected at first sight of the city. Such massive roads can thus help to connect the ordinary with the extraordinary, they help to dampen the excessiveness of a city. While my analysis engages with Beijing, this observation may well be applicable also for other places, and are not necessarily confined to ring roads either.[1] I will first present a brief history of the ring roads, and show how they are included in the city planning of the government. Then I will show how they serve as cognitive markers, and thus help to navigate, and thus live in, the city. They have also, as I will show in the next section, become sites of contention—rappers address issues of growing inequalities, as do artists, and jokes are being made. These forms of popular appropriation turn the ring roads, and with them the city of Beijing, into something more mundane, more banal, and more human. This attests to how cities have become sites of contestation and negotiation. In the final section I cannot help but be seduced into a more metaphorical and maybe also more romantic reading of the ring roads: Inspired by a fiction documentary of filmmaker Bono Lee, titled *Beijing is coming*, I like to read the ring roads also as something without an end, a road on which one never arrives, thus symbolizing the predicament of contemporary China: that of dazzling and never-ending change toward a future yet unknown.

Historical rings

The first mystery I wanted to solve when doing research for this chapter was to discover the first ring road. Beijing now has six ring roads, the numbering starts with two, and goes up to six. The seventh ring road is mostly located in Hebei, the province surrounding Beijing. It closed up only in 2016 and was opened to the public in 2018 but looks more like a boat, rather than a ring (see Table 8.1 for a summary of the ring roads).

Whereas for those living in the center of Beijing the city stops at the fifth ring road, figures tell a completely different story: from the total Beijing population of 21,516,000 inhabitants, 51% lives *outside* of the fifth ring road. As I will show later, it is especially these fringes of the city where one is confronted with stark social, cultural, and economic inequality that haunts China.

Table 8.1: The Beijing ring roads[2]

	Length (km)	Date of completion	Population*
Ring road 2	32.7	1992	1,481,000 (6.9%)
Ring road 3	48.3	1999	2,573,000 (11.9%)
Ring road 4	65.3	2001	2,875,000 (13.4%)
Ring road 5	98.6	2003	3,607,000 (16.8%)
Ring road 6	187.7	2009	5,802,000 (26.9%)
Ring road 7	940.0	2016	5,177,000 (24.1%)

* refers to the population within second ring road, between the second and third ring roads, third and fourth ring roads, and so on.

But where is the first ring road? Some claim it to be the road around the Forbidden City, others refer to an old tramline that started in 1924 and moved from Tiananmen, through Xidan, Di'anmen, Dongdan, and back to Tiananmen, 17 kilometers long (*Gonghui Bolan*, 2011). As it turns out, according to one source, there has never been a first ring road (Cui, 2009). The construction of the third ring road started in 1958, as part of a city planning that was very much inspired by the Soviet Union. This was Beijing's first ring road to be build, building of the second ring road only started in the 1970s (Cui, 2009), although in the end it was closed up later than the second ring road. For a long time, only three parts were finished, in the north, east, and south—hence the name given to it, the 'third ring road' refers to these three parts of the ring road. Hence the nonexistence of a first ring road.

The ring roads are excessive, in length, in speed, in everything, pretty much like Beijing itself is an excessive city. They help to create order in the chaos of the city, and as such serve as governmental tools that help regulate and divide the distribution of people, buildings, radiating roads, and parks in Beijing. Compared to the old Beijing, a walled city with designated city gates, the roads give a sense of limitlessness, a forever expanding city. This is referred to as the pancake model (*tandabing* 摊大饼) (Ji, 2013), referring to the fear that the city gets bigger and bigger—a fear quite justified when we see the length of the sixth ring road (188 km) and that of the seventh road (940 km).

The classed logic of the ring roads is quite clear, the fifth ring road is the strongest marker of inclusion and exclusion: beyond this ring road we will find mostly (but, as I remarked earlier, not only) migrant workers and poor people, the people also that make the rapid speed of changes possible, the ones that have been building the new cityscape of Beijing. As

Li Zhong, general manager of a real estate company explains, "The ring roads of Chinese cities have become a representation of city centralization, as a psychological boundary, there is a strong feeling of 'inside the circle and outside the circle' (*quanliquanwai* 圈里圈外)" (Ji, 2013). House prices are also strongly connected to the location of the house vis-à-vis the ring road. The building of the fifth ring road has helped raise the prices of real estate in the areas surrounding the ring roads dramatically. The rings thus connote strongly class difference, in the words of playwright Zhou Liming (in Ji, 2004):

> "When your house is inside or outside the fourth ring road implies two different classes. Living in *Zhongguancun* means you belong to the IT circle, in *Guomao* to the finance circle, and living near the Imperial Palace means you are part of the powerful class of old Beijing. Living in 5th or 6th are always ants (*yizu* 蚁族) or losers (*diaosi* 屌丝)."

But the roads are about much more than class alone. There is also debate, for example, whether the ring roads do not create jams, following the logic of "the more you build the more you get stuck" (*Yue xiu yue du* 越修越堵). Urban researcher Yang Meng explains (Ji, 2013):

> "City ring roads are usually a forbidding kind of urban space. They brutally and violently demarcate the city, marking boundaries difficult for pedestrians and green areas to transgress. Although urban planning maps usually indicate a series of green corridors connecting the rings, in effect they have invariably become 'green deserts.' It is a case of transport functionality overriding every need for walking space."

Critiques aside, it comes as no surprise that for the government, the ring roads are part of their attempt to present a modern city to the world. In the years prior to the Olympics, they would do their utmost to make the roads and their direct surrounding look better, as one article states, "to give all the athletes and travelers a beautiful Beijing is the hope of all Beijing citizens. The comprehensive regulations of the west second ring road has started recently and will serve as an example for all" (Zhao, 2006). This cleaning up involved more strict regulations for advertisements, changing the electric wiring from above to underground, improving the lighting, and improving the buildings. The choice of color reflects a conscious navigation between the traditional and the modern: "The outside surface of the building: light green a style of simple ancient (*gupu* 古朴) but also modern (*xiandai* 现代)" (Zhao, 2006). In the end, the authorities aimed "To make the west second ring road a green wall and green necklace" (Zhao, 2006). The necklace metaphor has appeared more than once. The ring roads are considered the necklaces of Beijing.

But how do these necklaces appear in representations of the city? I observe four recurring tropes in media. First, following the hegemonic narratives of the city government, they signify Beijing as a modern expanding city of speed and progress. It is no coincidence that key architecture in the city, in particular the CCTV building from Rem Koolhaas next to the third ring road, and the Bird's Nest north of the fourth ring road, can be seen from the roads. They evoke an image of progress and high modernity. But in the news the roads also frequently feature as a sign of pollution, and images depict the roads in a hazy polluted sky. One Internet meme makes fun of this view. What we see is just fog plus a drawing of the CCTV building. Third, the ring roads signify an overtly busy and congested city, with endless lines of cars that hardly move. Finally, the ring roads allude to the complexity of the city: The maze of crisscrossing roads are hard to understand. This complexity meets with skepticism and sarcasm. For example, on the Internet, a photoshopped image mocks the complex crossing of Xizhimen, located at the northwest corner of the second ring road, which has also been jokingly referred to as the ninth miracle of the world (Li et al., 2014). What is depicted are endlessly looping roads, a concrete jungle, in which only roads and cars are rendered visible. These tropes attest to the importance of the ring roads; their significance goes far beyond merely transportation and mobility, instead, they serve as symbolic markers and as visual spectacles.

Together with landmarks like Tiananmen, the CCTV building, and the Bird's Nest, the ring roads are the quintessential elements used by the people to navigate the city. The ring roads give access to the city, and as such help to pacify or dampen the sense of excess that always haunts Beijing. While the fifth ring road serves as an important marker for class disjunctures, the second ring road proves to be the marker for the "old city center" and the "new Beijing." A study in 2001 discovered that people mainly refer to buildings that are located inside the second ring roads, and especially and mostly to Tiananmen Square, and then locate the ring roads accordingly (Gu and Song, 2001). When I asked students and teachers from the Beijing film academy in the spring of 2016 to draw me their personal map of Beijing, aside from their own home, plus Tiananmen Square and the Forbidden City, it was often the ring roads that were drawn (see Figure 8.2). People's impressions from the center are very clear, while the margins remains more vague (Gu and Song, 2001). With the further development of the Central Business District, the Olympic Green, and

Figure 8.2: Drawing exercise, June 20, 2016

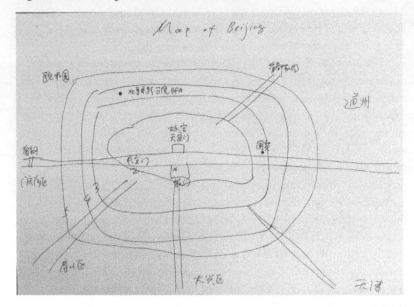

Source: By author

Zhongguancun, the high tech area of Beijing, it is likely that the public imagination regarding Beijing has also moved beyond the second ring road. The rings are deeply enmeshed in the urban planning policies and the crafting of a new Beijing by the local authorities. In the Beijing urban museum we are presented with an image of a well-planned city, planned according to different Five-Year Plans (for analysis of the museum and its movies, see de Kloet, 2016). The ring roads are part of that careful planning. What is obscured in such representations are the struggles, tensions, inequalities, and violence that accompanies the changes of the cityscape. Just as the people are usually absent in the shiny white scale models of real estate projects, so is everyday life, with all its contradictions, struggles, and tensions, removed from the Urban Museum. To grasp these dynamics, it helps to probe further into cultural expressions that are inspired by the ring roads.

Rings of resistance

The ring roads speak to the public imagination. They return in songs, television series, movies, jokes, art projects, and theatre plays. Such mediations of the city do not just display, but they also help to construct and reimagine the city. They help to alter, if not undermine, the narrative of progress and speed as propagated by the government, and turn the ring roads, as well as the city of Beijing, into a more human, a more manageable space. The circulation of memes as mentioned earlier, referring to pollution, congestion, and Beijing turning into a concrete jungle, already alludes to such proliferation of counter-narratives and images. In what follows, I will briefly analyse three such expressions in the domains of respectively, digital culture, popular culture, and art: a joke that circulated widely on social media platforms, a song that became a hit in 2011, and an art work from 2016.

A joke

As elsewhere, memes and jokes are constantly circulating on China's social media platforms, most prominently WeChat and Weibo. The speed with which they circulate makes it hard for the authorities to control them. One popular joke that circulated widely refers to the ring roads. In the joke, each ring road is read as signifying a specific part of life, for example, the second refers to one's mood, the third to life, and so on.

The story is:

> Mood, just like the 2nd ring road of Beijing, you'll never find an exit;
> Life, just like the 3rd ring road of Beijing, anything can happen;
> Love, just like the 4th ring road of Beijing, when it goes well, you may burst with passion, when it is stuck, you feel heartbroken;
> Career, just like the 5th ring road of Beijing, there's always a car in front of you. You wanna overtake? You never had the guts...
> Dream, just like the 6th ring road of Beijing, you heard of it, you never drive on it, several times you want to go, but don't know where the entrance is;
> Future, just like the 7th ring road of Beijing, you never know if it will be built or not, not reliable at all.

Here, the ring roads become larger than life, they stand for the important aspects of everyday life, ranging from your dreams to love life. The joke is an example of how such manifestations of government-led city planning are appropriated, turned into quite unexpected representations of space that are deeply embedded in the banal and the everyday.

A song

In 2011, pop music star MC Hotdog released together with comedy actor Yue Yunpeng the song titled "The song of the fifth ring road." The lyrics are above all silly and nonsensical; they sing "Ah, 5th ring, you have one more ring than the 4th ring" and keep on counting; as such, they fool around with the numbers of the ring roads. But the singers also refer to issues of congestion when they sing "There are always traffic jams, and my expression looks stupid, I have got used to just keeping driving aimlessly." The song became an instant hit, and was part of a movie titled *Pancake man* (*jianbingxia* 煎饼侠). The clip starts with a top-down view on the Forbidden City, as if to remind the viewer of the old closed city planning of Beijing, after which we are quickly guided to images of the ring roads.[3] From the four tropes analyzed earlier, three dominate: the ring road is depicted as a sign of progress, speed, and thus accelerated modernity, and these images are usually taken by night. But in daytime reality takes over, people go to work, and the roads transform into spaces of congestion and thus pollution. In an analysis of the song, the author Jiang Yeyu wonders, how come this has become the city song of Beijing? As he explains:

> The ring road has become an index to evaluate living standard and class. The best health care, education and transportation resources are within the fourth ring road. The fifth and sixth ring road becomes the hopeless choice of new immigrants in the city because of the house prices of the core region. 65% of the immigrant population lives between the fifth and sixth ring road. (Jiang, 2016)

He then uses James Scott's notion of the weapons of the weak—that are found in everyday life and popular culture—to explain the political significance of this song. He explains how the humorous style, the sound, and the lyrics all explain the popularity; its nonsense is directed, in his view, against mainstream discourse. As such, the song helps to give a voice to the discontent of the people toward the reality they face in Beijing. He writes, "Just like the last sentence in the lyrics—'what to do if you become the seventh ring'—you can only answer, 'you will have two more rings than the fifth ring', this expression articulates just the helplessness of the people toward social reality" (Jiang, 2016).

Figure 8.3: The protruding steel bars of unfinished villas

Photograph courtesy of Ma Lijiao

An art work

In the summer of 2014, the independent Second Floor art publishing institute in Beijing asked for creative works that engage with the space between the fifth and the sixth ring roads in Beijing.[4] Participants were expected to stay at least ten days in the village of their preference, for at least eight hours a day. In the year to follow, 40 projects were conducted in 40 different villages, towns, or neighborhoods. The project aimed to make urban life beyond the fifth ring road visible and tangible, to show how the migrant workers and disadvantaged people living there experience the city. For example, artist Ma Lijiao went to the Xiaojiahe East Village (see Figure 8.3). There, he first engaged with the local population by becoming a member of their WeChat groups, and thus acted as if he were one of them. This allowed him not only to get a sense of everyday life in the village, but also to communicate with the inhabitants. In the village, he acted as a student to gain the trust of migrant workers. He engaged with their struggles surrounding the unfinished real estate site there, a struggle that involved fights between the migrant workers living there and the owners of the property. By acting as a journalist, he managed to film the tensions and struggles, a film that became part of his art work later. As Deng and de Kloet argue:

Through his acting as a migrant worker, migrant workers emerge not as an anonymous horde of people, but as individuals with voices, thoughts and feelings. In his acting as a journalist and an art student, he interrogates the legitimacy of the 'right' of land use and exposes the conflicting ideas, if not possibility, of 'public space' in urbanizing Beijing. (2017: 37)

In the film, a female land renter says: "It's useless to seek help from the government. The government is on their side. They all know each other." As such, this work undermines the smooth narrative of development, of accelerated modernity, of the new Beijing; instead, it shows the struggles, the different forms of exclusion, and the tactics that are mobilized as to counter these inequalities. And for this work, the existence of the ring roads, and the particular classed meaning of the fifth ring road, serves as a catalyst to dig up these everyday tactics of resistance.

Forever being lost

How livable are megacities? How are we to counter feelings of excess, of being blasé, of alienation? The Beijing ring roads are quite unique markers that dominate the cognitive map of Beijing. They are both tools for the city authorities to control the city, as well as being used by its citizens to gain a sense of control. As such, they give access to the excessive city of Beijing, and turn it into a more ordinary city. These dialectics between hegemonic control and everyday appropriation—that refer back to Lefebvre's concepts of representations of space versus representational space—gain even more relief when we engage with cultural products that are inspired by the ring roads of Beijing. I have shown how in music, art, jokes, and everyday life the ring roads inspire reflection on, mostly, the growing disjunctures between the rich and the poor, on the massive population that has moved to areas beyond the fifth ring road, constituting 51% of the Beijing population, yet remaining by and large invisible. These are not homogenous areas either, for example, Tongzhou is known for its quite large artist population, and different villa villages have been built for the new rich in the outskirts as well, following a more American model of city planning. Despite their excessiveness, the ring roads turn Beijing in an ordinary city in the way Jennifer Robinson analyses the city and in the way Robert Park insists on the importance of individual uses and appropriations of the city. This prompts me to a plea for more close, ethnographic readings of life in between the ring roads, in the ways Park

Figure 8.4: Driving at night on the second ring road in *Beijing is coming* (Lee, 2008)

你可以开心一世 像走了很远
you can ride forever. Seems like you've travelled very far

Source: Lee (2008).

envisioned it a hundred years ago. This chapter presents a modest step in that direction.

But I have written little yet about this peculiar characteristic of a ring road: it allows you to keep on driving without ever arriving. This may yield Daoist associations with privileging the process and the way above the goal or destination. But to me, it mostly reflects the speed of changes taking place in the city of Beijing, as well as in other Chinese cities, and the unclear outcome of these changes. The title of Bono Lee's movie *Beijing is coming* refers directly to the Olympics, a ten-day event that was labeled in China as a coming out party—I still remember the slogan on t-shirts in that year: "The world gives us ten days, we will give the world 5,000 years." The title of the movie is ironic and can also be read in a more sexual way, a line of thinking I pursued elsewhere in more detail by giving a queer reading of the opening ceremony (de Kloet, 2008). The movie introduces Xiao Han, also known as Speedy Fourteen, someone born in the 1980s in China. He loves driving at night over the ring roads, overtaking as many cars as possible. While we see a car driving over the ring roads, with the camera zooming in time and again on the characteristic buildings that the car passes, Xiao Han is overtaking as many cars as he can. He explains:

> "[The night] is the time I usually take my ride. I guess the rings in Beijing are most suitable for cruising at this hour. Feels like you can go on and on, it feels so good. If you just

circle around the Second Ring, the Third Ring, or even the Fourth Ring, I tell you, you can ride forever. It seems like you have traveled very far. But in fact, you didn't go anywhere. Right, I particularly enjoy leaving other cars behind. It feels so great. And it makes you feel you are not stuck in the same place anymore. You know, Beijing is changing so fast right now, if you still want to see anything, you've got to drive faster." (Lee, 2008)

Faster and faster as to keep on pace with the changes of the city, as to avoid falling out, being excluded, being pushed outward, beyond the fifth or sixth road (see Figure 8.4).

On the ring roads in Beijing, we are in a loop that spins around forever, freezing time at night, forcing the city to become an always-returning spectacle of lights and cars, a moving theatre of buildings that pass by, and that almost all express a desire to be a historical but modern city, a prosperous and world–class city. The night makes these fantasies possible until the day breaks—and the cars come, with so many people, turning the roads into lanes for cars that look like ants, moving forward, to and from work, slowly but steadily, as part of the everyday routines that make up the social fabric of the city.

Acknowledgments

Thanks to Pei Randi for her help in data collection and translation and to her and Yiu Fai Chow and Leonie Schmidt for discussing the significance of the ring roads of Beijing. Thanks to Deng Liwen for allowing me use her work on the 5+1 project. I thank Bono Lee for sharing his movie *Beijing is coming* with me in that magic year of 2008. This research has been supported by a consolidator grant from the European Research Council (ERC-2013-CoG 616882-ChinaCreative).

Notes

[1] When it comes to ring roads, also other cities have these, Houston, Texas, for example, has three, like Tokyo and Shanghai, and Amsterdam has one.

[2] Data taken from http://baike.baidu.com/link?url=L2-iVJs46uR3NI9JM63LdSc4M ovQb2kkaz6DfXR7Pq0VqtxYE3ff9UIIVCrP6QjTcAhBFgpW4IQ6eOVI7ksca_ (on the ring roads); and http://club.dituhui.com/t/55604c3f695a323043010000 (on population distribution).

[3] See: https://www.youtube.com/watch?v=aobXmIzKosM.

[4] See, for a more substantial analysis, Deng and de Kloet (2017).

References

Cui, J. (2009) "北京二环快速路规划建设的回想", ["Recalling Beijing 2rd ring road expressway planning and construction"], 北京规划建设 [*Journal of Beijing Planning and Construction*], 6: 94–7.

de Kloet, J. (2008) "Pyjamas, nylon stockings and other Olympic dreams," *Wear—The Journal of HomeShop*, 1(1): 24–8.

de Kloet, J. (2016) "Rescuing history from the city," in C. Lindner and S. Jordan (eds.) *Cities interrupted: Urban space and visual culture*, London: Bloomsbury, pp. 31–48.

Deng, L. and de Kloet, J. (2017) "Keep on dreaming: Art in a changing Beijing," *IIAS Newsletter*, 76: 36–7. Available at: https://iias.asia/sites/default/files/IIAS_NL76_3637.pdf.

Gonghui Bolan (xiaxunkan) (2011) "北京的 一环路 在哪里?" ["Where is Beijing's 1st ring road?"] 工会博览 （下旬刊) [*A view of labor unions*], 9: 41.

Gu, C. and Song, G. (2001) "北京城市意象空间及构成要素研究. 地理学报" ["Research on Beijing city image space and constituent elements"], 地理学报 [*Journal of Geographical Sciences*], 1: 64–74.

Ji, X. (2004) "请问你在北京住几环？话剧《环路男女》侧记. 南方周末" ["Which ring do you live on? A report on the play 'Ring road man and women'"], *Southern Weekend*, July 11. Available at: www.infzm.com/content/102209.

Ji, X. (2013) "关于北京 '七环路' 的4个猜想. 中国经济导报" ["Four hypotheses about Beijing 7th ring road"], *Zhongguo Jingji Daobao* [*China Economic Review*], June 15.

Jiang, Y. (2016) "《五环之歌》怎么成 '北京市歌'Ifeng.com" ["How did the song of 5th ring become Beijing city song?"], 凤凰网, April 13. Available at: http://hainan.ifeng.com/a/20160413/4452930_0.shtml.

Lee, B. (2008) *Beijing is coming*. Movie.

Lefebvre, H. (1991) *The production of space*, trans. D. Nicholson-Smith, Oxford: Blackwell, first published in 1974.

Li, L., Lu , and Zhang Y. (2014) "二环城市快速路与北京城市发展. 城市发展研究" ["The 2rd fast ring road and Beijing city development"]. 城市发展研究 [*Urban Studies*], 7: 32–41.

Park, R. E. (1915) "The city: Suggestions for the investigation of human behavior in the city environment," *The American Journal of Sociology*, 20(5): 577–612.

Robinson, J. (2006) *Ordinary cities: Between modernity and development*, Abingdon: Routledge.

Schmidt, L. (2012) "Urban Islamic spectacles: Transforming the space of the shopping mall during Ramadan in Indonesia," *Inter-Asia Cultural Studies*, 13(3): 384–407.

Simmel, G. (2002) "The metropolis and mental life," in G. Bridge and S. Watson (eds) *The Blackwell City Reader*, Oxford: Blackwell, pp. 11–19.

Zhao Z. (2006) "浅灰色 '西二环路再为北京'添彩" ["'Light Gray' West 2rd ring road will add more color for Beijing"], 中华建筑报 [*China Construction News*], August 24.

9

Pathways to Urban Residency and Subjective Well-Being in Beijing

Juan Chen and Shenghua Xie

Introduction

Urbanization is a risk factor for subjective well-being, and the situation in China is evidence of this general rule (Harpham, 1994; Marsella, 1998; Vlahov and Galea, 2002; Gong et al., 2012). Over the last three decades, China has witnessed the largest peacetime human migration in history and a simultaneous acceleration of urban expansion. In 1978, 17.92% of the population lived in urban areas; by 2016, the proportion had risen to 57.35% (National Bureau of Statistics of China, 2017). Between 1978 and 2010, the total number of cities in China increased from 193 to 658. Of these, the number of megacities increased from 2 to 16; large cities, from 27 to 124; medium-sized cities, from 35 to 138; and small cities, from 129 to 380. The number of townships leapt during the same period from 2,173 to 19,410 (Central Committee of the Communist Party and State Council of China, 2014). Despite the rapid growth in migration and urbanization, happiness in China plummeted (Brockmann et al., 2009). Many studies have reported high psychological distress among urban residents (Gong et al., 2012). In order to deal with this issue, it is necessary to investigate more closely how the process of urbanization is affecting the subjective well-being of millions of residents who are either new arrivals or established residents in the expanding cities.

Size of population, sources of population, and the distribution of population within the city are the first things that we should establish when researching a city (Park, 1915). In the past 30 years, the rapid migration and city expansion in China have led to significant changes in the urban population composition and characteristics (Chen and Chen, 2015). Studies on China's migration and urbanization have primarily focused on migrants who leave rural areas to work in urban centers. The rural-to-urban migrant population is of great interest and concern. However, Webb (1984) suggests that the rural–urban division is not sufficiently nuanced and has limited utility: the region being studied must be defined by more relevant criteria, especially the detailed composition of the population. In an effort to establish such criteria, this chapter draws attention to urban populations with divergent pathways to urban residency. We differentiate and include in our analysis a number of modes of residency change other than rural-to-urban migration that are occurring on a major scale in China, including that of urban-to-urban migrants from townships and small cities to large metropolises who may or may not have obtained urban *hukou* in the host city, and in situ urbanized rural residents who became urban residents not because they decided to try their luck in the city but because their land was reclassified as urban.

The following discussion and analysis focus on the different pathways by which an individual can become an urban resident of Beijing and the consequences of these pathways on four measures of subjective well-being: self-rated physical health, self-rated mental health, life satisfaction, and perceived social standing. Beijing, the capital city of China, continues to experience massive migration inflow and rapid urban expansion. The municipality of Beijing currently comprises 16 administrative subdivisions, including two inner city districts (Chongwen and Xuanwu were incorporated into Dongcheng and Xicheng, respectively, on July 1, 2010) inside the second ring road, four urban districts between the second and fifth ring roads, six inner suburban districts linked by the sixth ring road, and four outer suburban districts within the city limits (on November 13, 2015, two counties—Miyun and Yanqing—were upgraded to districts). The composition of Beijing's population has also changed considerably (Figure 9.1). By the end of 2014, the total population in Beijing had reached 21.5 million—an increase of 57.8% from 2000 (13.6 million) and nearly three times the population of 1978 (8.7 million). Of the total population, 86.4% (18.6 million) reside in urban districts or suburban townships and 38.1% (8.2 million) do not have Beijing urban or rural *hukou* (Beijing Municipal Bureau of Statistics, 2015). As such, Beijing is an ideal subject for a case study exploring the link between the pathways to urban residency and the subjective well-being of urban residents in China.

Figure 9.1: Population composition in Beijing, 1978–2014

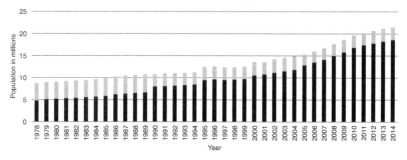

a. Urban and rural populations in Beijing

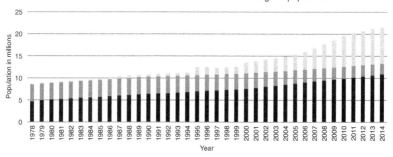

b. Urban hukou, rural hukou, and migrant populations

Source: Beijing Municipal Bureau of Statistics (2015).

Urbanization and subjective well-being

A city is not a mere aggregate of individuals and social arrangements but an institution possessing a moral organization and a physical organization that mutually interact in characteristic ways to change one another (Park, 1915). Consequently, urbanization, which brings about changes in city size, population structure, lifestyle, and social relations, is likely to influence the health and well-being of urban residents. Vlahov and Galea (2002) argue that this influence can be observed in the physical environment, the social environment, and access to health and social services.

Though cities often have better health-care facilities and health and social services, they also pose a risk to subjective well-being because of factors such as ambient air pollution, occupational injuries, traffic hazards, poor diet, and reduced physical activity (Macintyre et al., 2002; Moore et al., 2003; Galea et al., 2005; WHO, 2008; WHO and UN-Habitat, 2010; Gong et al., 2012; Li et al., 2012). Such negative effects are experienced both directly (such as through exposure to polluted air and water) and indirectly (through the perception of risk and attendant chronic stress, for example) (Peek et al., 2009; Chen et al., 2013). To date, empirical research has consistently demonstrated that living in very dense cities lowers various dimensions of subjective well-being (Morrison, 2011; Chen et al., 2015).

Urbanization, which substantially modifies the social environment, may have both salutary and pernicious effects on residents' subjective well-being. Salutary effects include good neighborhood relations and well-established social networks, which are positively associated with the subjective well-being of urban residents. On the other hand, awareness of low socioeconomic status, lack of social capital, and social segregation may negatively affect individuals' subjective well-being (Vlahov and Galea, 2002; Gruebner et al., 2017). Furthermore, social environment factors may have distinct effects on different subgroups in cities. For example, in China, the positive effect of neighborhood on subjective well-being have been found to be stronger for long-term local residents than for rural-to-urban migrants (Chen and Chen, 2015; Liu, Zhang, Liu et al., 2017; Liu, Zhang, Wu et al., 2017).

Though previous studies have provided extensive evidence of urbanization's influence on subjective well-being, few studies have examined the potential effects of an individual's particular means of achieving urban residency on subjective well-being. Since the city is often defined by the size, distribution, and concentration of its population, it is very important to compare the idiosyncrasies in the evolution of city populations (Park, 1915). The distribution of population in cities is not only determined by occupations and economic conditions but also by pathways to urban residency, a fact that can be proved by the number of specific areas in Chinese cities that are occupied by a particular subgroup, such as migrants, landless peasants, and locals. In addition, a comparison of neighborhood effects on the subjective well-being of local residents and that of rural-to-urban migrants reflects the role played by different pathways to urban residency in determining subjective well-being.

An individual's pathway to urban residency is an important indicator of lifestyle changes: different migration and urbanization routes result in different assimilation outcomes (Rumbaut, 1997). Certain approaches may lead to smooth integration into urban life, whereas others may be associated with various institutional barriers that prevent urban integration. Compared to objective measures such as employment, income, wealth, and housing, subjective well-being (individuals' own perception of their comparative health, happiness, and prosperity) is a broader indicator of well-being (Kingdon and Knight, 2006). A measure of subjective well-being not only reflects current social circumstances but also incorporates an assessment of individuals' backgrounds and their future prospects (Singh-Manoux et al., 2003).

Pathways to urban residency in China

Urbanization in China is the result of two distinct but interrelated phenomena. The first is the growth of cities and towns due to the influx of migrant labor, particularly from rural areas. The second is in situ urbanization, whereby villagers become urban residents not because they decided to move to the city but because their land was reclassified as urban. The uncontrolled expansion of Chinese cities has rapidly devoured millions of hectares of formerly agricultural land and produced thousands of urban villages (Liu et al., 2010; Chen et al., 2012; Chung and Unger, 2013). Large swathes of the population did not go to the city; the city came to them (Chen et al., 2014, 2015). The massive demographic shift in China was, therefore, the result not only of the migration of over 200 million rural residents who left their homes to start new lives in cities as migrant laborers (Chan, 2013), but also of the reclassification of 200 million former villagers as residents of new urban districts (Friedmann, 2005; Lin, 2007; Liu et al., 2010).

Hukou, the Chinese household registration system, still plays a major role in the migration and urbanization process in China. Official changes in *hukou* status and welfare entitlements for in situ urbanized rural residents have often lagged far behind the conversions of farmland (Ong, 2014). The *hukou* system does not simply separate migrants and urban residents according to their *hukou* status; its ramifications are more complex. Although the majority of migrants have rural or urban *hukou* according to their hometown registration, there are institutionalized and non-institutionalized channels that allow some rural *hukou* holders to acquire urban *hukou* and some urban *hukou* holders from townships and small cities to acquire *hukou* in the host city. These channels include the pursuit of higher education followed by employment in government or state-owned enterprises, membership in the Chinese Communist Party (CCP) and/or the People's Liberation Army (PLA), influential family connections (Wu and Treiman, 2004), and the purchase of a house in the city.

Given these various pathways to urban residency, Beijing urban *hukou* holders include not only those who were born into local urban families but also former Beijing rural residents; migrants with rural origins; urban migrants from other cities who acquired Beijing urban *hukou* through the channels of education, employment, family connections, and home ownership; and in situ urbanized Beijing rural residents who acquired urban status. Those without Beijing urban *hukou* include Beijing rural *hukou* residents, urban migrants from other cities, and rural migrants from other cities and provinces. Such divergent pathways to urban residency are not unique to Beijing; they are also common to other large cities and megacities in China.

How do people's various pathways to urban residency affect subjective well-being? This is a particularly urgent question given the massive population flow and the rapid city expansion in China. Drawing on two waves of a household survey in Beijing, this chapter attempts to address this knowledge gap. In the following sections, we describe our survey data, explain the methods, and present results demonstrating the consequences of various pathways to urban life on individuals' subjective well-being.

Data from a household survey in Beijing

Data for this study came from two waves of a face-to-face household survey we completed in collaboration with the Research Center for Contemporary China at Peking University in Beijing in 2013 and 2015. The survey target population consisted of permanent residents and migrants aged 18 or older residing in the urban area of Beijing, regardless of their officially registered *hukou* status. The surveyed area included the six established urban districts within the fifth ring road (Dongcheng, Xicheng, Haidian, Chaoyang, Fengtai, and Shijingshan) and the centers of the six new urban districts (Changping, Shunyi, Tongzhou, Daxing, Fangshan, and Mentougou) connected by the sixth ring road. We employed spatial probability sampling technology to reach the target population.[1] Figure 9.2 displays the spatial distribution of the 80 primary sampling units (PSUs), with 59 in the six established urban districts and 21 in the centers of the six new urban districts.

We sampled a total of 4,530 household addresses for the 2013 wave and completed 2,558 interviews (a response rate of 56.5%). Similarly, a total of 4,572 household addresses were sampled in 2015 and 2,610 interviews were completed (a response rate of 58.4%).[2] Approval was granted for the ethical review of research projects involving human subjects by The Hong Kong Polytechnic University. Survey weights were developed to adjust for unequal probabilities of selection. Post-stratification weights were calculated based on the age and gender distribution of the population of Beijing reported in the 2010 Chinese Population Census (National Bureau

Figure 9.2: Spatial distribution of 80 primary sampling units for the household survey in Beijing

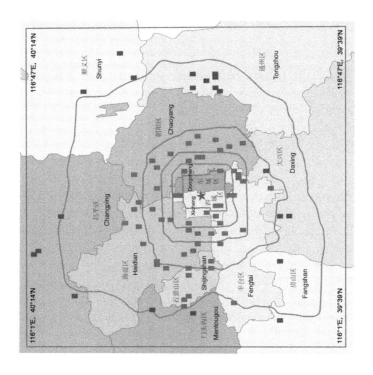

Source: Author, based on own data

of Statistics of China, 2012). We pooled the two waves of data for a final sample of 5,168. A total of 227 cases were excluded due to missing data on variables used in this study, leaving a sample of 4,941 for the analysis.[3]

Diverse pathways to urban residency in Beijing

The respondents' pathways to Beijing urban residency were coded according to eight categories:

1. Beijing-born urban *hukou* residents (those who were born in Beijing with Beijing urban *hukou*);
2. Beijing rural residents who obtained urban *hukou* (former Beijing rural *hukou* holders who acquired Beijing urban *hukou* through the channels of education, employment, family connections, or home ownership);
3. Beijing in situ urbanized rural residents (those in situ urbanized Beijing rural residents who acquired urban status);
4. Beijing rural *hukou* residents (those with Beijing rural *hukou*);
5. urban migrants who obtained Beijing urban *hukou* (migrants from other cities who acquired Beijing urban *hukou* through the channels of education, employment, family connections, or home ownership);
6. rural migrants who obtained Beijing urban *hukou* (migrants with rural origins who acquired Beijing urban *hukou* through the channels of education, employment, family connections, or home ownership);
7. urban migrants without Beijing urban *hukou* (those with urban *hukou* in other cities and provinces); and
8. rural migrants without Beijing urban *hukou* (those with rural *hukou* in other cities and provinces).

Figure 9.3 shows the composition of the survey respondents according to their pathways to urban residency in Beijing. Only about one third of the respondents are Beijing-born urban *hukou* residents. Urban and rural migrants from cities and provinces outside Beijing who do not have Beijing urban *hukou* account for another third, and the last third is composed of former Beijing rural *hukou* holders, rural-to-Beijing migrants, and urban-to-Beijing migrants who have obtained Beijing urban *hukou* (about 4% for each group), Beijing in situ urbanized rural residents with urban *hukou* (8.23%), and Beijing rural residents without urban *hukou* (8.76%).

Figure 9.3: Diverse pathways to urban residency in Beijing

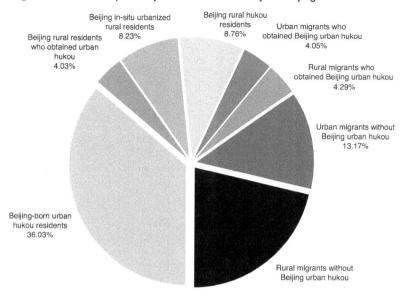

Source: Author, based on own data

Disparities in subjective well-being and sociodemographic characteristics

Table 9.1 outlines the descriptive statistics on the four measures of subjective well-being according to the eight pathways to urban residency in Beijing. Subjective well-being was assessed using four measures: self-rated physical health, self-rated mental health, life satisfaction, and perceived social standing. Self-rated physical health was assessed by the respondents' answer to the question: "In general, how would you rate your overall physical health status?" Responses were measured on a five-point scale where 1 = "very poor," 2 = "poor," 3 = "fair," 4 = "good," and 5 = "very good." Self-rated mental health was assessed by the respondents' reports of their current mental health status using the same five-point scale. The two variables were further dichotomously coded with 1 indicating "good/ very good." Life satisfaction was determined by responses to the question "Are you satisfied (*manyi*) with your current life?" For this question, a seven-point scale was used as a continuous variable with 1 indicating "very unsatisfied" and 7 indicating "very satisfied." To measure perceived social standing, the respondents were asked to rank their relative socioeconomic position, with 0 indicating "at the bottom" and 10 indicating "at the top." The measure was coded as a continuous variable ranging from 0 to 10.

Table 9.1: Descriptive statistics of subjective well-being and sociodemographic characteristics by pathways to urban residency in Beijing

	Beijing-born urban and rural residents				Urban and rural migrants to Beijing			
	Beijing-born urban hukou residents	Beijing rural residents who obtained urban hukou	Beijing in situ urbanized rural residents	Beijing rural hukou residents	Urban migrants who obtained Beijing urban hukou	Rural migrants who obtained Beijing urban hukou	Urban migrants without Beijing urban hukou	Rural migrants without Beijing urban hukou
Subjective well-being								
Self-rated physical health (good/very good, %)	62.79	53.60	60.69	49.27	65.40	51.24	70.58	71.90
Self-rated mental health (good/very good, %)	75.38	72.75	82.22	66.27	77.40	66.75	81.70	74.01
Life satisfaction (1–7, mean)	4.80 (0.05)	5.02 (0.10)	4.66 (0.08)	4.92 (0.10)	4.94 (0.10)	4.99 (0.11)	4.65 (0.05)	4.42 (0.05)
Perceived social standing (0–10, mean)	4.84 (0.07)	4.84 (0.13)	4.48 (0.10)	4.29 (0.14)	5.12 (0.10)	4.86 (0.11)	4.78 (0.07)	4.22 (0.07)
Demographic characteristics								
Age (18–93, mean)	46.33 (0.48)	53.38 (1.55)	51.80 (0.98)	50.54 (1.06)	44.08 (1.35)	61.25 (1.84)	36.96 (0.61)	36.04 (0.50)
Gender (female, %)	42.57	48.11	48.34	48.58	48.66	49.95	42.59	43.89
Marital status (married, %)	77.69	83.63	85.98	80.56	80.27	79.73	68.92	70.76
Ethnicity (ethnic minority, %)	5.10	7.40	4.10	4.08	5.98	1.88	5.84	4.08

	Beijing-born urban and rural residents				Urban and rural migrants to Beijing			
	Beijing-born urban *hukou* residents	Beijing rural residents who obtained urban *hukou*	Beijing in situ urbanized rural residents	Beijing rural *hukou* residents	Urban migrants who obtained Beijing urban *hukou*	Rural migrants who obtained Beijing urban *hukou*	Urban migrants without Beijing urban *hukou*	Rural migrants without Beijing urban *hukou*
Socioeconomic status								
Years of schooling (0–27, mean)	12.58 (0.14)	11.11 (0.33)	9.40 (0.23)	9.43 (0.31)	15.27 (0.37)	9.34 (0.63)	13.82 (0.19)	10.26 (0.20)
Employment sector ownership (public[a], %)	30.58	29.06	23.20	18.87	44.31	24.21	13.44	8.00
Party membership (CCP[b] member, %)	22.21	30.37	11.80	6.95	45.72	35.09	15.81	5.46
Household wealth index (0–7, mean)	3.40 (0.06)	3.30 (0.11)	2.97 (0.07)	3.02 (0.12)	3.38 (0.10)	2.93 (0.12)	3.15 (0.07)	2.62 (0.08)
Homeownership (homeowner in Beijing, %)	80.02	89.15	91.52	90.84	68.71	71.90	33.37	16.01
Years living in Beijing (0.5–86, mean)	–	–	–	–	20.43 (1.45)	38.22 (1.99)	8.78 (0.31)	7.99 (0.28)
Place of residence (new urban districts, %)	17.34	44.24	48.29	58.59	11.44	17.49	23.53	27.84
Sample N	1,861	199	411	388	211	213	673	985
Weighted percentage	36.03	4.03	8.23	8.76	4.05	4.29	13.17	21.43

Notes: Total sample N = 4,941. Means/percentages are reported; standard errors in parentheses.
Survey design effects (strata, clusters, and individual weights) are adjusted in the estimations.
a Government, state-owned enterprises, and public institutions (*shiye danwei*).
b Chinese Communist Party.

Figure 9.4: Differences in subjective well-being by pathways to urban residency in Beijing

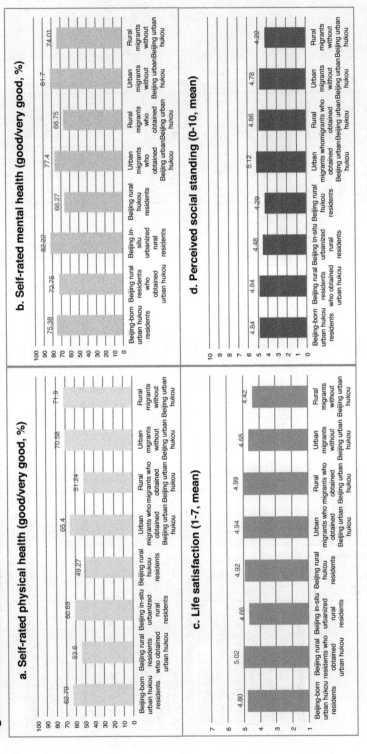

To better illustrate the differences in subjective well-being by pathways to urban residency in Beijing, we have presented the findings as a chart in Figure 9.4. In keeping with the "healthy migrant phenomenon," rural migrants without Beijing urban *hukou* report the best self-rated physical health (Chen, 2011). Their reported life satisfaction and perceived social standing, however, are the lowest of the eight groups. Beijing in situ urbanized rural residents have the best self-rated mental health, and Beijing rural *hukou* residents the worst self-rated physical health and self-rated mental health. Urban migrants who have obtained Beijing urban *hukou* do well on perceived social standing.

Table 9.1 also includes descriptive statistics on the demographic characteristics, socioeconomic status, length of residence in Beijing, and place of residence in Beijing of the various groups. Demographic characteristics included in the survey were age (years), gender (1 = female), marital status (1 = married), and ethnicity (1 = ethnic minority). Measures of socioeconomic status were education (years of schooling), employment sector (1 = public, including government, state-owned enterprises, and public institutions [*shiye danwei*]), party membership (1 = Chinese Communist Party member), household wealth (determined by a scale, ranging from 0 to 7, based on ownership of a number of consumer items, such as an LCD TV and a car), and homeownership (1 = home owner in Beijing). Migrants' length of residence in Beijing was measured in years ranging from 0.5 (6 months) to 86. The respondents' place of residence in Beijing was coded as a dichotomous variable with 1 indicating new urban districts.

The disparities in socioeconomic measures are the most prominent. As shown in Figure 9.5, rural migrants without Beijing urban *hukou* are the least likely to be employed in government, state-owned enterprises, or other public institutions; to be a CCP member; or to own a house in Beijing. In contrast, urban migrants who have obtained Beijing urban *hukou* report the highest level of education and are the most likely to be a CCP member and to work in government, state-owned enterprises, or other public institutions. Not surprisingly, about 90% of current or former Beijing rural residents are homeowners in Beijing.

We next examined the relationships between the eight pathways to Beijing urban residency and the four measures of subjective well-being among the whole sample. The logistic regressions were modeled on self-rated physical health and self-rated mental health. Ordinary least squares (OLS) regressions were estimated on life satisfaction and perceived social standing. Demographic characteristics, socioeconomic status, place of residence in Beijing, and year of the survey were included as control variables. Table 9.2 presents the regression results.

Figure 9.5: Disparities in socioeconomic status by pathways to urban residency and subjective well-being residency in Beijing: Associations between pathways to urban

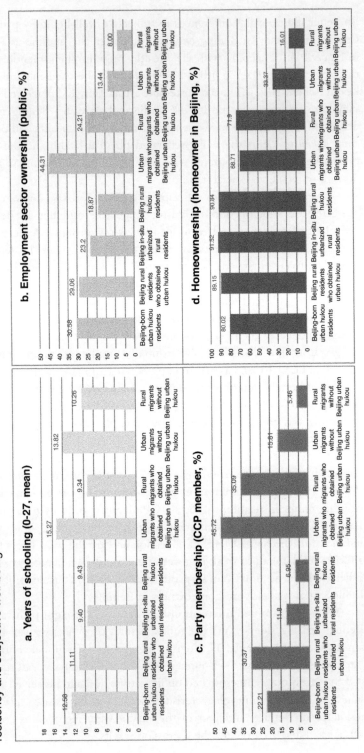

a. Years of schooling (0-27, mean)

b. Employment sector ownership (public, %)

c. Party membership (CCP member, %)

d. Homeownership (homeowner in Beijing, %)

Table 9.2: Multiple regressions on subjective well-being of the whole sample (N = 4,941)

	Model 1	Model 2	Model 3	Model 4
	Self-rated physical health[1]	Self-rated mental health[1]	Life satisfac-tion[2]	Perceived social standing[2]
Demographic characteristics				
Age (18–93)	−0.028	−0.056[***][*]	−0.036[***]	−0.038[***]
	(0.015)	(0.016)	(0.008)	(0.011)
Age (squared)	0.000	0.000[**]	0.000[***]	0.000[***]
	(0.000)	(0.000)	(0.000)	(0.000)
Gender (female)	0.071	0.072	0.155[***]	0.121[*]
	(0.078)	(0.081)	(0.038)	(0.048)
Marital status (married)	−0.098	0.265[*]	0.124[*]	0.096
	(0.107)	(0.119)	(0.053)	(0.062)
Ethnicity (ethnic minority)	−0.238	−0.161	−0.014	0.033
	(0.141)	(0.178)	(0.093)	(0.117)
Socioeconomic status				
Years of schooling (0–27)	0.034[**]	0.028[*]	0.026[***]	0.049[***]
	(0.012)	(0.012)	(0.007)	(0.009)
Employment sector ownership (public[a])	0.202	0.227	0.061	0.154[*]
	(0.109)	(0.117)	(0.057)	(0.071)
Party membership (CCP[b] member)	−0.037	−0.003	0.081	0.164[*]
	(0.104)	(0.118)	(0.050)	(0.064)
Household wealth index (0–7)	0.073[*]	0.070[*]	0.090[***]	0.145[***]
	(0.029)	(0.033)	(0.020)	(0.026)
Homeownership (homeowner in Beijing)	−0.040	0.019	0.118	0.290[***]
	(0.106)	(0.143)	(0.061)	(0.073)
Pathways to Beijing urban residency				
Beijing-born urban hukou residents (reference)	–	–	–	–
Beijing rural residents who obtained urban *hukou*	−0.191	−0.061	0.075	−0.044
	(0.193)	(0.241)	(0.089)	(0.137)
Beijing in situ urbanized rural residents	0.160	0.637[**]	−0.123	−0.158
	(0.153)	(0.198)	(0.092)	(0.106)
Beijing rural *hukou* residents	−0.377[*]	−0.223	0.114	−0.329[*]
	(0.155)	(0.176)	(0.104)	(0.136)

	Model 1	Model 2	Model 3	Model 4
	Self-rated physical health[1]	Self-rated mental health[1]	Life satisfaction[2]	Perceived social standing[2]
Urban migrants who obtained Beijing urban *hukou*	−0.043	−0.022	0.060	0.115
	(0.154)	(0.174)	(0.096)	(0.101)
Rural migrants who obtained Beijing urban *hukou*	−0.063	−0.258	0.023	0.021
	(0.191)	(0.195)	(0.113)	(0.112)
Urban migrants without Beijing urban *hukou*	0.137	0.316[*]	−0.010	0.152
	(0.135)	(0.144)	(0.065)	(0.092)
Rural migrants without Beijing urban *hukou*	0.341[*]	0.005	−0.079	−0.082
	(0.156)	(0.165)	(0.078)	(0.110)
Place of residence in Beijing (new urban districts)	0.054	−0.073	0.180[**]	−0.077
	(0.137)	(0.144)	(0.067)	(0.083)
Year of survey (2015)	−0.113	0.380[**]	0.007	0.096
	(0.109)	(0.122)	(0.060)	(0.080)
Constant	1.060[**]	1.543[***]	4.352[***]	3.890[***]
	(0.404)	(0.419)	(0.219)	(0.278)
Wald F statistics	10.01	5.13	10.68	13.00
	(19, 156)	(19, 156)	(19, 156)	(19, 156)

Notes:

Coefficients are reported; standard errors in parentheses; * $p < 0.05$, ** $p < 0.01$, *** $p < 0.001$.

Survey design effects (strata, clusters, and individual weights) are adjusted in the estimations.

1   Logistic regression.

2   Ordinary least squares (OLS) regression.

a   Government, state-owned enterprises, and public institutions [*shiye danwei*].

b   Chinese Communist Party.

Table 9.3: Multiple regressions on subjective well-being of the four migrant groups (N = 2,082)

	Model 1	Model 2	Model 3	Model 4
	Self-rated physical health[1]	Self-rated mental health[1]	Life satisfaction[2]	Perceived social standing[2]
Demographic characteristics				
Age (18–93)	−0.030	−0.070*	−0.055***	−0.038*
	(0.028)	(0.029)	(0.013)	(0.016)
Age (squared)	0.000	0.001*	0.001***	0.001**
	(0.000)	(0.000)	(0.000)	(0.000)
Gender (female)	−0.047	0.074	0.154*	0.164*
	(0.107)	(0.114)	(0.059)	(0.077)
Marital status (married)	0.116	0.472*	0.352***	0.133
	(0.167)	(0.188)	(0.073)	(0.094)
Ethnicity (ethnic minority)	0.081	0.086	0.161	0.098
	(0.282)	(0.308)	(0.161)	(0.161)
Socioeconomic status				
Years of schooling (0–27)	0.021	0.010	0.017	0.062***
	(0.018)	(0.019)	(0.010)	(0.014)
Employment sector ownership (public[a])	0.159	0.385	0.200*	0.307**
	(0.191)	(0.209)	(0.092)	(0.102)
Party membership (CCP[b] member)	0.098	0.177	0.076	0.052
	(0.173)	(0.173)	(0.085)	(0.107)

	Model 1	Model 2	Model 3	Model 4
	Self-rated physical health[1]	Self-rated mental health[1]	Life satisfaction[2]	Perceived social standing[2]
Household wealth index (0–7)	0.077	0.105*	0.080**	0.133***
	(0.042)	(0.051)	(0.025)	(0.035)
Homeownership (homeowner in Beijing)	−0.323*	−0.117	−0.048	0.139
	(0.155)	(0.187)	(0.080)	(0.090)
Pathways to Beijing urban residency				
Urban migrants who obtained Beijing urban hukou (reference)	–	–	–	–
Rural migrants who obtained Beijing urban hukou	0.555	0.701	−0.194	−0.489*
	(0.390)	(0.489)	(0.252)	(0.234)
Urban migrants without Beijing urban hukou	0.030	0.639*	−0.126	−0.246
	(0.289)	(0.310)	(0.169)	(0.197)
Rural migrants without Beijing urban hukou	0.165	0.315	−0.300	−0.445*
	(0.320)	(0.326)	(0.177)	(0.202)

	Model 1	Model 2	Model 3	Model 4
	Self-rated physical health[1]	Self-rated mental health[1]	Life satisfaction[2]	Perceived social standing[2]
Interactions: Years living in Beijing (0.5–86)				
x Urban migrants who obtained Beijing urban *hukou*	-0.005	0.003	-0.002	-0.009
	(0.009)	(0.010)	(0.005)	(0.006)
x Rural migrants who obtained Beijing urban *hukou*	-0.021*	-0.027*	0.000	0.004
	(0.011)	(0.012)	(0.006)	(0.007)
x Urban migrants without Beijing urban *hukou*	-0.000	-0.014	0.003	0.015
	(0.015)	(0.013)	(0.005)	(0.008)
x Rural migrants without Beijing urban *hukou*	-0.002	-0.020	0.008	0.015
	(0.011)	(0.012)	(0.008)	(0.011)
Place of residence in Beijing (new urban districts)	0.162	0.119	0.143	-0.059
	(0.173)	(0.195)	(0.086)	(0.103)
Year of survey (2015)	-0.081	0.354*	-0.000	0.129
	(0.152)	(0.160)	(0.073)	(0.092)

	Model 1	Model 2	Model 3	Model 4
	Self-rated physical health[1]	Self-rated mental health[1]	Life satisfaction[2]	Perceived social standing[2]
Constant	1.220	1.461	4.868***	3.864***
	(0.762)	(0.743)	(0.380)	(0.455)
Wald F statistics	5.57	3.27	6.71	9.53
	(19, 156)	(19, 156)	(19, 156)	(19, 156)

Notes:
Coefficients are reported; standard errors in parentheses; * $p < 0.05$, ** $p < 0.01$, *** $p < 0.001$.
Survey design effects (strata, clusters, and individual weights) are adjusted in the estimations.
1   Logistic regression.
2   Ordinary least squares (OLS) regression.
a   Government, state-owned enterprises, and public institutions (shiye danwei).
b   Chinese Communist Party.

176

Figure 9.6: Predicted self-rated physical and mental health and years living in Beijing among the four migrant groups

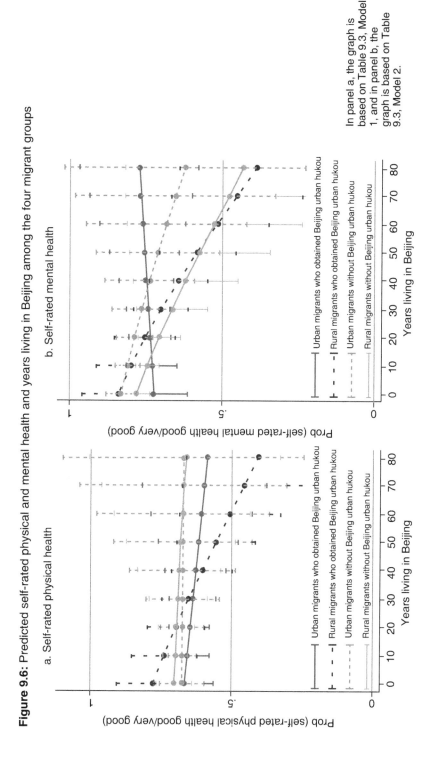

In panel a, the graph is based on Table 9.3, Model 1, and in panel b, the graph is based on Table 9.3, Model 2.

As Table 9.2 demonstrates, education and household wealth are consistent predictors for all four measures of subjective well-being. Being a homeowner in Beijing is significantly associated with higher perceived social standing. Controlling for sociodemographic factors, in situ urbanized rural residents who have obtained Beijing urban *hukou* fare better in terms self-rated mental health than Beijing-born urban *hukou* residents; however, Beijing rural *hukou* residents still report worse self-rated physical health and lower perceived social standing than Beijing-born urban *hukou* residents. The ratings of urban and rural migrants who have obtained Beijing urban *hukou* are not significantly different than those of Beijing-born urban *hukou* residents. Urban migrants without Beijing urban *hukou* are likely to have better self-rated mental health, whereas rural migrants without Beijing urban *hukou* reported better self-rated physical health.

Finally, we examined the interactions between pathways to urban residency and length of residence in Beijing among the four migrant groups. The results are reported in Table 9.3 and illustrated in Figure 9.6. For rural migrants who obtained Beijing urban *hukou*, the number of years living in Beijing clearly contribute to a decrease in self-rated physical health and self-rated mental health. For urban and rural migrants without Beijing urban *hukou*, there is also a downward trend in the scores for self-rated mental health, but it is not statistically significant.

Conclusion

As a result of a rapid migration and urbanization process, China has experienced significant changes in the composition of its urban population in the past 30 years. Based on two waves of a household survey in Beijing undertaken in 2013 and 2015, our study draws attention to the associations between pathways to urban life and measures of subjective well-being. Only about one third of the survey respondents were Beijing-born urban *hukou* residents; the rest followed different pathways to urban residency in Beijing. While rural-to-urban migrants have been extensively studied, urban-to-urban migrants and in situ urbanized rural residents account for half of the urban population growth in Beijing.

The respondents who obtained Beijing urban *hukou* but were formerly Beijing rural residents, rural-to-Beijing migrants, and urban-to-Beijing migrants reported levels of subjective well-being that were very similar to those of Beijing-born urban *hukou* residents. In fact, Beijing in situ urbanized rural residents reported better mental health. The respondents who still have Beijing rural *hukou* experienced poorer physical health and lower perceived social standing. These results indicate the health and welfare benefits that accompany Beijing urban *hukou*. The addresses of the Beijing rural *hukou* residents in our study have most likely been recently converted from rural to urban, but their *hukou* status has not changed accordingly, so they have not acquired the social benefits associated with urban *hukou*. There must be renewed effort to ensure that their *hukou* status is changed and that they receive access to the urban welfare and health-care systems.

The self-rated physical health of the rural migrants without Beijing urban *hukou* appears to support the theory of the "healthy migrant phenomenon," but self-rated mental health is a different story (Chen, 2011). These results may be caused by the "salmon bias" (that is, many migrants choose to return to their hometown if they have a serious health problem) (Lu and Qin, 2014). Conversely, urban-to-Beijing migrants report better mental health but not better physical health. For the rural migrants who had obtained Beijing urban *hukou* in our study, the years spent living in Beijing were negatively associated with self-rated physical and mental health. It is necessary to reach out to the migrant population and provide equal access to health services in Beijing so that they can maintain their initial health advantages and reduce future health-care expenses. In addition to changing the restrictive *hukou* system, the government should adopt policies that promote universal coverage of social security and health-care systems to reduce the urban–rural divide.

According to Park (1915), the distribution, concentration, and segregation of the population in cities establish "moral regions," making the city a mosaic of small worlds. This is also true for residents in urban China since subgroups in cities such as rural-to-urban migrants, urban-to-urban migrants, and in situ urbanized rural residents each provide distinctive evaluations of subjective well-being. However, the link between urbanization and subjective well-being in urban China also has some unique traits. Among them, the role of pathways to urban residency is of particular note. Previous studies on urbanization and mental health often focus on the influence of the physical environment, the social environment, and access to health and social services. This study, however, suggests that the pathway to urban residency also influences subjective well-being. The findings of this study therefore suggest that not only the present situation of urban residents but also their backgrounds should be considered in policy making to enhance subjective well-being in urban China.

To conclude, our findings draw attention to the changing composition of urban population, the various pathways to urban residency, and the effect of divergent pathways on individuals' subjective well-being. The study also demonstrates that in order to improve subjective well-being in urban China, it is necessary to reform the divisive *hukou* system and the associated unequal distribution of social and economic resources and welfare benefits.

Notes

[1] The spatial probability sampling procedure progressed in several stages. Primary sampling units (PSUs), which are cells of spatial grids defined as half square minutes (HSMs) of latitude and longitude, were first selected from a spatial sampling frame of Beijing, using the probability-proportionate-to-size (PPS) method. Secondary sampling units (SSUs) were then randomly selected within PSUs. Because spatial sampling units are unnatural blocks (squares defined by precise coordinates), the samplers used geographical positioning system receivers to identify unit boundaries. All households residing within these small "spatial blocks" were enumerated. Within each household, one respondent who had resided in Beijing for more than six months was selected using the Kish grid—a pre-assigned table of random numbers commonly used in survey research to determine which person in the household to interview (Landry and Shen, 2005).

[2] In order to achieve a confidence level of 95% and an absolute sampling error of not greater than 5%, we had to obtain a valid sample of 2,500 respondents in each wave, which would ensure the appropriate estimation of the population parameters.

[3] The analysis applied both survey and post-stratification weights, and addressed the problems inherent in a multilayered clustered sampling design by using the "svy" (survey) commands in Stata 14.0, which estimate appropriately corrected standard errors in the presence of stratification and clustering.

Acknowledgments

The 2013 and 2015 waves of the household survey in Beijing were funded by the General Research Fund of the Research Grants Council of Hong Kong (PolyU5411/12H). The author is grateful for the research collaboration of the Research Center for Contemporary China (RCCC) at Peking University during the implementation of the survey. The research undertaken for this chapter also received funding from the Li & Fung China Social Policy Research Fund.

References

Beijing Municipal Bureau of Statistics (2015) *Beijing statistical yearbook 2015*, Beijing: China Statistics Press.

Brockmann, H., Delhey, J., Welzel, C., and Yuan, H. (2009) "The China puzzle: Falling happiness in a rising economy," *Journal of Happiness Studies*, 10(4): 387–405.

Central Committee of the Communist Party and State Council of China (2014) *National new-type urbanization plan (2014–2020)*. Available at: www.gov.cn/zhengce/2014-03/16/content_2640075.htm.

Chan, K. W. (2013) "China: Internal migration," in I. Ness and P. Bellwood (eds.) *The encyclopedia of global human migration*, Oxford: Blackwell.

Chen, J. (2011) "Internal migration and health: Re-examining the healthy migrant phenomenon in China," *Social Science & Medicine*, 72(8): 1294–1301.

Chen, J. and Chen, S. (2015) "Mental health effects of perceived living environment and neighborhood safety in urbanizing China," *Habitat International*, 46: 101–10.

Chen, J., Chen, S., and Landry, P. F. (2013) "Migration, environmental hazards, and health outcomes in China," *Social Science & Medicine*, 80: 85–95.

Chen, J., Chen, S., Landry, P. F., and Davis, D. S. (2014) "How dynamics of urbanization affect physical and mental health in urban China," *China Quarterly*, 220: 988–1011.

Chen, J., Davis, D. S., Wu, K., and Dai, H. (2015) "Life satisfaction in urbanizing China: The effect of city size and pathways to urban residency," *Cities*, 49: 88–97.

Chen, J., Wu, K., and Sung-Chan, P. L. P. (2012) "Families on the move in China: Challenges, strategies, and implications," *China Journal of Social Work*, 5(2): 109–22.

Chung, H. and Unger, J. (2013) "The Guangdong model of urbanisation: Collective village land and the making of a new middle class," *China Perspectives*, 3(95): 33–41.

Friedmann, J. (2005) *China's urban transition*, Minneapolis: University of Minnesota Press.

Galea, S., Ahern, J., Rudenstine, S., Wallace, Z., and Vlahov, D. (2005) "Urban built environment and depression: A multilevel analysis," *Journal of Epidemiology and Community Health*, 59(10): 822–7.

Gong, P., Liang, S., Carlton, E. J., Jiang, Q., Wu, J., Wang, L., and Remais, J. V. (2012) "Urbanisation and health in China," *The Lancet*, 379(9818): 843–52.

Gruebner, O., Rapp, M. A., Adli, M., Kluge, U., Galea, S., and Heinz, A. (2017) "Cities and mental health," *Deutsches Arzteblatt International*, 114(8): 121–7.

Harpham, T. (1994) "Urbanization and mental health in developing countries: A research role for social scientists, public health professionals and social psychiatrists," *Social Science & Medicine*, 39(2): 233–45.

Kingdon, G. G. and Knight, J. (2006) "Subjective well-being poverty vs. income poverty and capabilities poverty?" *Journal of Development Studies*, 42(7): 1199–224.

Landry, P. F. and Shen, M. (2005) "Reaching migrants in survey research: The use of the global positioning system to reduce coverage bias in China," *Political Analysis*, 13(1): 1–22.

Li, X., Wang, C., Zhang, G., Xiao, L., and Dixon, J. (2012) "Urbanisation and human health in China: Spatial features and a systemic perspective," *Environmental Science and Pollution Research*, 19(5): 1375–84.

Lin, G. C. S. (2007) "Reproducing spaces of Chinese urbanisation: New city-based and land-centred urban transformation," *Urban Studies*, 44(9): 1827–55.

Liu, Y., He, S., Wu, F., and Webster, C. (2010) "Urban villages under China's rapid urbanization: Unregulated assets and transitional neighbourhoods," *Habitat International*, 34(2): 135–44.

Liu, Y., Zhang, F., Liu, Y., Li, Z., and Wu, F. (2017) "The effect of neighbourhood social ties on migrants' subjective wellbeing in Chinese cities," *Habitat International*, 66: 86–94.

Liu, Y., Zhang, F., Wu, F., Liu, Y., and Li, Z. (2017) "The subjective wellbeing of migrants in Guangzhou, China: The impacts of the social and physical environment," *Cities*, 60A: 333–42.

Lu, Y. and Qin, L. (2014) "Healthy migrant and salmon bias hypotheses: A study of health and internal migration in China," *Social Science & Medicine*, 102: 41–8.

Macintyre, S., Ellaway, A., and Cummins, S. (2002) "Place effects on health: How can we conceptualise, operationalise and measure them?" *Social Science & Medicine*, 55(1): 125–39.

Marsella, A. J. (1998) "Urbanization, mental health, and social deviancy: A review of issues and research," *American Psychologist*, 53(6): 624–34.

Moore, M., Gould, P., and Keary, B. S. (2003) "Global urbanization and impact on health," *International Journal of Hygiene and Environmental Health*, 206(4/5): 269–78.

Morrison, P. S. (2011) "Local expressions of subjective well-being: The New Zealand experience," *Regional Studies*, 45(8): 1039–58.

National Bureau of Statistics of China (2012) *Tabulation on the 2010 population census of the People's Republic of China*, Beijing: China Statistics Press.

National Bureau of Statistics of China (2017) *China statistical yearbook, 2017*, Beijing: China Statistics Press.

Ong, L. H. (2014) "State-led urbanization in China: Skyscrapers, land revenue and 'concentrated villages'" *China Quarterly*, 217: 162–79.

Park, R. E. (1915) "The city: Suggestions for the study of human nature in the urban environment," *The American Journal of Sociology*, 20(5): 577–612.

Peek, M. K., Cutchin, M. P., Freeman, D., Stowe, R. P., and Goodwin, J. S. (2009) "Environmental hazards and stress: Evidence from the Texas City Stress and Health Study," *Journal of Epidemiology and Community Health*, 63(10): 792–8.

Rumbaut, R. G. (1997) "Assimilation and its discontents: Between rhetoric and reality," *International Migration Review*, 31(4): 923–60.

Singh-Manoux, A., Adler, N. E., and Marmot, M. G. (2003) "Subjective social status: Its determinants and its association with measures of ill-health in the Whitehall II study," *Social Science & Medicine*, 56(6): 1321–33.

Vlahov, D. and Galea, S. (2002) "Urbanization, urbanicity, and health," *Journal of Urban Health: Bulletin of the New York Academy of Medicine*, 79(4): S1–S12.

Webb, S. D. (1984) "Rural–urban differences in mental disorder," in H. Freeman (ed.) *Mental Health and the Environment*, London: Livingstone-Churchill, pp. 226–49.

WHO (World Health Organization) (2008) *Our cities our health our future: Acting on social determinants for health equity in urban settings: Report to the WHO Commission on Social Determinants of Health from the Knowledge Network on Urban Settings*, Kobe: WHO Centre for Health Development.

WHO (World Health Organization) and UN-Habitat (United Nations Human Settlements Programme) (2010) *Hidden cities: Unmasking and overcoming health inequities in urban settings*, Kobe: WHO, Centre for Health Development and Nairobi: UN-Habitat.

Wu, X. and Treiman, D. J. (2004) "The household registration system and social stratification in China: 1955–1996," *Demography*, 41(2): 363–84.

10

A Study of Socio-spatial Segregation of Rural Migrants in Shenzhen

A Case of Foxconn

Zhigang Li, Shunxian Ou, and Rong Wu

Many years ago
  He took his luggage
  Entered this
  Glorious city
  Daring and energetic.
  Many years later
  Holding his own ash in hand
  He stands at
  Crossroad of the city
  Feel lost
  "Urban Farmer" by Mr. Lizhi Xu (1990–2014)[1]

Introduction

> "The city, in short, shows clearly the good and evil in human nature. This fact majorly justifies the view of making the city a laboratory or clinic in which human nature and social processes may be conveniently and profitably studied." (Park,1915: 612)

Cities such as Chicago or Shenzhen can be "laboratory specimens", amenable to measurement, dissection, experiment, and other contrivances (Gieryn, 2006: 10). In this study, we examine the socio-spatial segregation of migrants in Shenzhen, the laboratory of post-reform China's market-oriented and open-door policies. Similar to Chicago in the early 1900s, Shenzhen has experienced a tremendous transformation from a rural area in the 1970s to a globalizing city in the early 21st century, with the accumulation of millions of migrants. Nevertheless, as stated by Latour and Woolgar (1986), the modality of "laboratory" is largely constructed and contextualized. From a comparative perspective (Robinson, 2005), Shenzhen's socio-spatial landscape in the 21st century could by no means be the same as that of Chicago 100 years ago. Today, "time-space compression" has become prominent, along with the flow of capital, investments, and products on the global scale; regions or cities of the global South such as Shenzhen have become the hotspots of growth and migrant accumulation. Based on this, Shenzhen is undergoing the concomitant impact of globalization, migration, and urbanization—the speed, scales, and effects of which are far beyond that of Chicago in the early 1900s. Moreover, the making of Shenzhen is largely a state-led experiment, to explore new ways of China's market-oriented reform, and against a specific context of urban–rural dualism.

Park focused on two issues, migration and segregation, which are still the dominant forces underlying the development of cities in the early 21st century. In China, according to the 2014 national survey, there are more than 274 million migrant workers, and the urbanization of rural migrants has become a national strategy. The arrival of migrants contributed to the miraculous explosion of Shenzhen from a collection of villages to a globalizing city of more than 12 million residents within three decades. Shenzhen has often been taken as the youngest, the most promising, and the most entrepreneurial city in China. The electronic products of Shenzhen, such as PCs, notebooks, and cell phones, have outnumbered other Chinese cities, and it is often labeled a "world factory." Shenzhen, however, is also a dual city. The segregation or division of those who hold local household registrations (*hukou*) or land ownership rights (collective ownerships), that is the locals, and those without them, that is, rural migrants, is remarkable, as evidenced by the inequalities of living space, consumption, and everyday practices. Unlike Chicago, in which migrant segregation is largely associated with the dimensions of ethnicity, social status, and lifestyle, the migrant segregation of Shenzhen is mainly driven by globalization, the Chinese state, and Shenzhen's status as a world factory.

Following the lines of Park, "We may think of it [the city] as a mechanism—a psychophysical mechanism—in and through which private and political interests find corporate expression" (Park, 1915: 578). Are there important socio-spatial divisions between migrants and locals in Shenzhen? What are the psychophysical impacts on rural migrants? How is it different from elsewhere and at other times, such as Park's early twentieth-century Chicago? What are the implications of these differences for urban theory in general and for migrant segregation in particular? To address these questions, we will first measure and evaluate the extent of segregation in Shenzhen, and then focus on a specific case, Foxconn, to examine the psychophysical effects of segregation.

This chapter will be organized as follows. First, we will examine the literature of migrant segregation in post-reform Chinese cities. The growth of the literature on this topic suggests the *problématique* urbanization of post-reform China in the early 21st century. Beyond the qualitative or descriptive analysis of most extant studies, we need to take a further measurement of migrant segregation with some quantitative methods. The empirical section will focus on Shenzhen, and apply the methods of factory ecology to the new census, the sixth census of China, in 2010, to identify the socio-spatial landscape of migrants in Shenzhen. We focus on various types of migrants and patterns of segregation. Thereafter, we develop an ethnographic study of Foxconn, a typical case of industrial clusters, to interrogate the subjective feelings of migration and understand the physical and psychological interactions. At the end, we return to the discussions of migration, segregation, and the city as a psychophysical mechanism.

The literature on migrant segregation in post-reform urban China

An avalanche of literature has shed light on the rise of migrant enclaves and resultant segregation in post-reform Chinese cities (Wu et al., 2014), including spatial structure (Feng et al., 2007), the housing conditions of migrants (Wu, 2002), social integration (Li and Song, 2009; Li and Wu, 2013), and so on. They articulate a poor, marginalized, and limited living space for rural migrants, especially in large cities such as Beijing, Shanghai, and Guangzhou. Across various contexts, the marginal, segregated, or even the discriminatory status of rural migrants has been noted (Ren and Qiao, 2010; Fan et al., 2011). Both social and spatial segregation have been identified for rural migrants (Shen, 2017; Liu et al., 2014). Most literature concentrates on urban villages (Li and Wu, 2013; Liu et al., 2012). As stated by Wu et al. (2013), their informality has been created by the institutional division of urban–rural land market and land management system, together with the poor provision of migrant housing. Extant literature also articulates the difference between the new- and old-generation migrants. For example, Liu et al. (2012) found that new-generation migrants have larger social networks than the old-generation migrants in Guangzhou.

We know, however, relatively little about another type of migrant enclaves, that is, factory or collective dormitories. Built by factories or companies, these dormitories have also become the spatial clusters of rural migrants, housing millions of migrant workers. The lifestyle of migrants living in such enclaves could be very different to that of urban villages, and their effects on rural migrants, such as the resultant segregation, subjective feelings, and attachment remains a question to address. The social and spatial integration of migrants have also become a source of major concern. It has been found that some migrants can integrate into such cities as Guangzhou (Wissink et al., 2014) but Chen and Wang (2015) have articulated the structural and institutional constraints that prevent migrants from getting access to opportunities and resources. Also, it has been observed that migrants have different levels of interaction across various types of neighborhoods—stronger in old and deprived neighborhoods than in new commodity housing neighborhoods (Wang et al., 2016). Moreover, neighborhoods also have an impact on the characteristics of the social networks of migrants, and their integration in cities. For instance, the social networks of various migrants are different, as some are homogeneous, while others have mixed social networks (Wissink et al., 2014).

Most literature, however, focuses on Beijing, Shanghai, and Guangzhou and most studies target residential communities or urban villages. Such enclaves as industrial clusters or dormitories have been largely ignored, while the subjective feelings of migrants living in the industrial clusters have been barely explored. To address these research gaps, the following sections will focus on Shenzhen and examine its psychophysical mechanism, as well as the subjective feelings of migrants about the city and the industrial enclaves.

Shenzhen: China's migrant city and its migrant segregation

Shenzhen's growth is linked to the arrival of millions of rural migrants from across the country after late 1970s, when China started to implement its market reform and open-door policies. In about three decades, more than 10 million migrants have come to Shenzhen and made it one of the most prosperous cities in the world (Wang and Wu, 2010). Shenzhen is socially stratified: the first ladder is the formal or permanent migrants, about 2 million people in 2015; the second ladder is the urban natives, just about 300,000; and at the bottom are the "outsiders", that is, those informal or temporary migrants. Like the case of other Chinese cities, the first two groups hold Shenzhen *hukou* and most have such advantages as better welfare, market participation, and mobility. The elites include the "new rich," entrepreneurs or professionals working in joint ventures, private companies, factories, governments, or other formal institutions. The natives are mostly villagers who sell or rent their lands/houses and belong to collective institutions in the village (*cunweihui*). The outsiders are rural migrants mainly working in the service, industry, or other low-end sectors. With lower economic, social, and political capital, they live in factory clusters, urban villages, or low-rent affordable housing. But this social ladder is by no means crystallized or fixed, as migrants strive to integrate into Shenzhen and become "permanent" residents, a dream for most of them. Above all, Shenzhen is characterized by a remarkable socio-spatial segregation between rich and poor, between Shenzhen *hukou* holders and rural migrants, and between the dwellers on commodity housing estates and factory clusters or urban villages.

With the increasing accessibility of data such as national censuses, scholars have been better able to examine the socio-spatial landscape of Shenzhen (Wang et al., 2009; Hao, 2014; Hao et al., 2013; Lai et al., 2014;). First, we will use the newest census, that is, the sixth national census, 2010, to measure segregation and examine its factorial ecology. The research area includes all districts: six inner districts and four outer districts (Figure 10.1), covering all the 57 subdistricts, a total area of 1996.85 square kilometers, and the total population was 10.35 million in 2010. An analysis of the census generated 64 variables and four main categories were identified (Table 10.1): migrants, elites, natives, and professionals.

In detail, the first main category is "migrant," which has 43 variables with high loadings. It is highly related to such variables as "male" (0.960) and "female" (0.925). There is a positive relationship with the variables that indicate migration status, that is, "*hukou* in other county (city, district)"

Figure 10.1: Location and map of Shenzhen

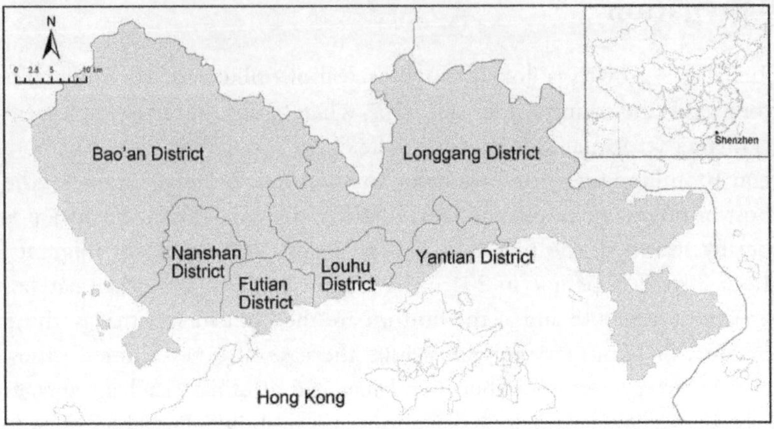

Source: Author

(0.964), "*hukou* unsettled" (0.694), "left registered place below 2 years" (0.979), and so on. As shown in Table 10.2, this group is marked by lower educational attainments, such as "middle school or lower levels" (0.967). Their income is largely derived from manual labor or other work, as its high loadings with the variables of "salary" (0.981) and "working time per week is above 40 hours" (0.982), which also indicates a hard–working lifestyle. Moreover, with regard to housing conditions, the factor has high loadings with the variables of "rent—cheap rental housing" (0.817) and "rent—other housing" (0.974), as rural migrants often live either in cheap rental housing or in the self-built housing of local villagers. The rent is cheap, and there is a high loading with the variable of "monthly rental below 1,000 yuan" (0.969). There is often limited living space, as there are high loadings of "house area below 50 square meters" (0.982). Above all, "migrant" has become the major factor or the prominent feature of Shenzhen's social space.

The second category is "elite," which is positive with high loadings of 31 variables. This group is featured by "income from property" (0.684) and housing conditions are characterized by "purchase—commodity housing" (0.694), "purchase—secondhand housing" (0.884), and "purchase—affordable housing" (0.418). Most of their houses were built in the period "1980–2000" (0.606) that is, housing built after the market reform but before the recent real estate boom. The properties also appear to be more comfortable, as there is a high loading of "house area, 50–110 square meters" (0.870). Specifically, the loadings of the variables of welfare in this group are prominent, such as "pension" (0.412), "insurance for unemployemnt" (0.436), and "lowest living security funding" (0.486).

Table 10.1: The loadings and factors of Shenzhen's factorial ecology

Variable Migrant	Main factor			
	Elite	Native	Professional	
Demographic variables				
Male	0.960	0.271	0.046	−0.015
Female	0.925	0.352	0.077	0.034
Age above 18	0.732	0.636	0.161	−0.015
Age above 18–64	0.964	0.255	0.038	0.006
Age above 65	0.247	0.649	0.583	0.214
Single	0.978	0.109	−0.029	0.054
Couple	0.912	0.367	0.097	−0.031
Divorce	0.184	0.758	0.428	0.337
Others	0.476	0.706	0.304	−0.009
Hukou status				
Hukou in Shenzhen	0.036	0.446	0.816	0.204
Hukou in other county (city, district)	0.964	0.244	−0.065	−0.024
Hukou unsettled	0.694	0.464	0.006	−0.052
Hukou at registered place	0.002	0.339	0.859	0.201
Left registered place below 2 years	0.979	0.093	0.089	0.015
Left registered place 2–6 years	0.904	0.388	0.000	0.016
Left registered place above 6 years	0.584	0.726	0.046	−0.034
Left registered place to do industry or business	0.981	0.158	−0.072	−0.024
Left registered place to change job	0.404	0.642	0.351	0.218
Left registered place to study	0.467	0.501	0.149	0.093
Left registered place to join family	0.464	0.812	0.047	−0.129
Left registered place to join relatives	0.668	0.501	0.103	0.148
Left registered place to relocate housing	−0.045	0.550	0.671	0.200
Left registered place to set *hukou*	−0.060	0.669	0.335	0.109
Left registered place to marry	0.215	0.874	0.235	0.076
Left registered place for other reasons	0.637	0.601	0.068	0.036
Born in Shenzhen	0.527	0.608	0.503	−0.003
Born in other cities, villages of Guangdong province	0.711	0.649	0.126	0.081
Born in the East region	0.956	0.200	0.065	0.057
Born in the Middle region	0.976	0.173	−0.004	0.016
Born in the West region	0.975	0.052	−0.042	−0.091
Collective *hukou*	0.005	−0.186	−0.575	0.012
Non-agricultural *hukou*	−0.540	0.076	0.736	0.273
Educational attainment				
Middle school or lower level	0.967	0.212	−0.053	−0.054
College or higher level	0.229	0.516	0.605	0.339
Employment				

Variable Migrant	Main factor			
	Elite	Native	Professional	
Non-working	0.568	0.732	0.323	0.111
Salary	0.981	0.175	−0.002	−0.008
Pension	−0.150	0.412	0.718	0.355
Insurance for unemployment	−0.091	0.436	0.421	0.241
Lowest living security funding	0.088	0.486	0.253	−0.077
Income from property	0.564	0.684	0.213	0.121
Raised by other family members	0.620	0.718	0.224	0.041
Income from other resources	0.652	0.619	0.158	0.068
Working time per week below 20 hours	0.640	0.166	0.009	0.010
Working time per week 20–40 hours	0.615	0.250	0.098	0.199
Working time per week above 40 hours	0.982	0.170	−0.005	−0.014
Tenure				
Rent—cheap rental housing	0.817	0.146	−0.078	−0.075
Rent—other housing	0.974	0.096	−0.066	−0.029
Self-built housing	0.689	0.327	−0.190	−0.415
Purchase—commodity housing	0.047	0.694	0.598	0.169
Purchase—secondhand housing	0.023	0.884	0.256	0.136
Purchase—affordable housing	0.008	0.418	0.363	0.086
Purchase—public housing	−0.309	0.075	0.380	0.531
Other tenures	0.825	0.112	−0.017	−0.250
Housing				
Number of housing per household	−0.432	0.093	0.711	0.024
Monthly rental below 1,000 yuan	0.969	0.046	−0.101	−0.166
Monthly rental 1,000–2,000 yuan	0.050	0.494	0.160	0.729
Monthly rental 2,000–3,000 yuan	−0.104	0.160	0.252	0.859
Monthly rental above 3,000 yuan	−0.059	0.082	0.240	0.808
House built before 1979	0.846	0.036	−0.110	−0.181
House built 1980–2000	0.680	0.606	0.146	0.160
House built after 2000	0.960	0.077	0.003	−0.101
House area below 50 square meters	0.982	0.021	−0.078	−0.058
House area 50–110 square meters	0.308	0.870	0.272	0.098
House area above 110 square meters	0.344	0.386	0.675	0.051

The third category is "native," as there are high loadings with the variables of "*hukou* in Shenzhen" (0.816), "*hukou* at the registered place" (0.859), "born in Shenzhen" (0.503), and "non-agricultural *hukou*" (0.736). This group is characterized by higher education ("college or higher level," 0.605), retirement ("pension," 0.718), and most purchased commodity houses (0.598). Their housing conditions are considerably better than those of other groups, as there are high loadings for such variables as "room number per household" (0.711), and "house area above 110 square meters" (0.675).

The last category is "professionals," with high loadings on five variables: "self-built housing" (−0.415), "purchase—public housing" (0.531), "monthly rental 1,000–2,000 yuan" (0.729), "monthly rental 2,000–3,000 yuan" (0.859), and "monthly rental above 3,000 yuan" (0.808). Compared with the first group, migrants, professionals may have initially been migrants, who have been able to assimilate or integrate successfully into the local society. This group are differentiated from migrants, both socially and spatially, as they often no longer stay in urban villages ("self-built housing," −0.415) and have access to the welfare system ("pension," 0.355).

The Index of Dissimilarity (ID), P index, and Location Quotient (LQ) are used to measure the segregation and interaction between migrants and locals. All the three indices have been widely used in related studies and in various contexts (Johnston et al., 2011). The status of locals and migrants depend on *hukou* status. Thus, migrants here refer to non-Shenzhen *hukou* holders, and locals refer to Shenzhen *hukou* holders, as per the census.

First, there is evident segregation between "locals" and "non-local *hukou* holders" (0.430) (Figure 10.2). As a larger ID indicates a higher level of segregation, compared to the IDs of Beijing, Shanghai, or Guangzhou, the level of migrant segregation in Shenzhen is relatively high. Figure 10.2 also shows the IDs between locals and migrants with different lengths of migration. Along with the increase in migration time, the levels of segregation decrease. For instance, the segregation between locals and migrants who left the place of *hukou* registration for less than two years is 0.400, while for those who left the place of *hukou* registration more than six years ago it is 0.324. This result suggests a trend toward spatial integration or assimilation after a prolonged stay in Shenzhen.

The P index reports the interaction between migrants and locals (Table 10.2), and a larger P indicates higher frequency of interactions. The P index between the locals and migrants is 0.134, such that there are few interactions between the two groups. Those who left their place of *hukou* registration less than two years ago have the smallest P index, and their interaction with the locals is the weakest. By comparison, those who left their place of *hukou* registration between two and six years ago have a higher frequency of interaction with locals (0.269), and higher interactions with recent migrants, that is, those who have left their place of *hukou* registration for less than two years (0.278).

Figure 10.2: Index of Dissimilarity for migrants

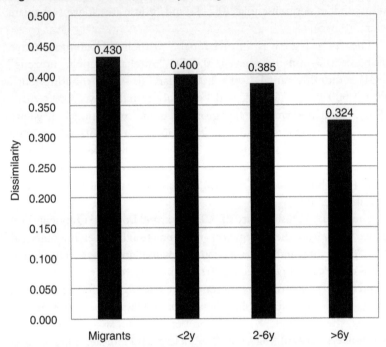

Notes:

"Migrants" refer to all migrants to Shenzhen.

"<2y" refers to migrants who had left their place of *hukou* registration for no more than two years;

"2–6y" refers to migrants who had left their place of *hukou* registration for two to six years; and

">6y" refers to migrants who had left their place of *hukou* registration for more than six years.

Table 10.2: P index for locals and migrants

	Locals	<2y	2–6y	>6y
Locals	–	–	–	–
<2y	0.112	–	–	–
2–6y	0.269	0.278	–	–
>6y	0.209	0.174	0.193	–

Notes:

"<2y" refers to migrants who had left their place of *hukou* registration for no more than two years;

"2–6y" refers to migrants who had left their place of *hukou* registration for two to six years; and

">6y" refers to migrants who had left their place of *hukou* registration for more than six years.

Figures 10.3 to 10.7 show the results of LQ for different types of residents in Shenzhen. Most locals live in the central areas, such as Nanshan, Futian, and Luohu (Figure 10.3) but most migrants live in Bao'an and Longgang, the suburban districts (Figure 10.4). This resonates with the findings in Shanghai, which show a clear segregation between the inner city and suburbs (Wu, 2002). Some clusters of locals can be identified in the suburbs, such as Longcheng subdistrict of Longgang District, Nan'ao subdistrict of Dapeng New District, and Guangming New District, which are the location of the local villages. As for the spatial distribution of migrants, we found larger LQ for such subdistricts as Guanlan subdistrict of Longhua New District, Shiyan subdistrict, Yongfu subdistrict, and Dalang of Bao'an District, which have accumulations of either development zones or industrial parks (Figure 10.4). In addition, with increased length of residence, the distance of the migrant clusters from the central city decreases (Figures 10.5–10.7). Moreover, migrants also concentrate in Yongfu subdistrict, Shiyan subdistrict of Bao'an District, Gongming subdistrict of Guangming New District, and Guanlan subdistrict of Longhua New District, where industrial and service job opportunities such as supermarkets, finance, and restaurants clustered during the last decades.

Above all, some suburban subdistricts became the major destinations of migrant workers, and these places are often closely linked to job opportunities or sectoral developments. What will be the psychological impacts of this spatial structure? What are the social and emotional experiences of the migrants living in suburban clusters?

Figure 10.3: The Location Quotient of locals

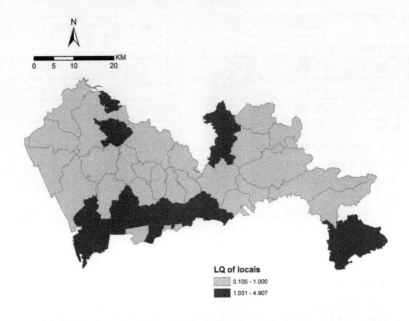

Figure 10.4: The Location Quotient of migrants

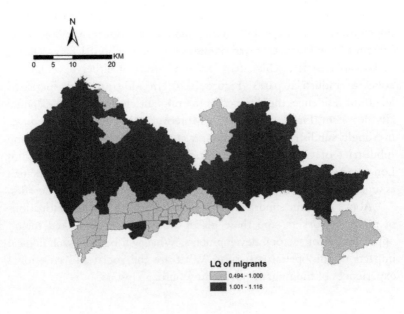

Figure 10.5: The Location Quotient of migrants living in Shenzhen below two years

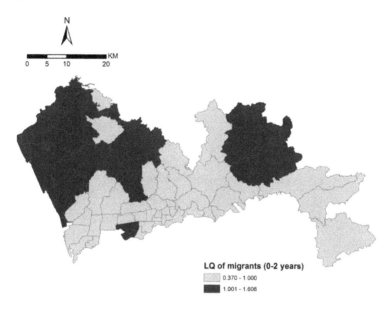

Figure 10.6: The Location Quotient of migrants living in Shenzhen between two and six years

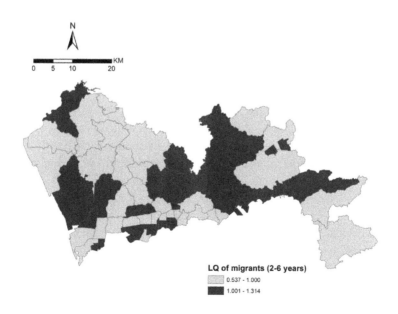

Figure 10.7: The Location Quotient of migrants living in Shenzhen above six years

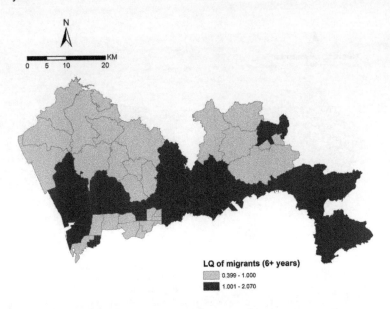

LQ of migrants (6+ years)

0.399 - 1.000

1.001 - 2.070

Foxconn and its psychophysical mechanism

Foxconn, which is located in Longhua District, is a typical example and it is one of the largest industrial clusters in Shenzhen (Chan et al., 2013). Its mother company, Foxconn Group, was set up by Terry Guo, the famous Taiwanese tycoon in 1988 (Figure 10.8). After three decades of high-speed growth, Foxconn Group had become the largest "original equipment manufacturer" (OEM) company in the world, which includes more than 30 industrial parks and clusters across China, covering more than 200 sub-branches and with about 1 million employees (Chan et al., 2013). As the first industrial cluster of Foxconn Group in Mainland China, Shenzhen Foxconn occupies some 2.3 square kilometers, with about 430,000 workers living and working in this "campus." As with *danwei* in pre-reform China, the cluster includes not only factories and warehouses, but also dormitories, banks, hospitals, and a library, a post office, an educational institute, bookstores, soccer fields, basketball courts, a track and field, swimming pools, cyber theatres, supermarkets, a collection of cafeterias and restaurants, and so on. Above all, Foxconn indicates a specific stage of China's cities in the early 21st century that is characterized by the world factory and the accumulation of millions of migrant workers.

Figure 10.8: The location and space of Foxconn, Shenzhen

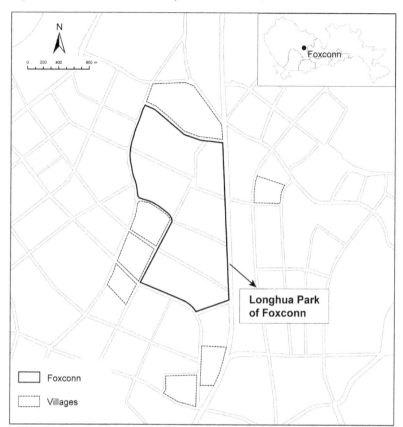

In 2013, we conducted fieldwork to interview 19 migrant workers who were working or had worked for Foxconn. Most (18) were born after 1980 and held rural *hukou*, coming from such regions as Guangdong, Guangxi, Hunan, Henan, Hebei, Anhui, Jiangxi, and other provinces. Among them, there are 12 men and 7 women; eight workers live in the dormitories of Foxconn, and ten workers live in the urban villages near Foxconn (Figure 10.8). Only one lived in commodity housing.

Most migrant workers followed the same experiential route, with four stages, namely: "migrate from rural to urban," "upgrade from informal job to formal job," "escape from Foxconn," and "stuck in Foxconn." Initially, these migrant workers "migrate from rural to urban" at the age of 18, normally with the help of employment agencies, schools, or relatives and other people from the same villages or towns. The process, however, is by no means a direct one:

"I came to Shenzhen, but I was cheated by the employment agency, all my money was taken away. They kept praising me, but cheated me, and they took all my money away. At the end, I only had my ID card in my hands. They introduced me to two small factories, asking me to do the interviews by myself. At the end, I almost had no money to buy a bus ticket." (Interview, April 14, 2013)

"We were all deceived by our school to come to work at Foxconn. They praised Foxconn as a paradise, and they talked about high salaries, easy tasks ... they told us that it is the only technology in need of girls' digital control, yet we have never been taught to do it." (Interview, April 21, 2013)

The relocation from rural villages to Shenzhen's suburbs is a process of integrating into globalization, which involves not only market forces such as job agencies and investors; it also includes both formal and informal institutions of the Chinese society, such as *guanxi* (social capital), training schools, and so on. It is a process full of challenges and difficulties, especially the psychological pressure originating from a change in the familiar surroundings of villages to heterogeneous urbanism.

The second stage is "upgrade from informal jobs to formal jobs." Before joining Foxconn, most of our interviewees had the experience of working in either sweatshops or small workshops. Comparatively, the work of Foxconn is relatively formal, with higher income and welfare conditions. However, the third stage is "escape from Foxconn," as they have been subjected to extreme work pressure and desperation (Cheng et al., 2011; Pun and Chan, 2012). To secure its unique status as the major manufacturer of electronics manufacturing and services for such leading brands as Apple, Sony, Samsung, Microsoft, and so on, Foxconn has set up this walled enclave and pushed its workers to their physical and psychological limits (for details, see Pun and Chan, 2012). Though some may be satisfied by the "stable" work of Foxconn, most migrants are not used to the modernized or even "militarized" management of Foxconn.

"I have worked at Foxconn for several years. I started feeling that I am just a talking machine, why keep doing this ... If you work in Foxconn, you just need to focus on the working plan, close your mouth, and keep doing it. After the working time, there is nothing to think about." (Interview, April 21, 2014)

Figure 10.9: Landscape of Foxconn

Foxconn's operation is marked by division of labor, mechanical repetition of each simple movement, and strict implementation. Every building and dormitory has a security checkpoint with guards standing by 24 hours a day, which gives migrants a feeling of having no freedom (Figure 10.9). Line leaders are also under pressure to treat workers harshly to reach productivity targets. Migrant workers feel that their status is even lower than machines, "even the air conditioning is set for machines, not for us." Moreover, the living space within the campus is just an extension of the workshop, the goal of which is just to reproduce the physical strength of workers at the lowest cost and time. For instance, the dormitory assignments are random and break up their social relations and social lives (Pun and Chan, 2012). Above all, the exhausting work, the boring everyday life, and strict control of time and space make for high pressure and frustrated young migrant workers—all these pushed them to escape. But *hukou* status and its lasting impact is a major barrier for migrant workers to escape and integrate into Shenzhen. They cannot access the same welfare or opportunities as locals, such as state financial support or bank loans, as it is hard for them to get support to run new businesses.

> "Now the condition at my hometown is improving; if you can find something profitable to do, it is easy to get bank loans at home. But in Shenzhen, it is so difficult to get it, you can only work for salaries." (Interview, April 21, 2013)

The fourth stage is "stuck in Foxconn." There are two ways to escape Foxconn. First, if migrant workers can learn and upgrade their skills, such as in relation to computer technology, designs, sales, and so on, they may be able to change jobs. But it is not easy to set aside money or time for training. Second, some may be able to start up a small business such as a factory or a shop.

> "I have no technology skills, no certificates, almost nothing, I have to keep working and learning. If I leave Foxconn now, there is nowhere to go. I want to move beyond the current life through my struggles [but] now I have to go to work every day." (Interview, April 20, 2013)

Some migrant workers may return to their hometowns to found a startup business but as both population and opportunities are now gravitating toward large cities such as Shenzhen, there are few opportunities for them to succeed.

> "Some returned home to start new businesses, after earning 100,000 to 200,000 yuan, they went back and opened shops or small businesses ... if you run a garage, there were no cars to fix; if you opened a restaurant or barbecue, there were no customers; at the end, you lose all your savings ... All the middle-aged or youngsters have gone out to work, and there are only kids and aged people left, so there is no market at all." (Interview, April 21, 2013)

Cultural obstacles are also a major issue. After three decades of urban–rural division, the villagers are of the opinion that working in cities is an advantage and it is a way of showing people's ability or quality. There are psychological pressures that push migrants to go back to Foxconn.

> "The overall condition in villages is better, but because of the old perspective of my father, who considers staying at home as cowardice ... my parents did not know that the working condition here is so harsh ... one of my friends went back

home to work, but none of his family members supported his decisions." (Interview, August 26, 2012)

"The business I was involved in needed an input of several thousand yuan, not too much, but I failed at the end. The product is in fact not appropriate, it is a 3D toy. These products should be sold in large cities, it is not for villagers." (Interview, April 21, 2013)

As such, migrants are stuck in a status of being neither urban nor rural. Foxconn is an enclave separating migrant workers from both urban and rural society. The modernism, Taylorism, assembly-line, and governmentality of the time, space, and everyday practices of migrant workers exacerbate their experiences of living and working in the clusters—yet, they could no longer return to their hometowns.

Discussions and conclusions

In this study, we examined the issue of migrant segregation in Shenzhen. We produced a panoramic view of the landscape of migrant segregation and explored the psychophysical impacts of Foxconn enclaves. We found that "migrant" stands out as the most prominent determinants of Shenzhen's factorial ecology, and there is marked segregation between locals and rural migrants. Shenzhen has been stratified, and this stratification has been materialized and exacerbated. Institutional factors such as *hukou* status stand out as the major determinant. Moreover, the segregation indices indicate that there are high levels of segregation between migrants and locals, and the P index indicates that there is limited interaction between locals and migrants.

Space matters to the segregation or integration of migrants. Our LQ analysis found that most locals live in the central city. In contrast, most migrants concentrate in the suburbs, especially those around development zones, industrial parks, or the job opportunities in the industrial or service sectors. Some subdistricts thus became the major clusters of migrant workers. As suggested by Shen (2017), migrants are stuck in the suburbs, and it is hard for them to relocate into the central city.

Two recent trends in urban development further exacerbate the situation. First, the rise in land use and real estate prices in the central city forces factories, supermarkets, and services to relocate to the suburbs, similar to the process of suburbanization in North America. Thus, job opportunities available to migrants are mainly concentrated in the suburbs.

Second, the process is interwoven with the redevelopment or gentrification of the central city, so that living costs for migrants within the central city have also generally increased, and the chances of relocation have further decreased. Accordingly, industrial clusters such as Foxconn have become the major living and working space for migrants in Shenzhen.

Industrial clusters accumulate not only international or transnational investments, products, and skills, they also accumulate migrant workers especially those new-generation migrants. Our case study of Foxconn shows that migrants have been stuck in these clusters. Rural migrants could neither integrate into Shenzhen nor return to their hometowns. At its extreme, in 2010, there were 18 cases of suicide at Foxconn, attracting public attention (Cheng et al., 2011; Pun and Chan, 2012).

Such tragedies indicate the psychological problems associated with such clusters as Foxconn. They relate to the concerns of Park regarding immobility, social isolation, and segregation in the US cities in the early 20th century (Park, 1915). The desperate dilemma of migrants stuck in Foxconn calls for further critical examinations of these factory enclaves, the everyday life of workers, and their subjective feelings in the early 21st century. Compared to the 1920s when Park examined Chicago, today's globalizing cities such as Shenzhen are entering a new era characterized by unprecedented local–global interactions and tremendous mobility. Its resultant impacts on the integration or segregation of migrants is becoming even more prominent, as people resort to cities to seek opportunities, fortunes, and dreams. Shenzhen's migrant segregation is closely linked to the status of the city as world factory, as most migrants concentrate in these industrial clusters, and struggle to survive and thrive. In this vein, our findings indicate the significance of China's new national strategies of "people's urbanization" to decrease the inequalities between locals and migrants, and help migrants integrate into cities.

Note

1   Mr. Lizhi Xu is a famous "workerpoet" (*da gong shiren*) of Shenzhen who once worked at Foxconn. He committed suicide in 2014 at the age of just 24. Permission to use the poem has been granted by Mr. Xu's family.

Acknowledgment

This research is funded by the National Science Foundation of China (41422103, 41771167). We appreciate the comments of Professor Bart Wissink on an earlier draft of this chapter. Our gratitude also goes to Miss Da Liu and Miss Feicui Gou (Wuhan University) for help in drawing some figures of this chapter.

References

Chan, J., Pun, N., and Selden, M. (2013) "The politics of global production: Apple, Foxconn and China's new working class," *New Technology, Work and Employment*, 28(2): 100–15.

Chen, Y. and Wang, J. (2015) "Social integration of new-generation migrants in Shanghai, China," *Habitat International*, 49: 419–25.

Cheng, Q., Chen, F., and Yip, P. (2011) "The Foxconn suicides and their media prominence: Is the Werther Effect applicable in China?" *BMC Public Health*, 11: 841–51.

Fan, C. C., Sun, M., and Zheng, S. (2011) "Migration and split households: A comparison of sole, couple, and family migrants in Beijing, China," *Environment and Planning A*, 43(9): 2164–85.

Feng J., Zhou Y. X., Logan, J., and Wu, F. (2007) "Restructuring of Beijing's social space," *Eurasian Geography and Economics*, 48(5): 509–42.

Gieryn, T. F. (2006) "City as truth-spot: Laboratories and field sites in urban studies," *Social Studies of Science*, 36(1): 5–38.

Hao, P. (2014) "Spatial evolution of urban villages in Shenzhen," in F. Wu, F. Zhang, and C. Webster (eds.) *Rural migrants in urban China: Enclaves and transient urbanism*, Abingdon: Routledge, pp. 202–19.

Hao, P., Geertman, S., Hooimeijer, P., and Sliuzas, R. (2013) "Spatial analyses of the urban village development process in Shenzhen, China," *International Journal of Urban & Regional Research*, 37(6): 2177–97.

Johnston, R., Poulsen, M., and Forrest, J. (2011) "Evaluating changing residential segregation in Auckland, New Zealand, using spatial statistics," *Tijdschrift Voor Economische En Sociale Geografie*, 102(1): 1–23.

Lai, Y., Peng, Y., Li, B., and Lin, Y. (2014) "Industrial land development in urban villages in China: A property rights perspective," *Habitat International*, 41: 185–94.

Latour, B. and Woolgar, S. (1986) *Laboratory life: The construction of scientific facts*, Princeton, NJ: Princeton University Press.

Li, S.-M. and Song, Y.-L. (2009) "Redevelopment, displacement, housing conditions, and residential satisfaction: A study of Shanghai," *Environment and Planning A*, 41(5): 1090–108.

Li, Z. and Wu, F. (2013) "Residential satisfaction in China's informal settlements: A case study of Beijing, Shanghai, and Guangzhou," *Urban Geography*, 34(7): 923–49.

Liu, Y., Dijst, M., and Geertman, S. (2014) "Residential segregation and well-being inequality between local and migrant elderly in Shanghai," *Habitat International*, 42: 175–85.

Liu, Y., Li Z., and Breitung, W. (2012) "The social networks of new-generation migrants in China's urbanized villages: A case study of Guangzhou," *Habitat International*, 36(1): 192–200.

Liu, Y., Wu F., Liu, Y., and Li, Z. (2017) "Changing neighbourhood cohesion under the impact of urban redevelopment: A case study of Guangzhou, China," *Urban Geography*, 38(2): 266–90.

Park, R. E. (1915) "The city: Suggestions for the investigation of human behavior in the urban environment," *The American Journal of Sociology*, 20(5): 577–612.

Pun, N. and Chan, J. (2012) "Global capital, the state, and Chinese workers: The Foxconn experience," *Modern China*, 38(4): 383–410.

Ren, Y. and Qiao, N. (2010) "Social integration for migrants: Process, measurement and determinants," *Population Research*, 34: 11–19 [in Chinese].

Robinson, J. (2005) "Urban geography: World cities, or a world of cities," *Progress in Human Geography*, 29(6): 757–65.

Shen, J. (2017) "Stuck in the suburbs? Socio-spatial exclusion of migrants in Shanghai," *Cities*, 60B: 428–35.

Wang, M. Y. and Wu, J. (2010) "Migrant workers in the urban labour market of Shenzhen, China," *Environment and Planning A*, 42(6): 1457–75.

Wang, Y. P., Wang, Y., and Wu, J. (2009) "Urbanization and informal development in China: Urban villages in Shenzhen," *International Journal of Urban and Regional Research*, 33(4): 957–73.

Wang, Z., Zhang, F., and Wu, F. (2016) "Intergroup neighbouring in urban China: Implications for the social integration of migrants," *Urban Studies*, 53(4): 651–68.

Wissink, B., Hazelzet, A., and Breitung, W. (2014) "Migrant integration in China: Evidence from Guangzhou," in F. Wu, F. Zhang, and C. Webster (eds.) *Rural migrants in urban China: Enclaves and transient urbanism*, Abingdon: Routledge, pp. 99–120.

Wu, F., Zhang, F., and Webster, C. (2013) "Informality and the development and demolition of urban villages in the Chinese peri-urban area," *Urban Studies*, 50(10): 1919–34.

Wu, F., Zhang, F., and Webster, C. (2014) *Rural migrants in urban China: Enclaves and transient urbanism*, Abingdon: Routledge.

Wu, W. (2002) "Temporary migrants in Shanghai: housing and settlement patterns," in J. R. Logan (ed.) *The new Chinese city: Globalization and market reform*, Oxford: Blackwell, pp. 212–26.

11

The Anxious Middle Class of Urban China

Its Emergence and Formation

Tai-lok Lui and Shuo Liu

Introduction

One of the most notable features of urbanization in China since the late 1990s is the rise of an urban middle class. While researchers continue to argue among themselves about the exact definition of the middle class in a post-socialist economy and how to draw the class boundary, few observers of contemporary China would disagree that many of the affluent managers, administrators, and professionals in the major cities are quickly acquiring a new social identity and leading new ways of life. From the proliferation of nightlife entertainment in urban hotspots to the consumption of luxurious items and/or foreign brands (on coffee consumption, see Henningsen, 2012; on taste and class identity, see Dong and Blommaert, 2016), from the drastic increase in car ownership to the growth of gated communities, the cityscape in contemporary China has undergone drastic changes in the course of urbanization and socioeconomic restratification. Social class constitutes an important dimension of the changing urban life in China. And the rise of a newly formed middle class in the major cities is both an agent in shaping the changing cityscape and an outcome of current urban development.

This chapter, drawing on our observations conducted in a suburban middle-class community in Beijing in 2007–17 (for details, see Lui and Liu, 2015, 2019) and the study of the middle class in Shanghai since the mid-1990s (see Lui, 2001, 2004, 2009), reports on the emergence and formation of an urban middle class in contemporary Chinese cities. It is argued that this middle class came into existence when China's economy was marketized and the social structure had undergone a major transformation as a result of such economic changes. Within a period of 20 to 25 years, China has witnessed the birth of a middle class in the context of the transition to a post-socialist economy, the formation of new class identities and lifestyles, and growing class-related anxieties. Of course, the rise of the middle class is only a part of the broader restratification processes in contemporary China. Equally significant are the influx of migrant workers into cities and the concomitant polarization in the urban social structure (for a survey of China's ongoing urban transformation, see He and Qian, 2017). But the newly formed middle class does put its footprints on contemporary Chinese cities. It is difficult to understand contemporary urbanism in China without acknowledging the role of the middle class. What follows is a discussion of the formation of this urban middle class, its social and cultural outlooks, and an analysis of how their class interests shape the social landscape of the Chinese cities.

Urbanization and social stratification

Urbanization and social stratification are two closely related socioeconomic processes and yet their interconnectedness has rarely been taken up by researchers from either the field of class analysis and/or social stratification on the one side, or that of urban sociology on the other. On the side of class analysis, the study of social class is often conducted at the national level (and thus the talk of American and British class structures). Few attempts have been made to contextualize the study of social class in the city.[1] However, it is ironic to see that actually quite a number of important monographs on the middle class are contextualized in particular urban communities. A notable example is Whyte's study of the "organization man" (1963). By situating the middle class in the suburban community, Whyte showed how social orderliness and conformity came to constitute the major features of the middle class's cultural and social outlook (also see Baumgartner, 1991).

Robert Park was clearly aware of the interconnection between urbanization and social stratification when he spelled out the agenda of urban research in his classical piece "The city: Suggestions for the investigation of human behavior in the urban environment," first published in 1915. He noted that "Physical and sentimental distances reinforce each other, and the influences of local distribution of the population participate with the influences of class and race in the evolution of the social organization" (Park, 1970: 10). The interaction between spatial restructuring under urbanization and the process of social stratification brings about what Park (1970: 10) described as "cities within cities." The gathering of people of similar socioeconomic and cultural characteristics, such as race and social class, is the result of, in Burgess's words (1970: 54), "a process of distribution … which sifts and sorts and relocates individuals and groups by residence and occupation."

Park showed strong interest in knowing such neighborhoods. He asked: "What is there in the subconsciousness … of this neighborhood which determines its sentiments and attitudes? … What is the social ritual, i.e., what things must one do in the neighborhood in order to escape being regarded with suspicion or looked upon as peculiar?" (Park, 1970: 11–12). And when he moved further, to the discussion of urbanites seeking "the same forms of excitement" (Park, 1970: 43), he came up with the idea of the moral region. The moral region emerges because of "the restrictions which urban life imposes" (Park, 1970: 44). Park emphasized that the existence of these moral regions (a typical example would be "the vice districts … found in most cities") was "part of the natural … life of a city" (Park, 1970: 43, 45). In a sense, they are special areas or neighborhoods within the city.

Park did not elaborate further on how he would like to look at the interaction between spatial restructuring and social stratification. But what we have noted above is perhaps quite relevant to our attempt to probe the connection between urbanization and class formation. The middle class emerges in an urban environment and it is interesting to see how a class identity is articulated and crystallized. But in order to examine the constitution of a class identity, we need to go beyond the social processes undergirding social stratification and the immediate community milieu. The overall political and ideological environment is also pertinent; and this is particularly significant in cases like China where the political regime remains authoritarian and the economy is undergoing a process of market transition. It is pertinent to examine how social class is constituted in the spatial context. The middle class chooses to stay in particular kinds of community, and these communities and the related styles of living express its class identity and culture. The first part of this process is about how the emerging middle class learns to live like a middle class. The second part is about how the middle class further adapts to the changing socioeconomic environment. The emergence of the middle class and the consolidation of a friendly institutional environment to this social class are no guarantees to managers, professionals, and administrators that they can lead stable and prosperous careers ever after. Indeed, experiences in postindustrial economies (see, for instance, Leicht and Fitzgerald, 2014, on the US) and newly industrialized economies in East Asia (see, for example, Lui, 2008, on Hong Kong; Yang, 2018, on South Korea) suggest that the once-conjectured steady upward developmental path of the middle class is probably more hypothetical than real. More importantly, the middle class also needs to face various challenges as the macro environment is experiencing rapid changes. As we shall see in the following discussion, soon after their arrival at the privileged positions, China's middle class find themselves encountering new challenges. Their responses to these challenges impact on the broader urban milieu.

Our research interest is about the emergence and formation of the middle class in contemporary urban China. Quite often, the immediate question to follow is about the political outlook of an emergent social class—are they agents of political change? The logic of such a kind of inquiry flows from defining the class boundary, identifying class interests, then explaining the manifestation (or the absence) of class consciousness, and finally examining the course of class action to be taken (Pahl, 1989; Crompton 2008). Such a "structure–consciousness–action" approach shows little interest in the process of articulation of class identity and class formation. As a result, the analysis of class jumps from one end (structure) to another (action) without knowing how the institutional as well as the more proximate socioeconomic, political, and cultural contexts would shape the formation of social class. It is our emphasis that, prior to an analysis of the political action of the middle class (if any), it is crucial for us to examine how a class identity is articulated and how class formation is carried out among the middle class. Without a closer look at the class formation process, it is difficult to understand how China's middle class is developing their identity, shared social perspective, and an articulation of common interests.

Socioeconomic changes in urban China have provided us with a good opportunity to observe the rise of a middle class as well as the way this social class is developing their culture and style of living. As we shall see in the following discussion, this emerging middle class rises to the occasion created by economic reform in a highly compressed socioeconomic and temporal environment. The middle class in contemporary China never seems to be able to enjoy a moment to settle down in the new environment. Very much like city life in China, the Chinese middle class is always in a state of continuous change. It is growing in numbers but is also cautiously finding its place in the changing milieu. The notion of middle-class identity is characterized by ambivalence (cf. Savage et al., 2001) and the emergent middle class is still overwhelmed by a sense of uncertainty and insecurity.

Ambiguity: A persistent feature of the middle class in contemporary China

Indeed, one of the most persistent features of the middle class in contemporary China is a sense of ambiguity in their self-perception. Such ambiguities condition the psychology of the Chinese middle class and give rise to a sense of anxiety among these professionals, managers, and administrators. This was the case when the notion of the middle class became popular in everyday life discourse in China in the late 1990s. And it remains the same in the context of growing affluence when more and more of the middle-class professionals, managers, and administrators have been able to consume international brand-name products, to own their apartment and car, and to go abroad for holidays. Ambiguity and anxiety are the keywords to understand the middle class in contemporary China.

But who belongs to the middle class in contemporary China? Similar to those debates on the middle class in other modern economies, such as the US or the UK and countries in continental Europe, and even those within East Asia, the label itself often carries different interpretations and usages.[2] It varies according to the theory of social class adopted by the researcher. It also varies in different stages of social development when new social classes emerge and come to the attention of news media and academic research. When China began its economic reform in the late 1970s and further pushed for marketization in the 1980s, the private entrepreneurs, the self-employed and small employers, and those managers in foreign enterprises were often seen as the rising social strata with their interests increasingly falling outside of the socialist socioeconomic system. Recently, the notion of a middle class has gradually become more focused and researchers have paid more attention to the difference between the capitalists (that is, private entrepreneurs) and what Goodman (2014a: 93) calls the intermediate middle class (what some researchers have labeled the new middle class), that is, those "whose place in society flows from their possession of skills, knowledge and organizational experience," like managers, administrators, and professionals. This can be seen as a recognition of the consolidation of the class structure, with the rich private entrepreneurs (as shown in their wealth and lifestyles) leading the kind of material life beyond the reach of most people. At the same time, this also illustrated the growing significance given to occupation as an indicator of one's situation in the labor market—marketable skills, knowledge, and organizational experience would determine one's life chances and the corresponding material rewards in the forms of salary and job-related benefits. Whereas previously in the early stage of market reform one's *danwei* (work-unit) was expected to be most crucial to the determination of fringe benefits (such as housing) obtained from the employer, nowadays *danwei* as such is no longer a determinant and an employee's position in the organizational hierarchy and/or his/her qualifications, skills, knowledge, and experience would be the key variables accounting for differentiation of pay and welfare/bonus package. It is in the course of this transition toward a more marketized labor market that the middle class emerges as a rising social class with the means to consume, to acquire domestic property, and to lead a new lifestyle.

The definitional controversy of the concept of the middle class continues despite a growing consensus about its classification on the basis of survey data. It is generally accepted that those under the categories of "managers," "professional and technical personnel," and "*banshi renyuan*" (office workers) can be grouped under the label of the middle class (also see Chen, 2013: 41–2; or in a slightly different label the "new middle class," see Li, 2015a). Based on the classification put forward by the Chinese Academy of Social Science (Lui and Liu, 2019), it is estimated that the percentage of the total population that can be categorized as middle class rose from 5% in 1978 to 15.9% in 2006. If the so-called 'old middle class' (the petty bourgeoisie or the so-called *geti* entrepreneurs in the context of contemporary China), is also included under a broad definition of the middle class, its share in the overall social structure reaches 25.4% in 2006.

Our discussion so far is about China's class structure at the national level. Hu (2011: 44) examined class structures at the city level on the basis of a reanalysis of a 1% sample of the census of the 2005 national population. His analysis suggests that the middle class ("managers," "professional and technical personnel," and "office workers") occupies a significant position in cities: 34.6% of the working population in Beijing belonged to the middle class and 29.9% in Shanghai, whereas in Guiyang it was 15.89% and for the entire country 10.71%. Media attention given to the urban middle class in major cities like Beijing, Shanghai, Guangzhou, and Shenzhen is a reflection of its significance in the urban setting.

At the macro level, China is undergoing sweeping changes in its social structure as a result of economic reform and marketization. As previously noted, in the past two decades we have witnessed the rise of the middle class, and the social structure is still undergoing rapid changes. However, from the standpoint of ordinary people in their everyday lives, the notion of the middle class continues to carry with it a sense of ambiguity. The usage of class (*jieji*) or stratum (*jieceng*) is still a matter to be handled cautiously.[3] The ideological underpinning of the term "social class" continues to alert people to the need of choosing the right words to locate themselves in the changing social hierarchy and to describe changes in the socioeconomic structure.[4] Whereas in the early 1990s the term was still strongly associated with class struggle of the Maoist era and thus most people consciously disassociated from the concept, the problem in the more recent periods has been that the term implied social antagonism and it simply did not fit in with the official discourse of China being a harmonious society (*hexie shehui*).

In a way, the current atmosphere is only slightly different from when we started our study of Shanghai's middle class in 1997–98 (Lui, 2001). It was the time when the notion of *bailing*, instead of the middle class, was used as a means of neutralization in an ideological environment where the notion of private property and the implications of individual possession and ownership of capital and/or property were still ambiguous. At that time, in our intensive interviews with respondents in Shanghai, most were very cautious in using the term of the middle class for self-description or identifying themselves as members of this emerging social class. Some underlined the fact that China was a socialist country and thus did not have the required socioeconomic conditions (such as the possession of personal wealth) for the formation of social class. Others suggested that they preferred the term intellectuals (*zhishi fenzi*) to *bailing*. Whereas the former implied substance (knowledge, for example), the latter was no more than a label for the well-off or a new category of big-spending consumers. At that time, when the expression *bailing* was applied, it primarily referred to those high-income occupations in foreign corporations and other employing organizations that were outside the *tizhi* (establishment). It was the emergence of such new social strata like *bailing* that caught people's attention and which were seen as symbols of the changing socioeconomic system in contemporary China: "Because of the essential changes brought about by the transformation from a 'status-based' cadre system to a 'contract-based' employment arrangement, we now have mental-labor, white-collar workers in our enterprises" (Zhu, 1998: 81).

In this connection, the research project on social stratification carried out by the Chinese Academy of Social Science in 1999 (Lu, 2002) can be seen as an attempt to find out how the social structure had been reshaped by economic reform. The suggestion of developing a new mapping of the class structure implied the recognition of fundamental changes in the way individuals' life chances were determined in the new socioeconomic environment. To some extent, this was also an acknowledgment of the fact that China had been restratified, while the official discourse continued to uphold China's status as a socialist society and thus social antagonism and conflict, if any, were not expected to be class-based. This was the period when the Chinese communist leadership began to rethink the party's positioning in the context of a social transformation in the country's economic and social structure. Jiang Zemin, who was then the Secretary General of the China Communist Party (CCP), spoke on his theory of "three represents" in 2000. A key feature of his speech touched on the formation of rising social strata brought about by economic reform. Those rising social strata on his list included not only *geti* and private entrepreneurs but also managers in foreign investments, technicians of enterprises in the field of new technology, administrative staff in intermediate organizations as well as those under the category of *ziyou zhiye* (free occupations) (Li, 2010: 10). Jiang saw the new challenge encountered by the CCP, whose past role and mission were that of being the vanguard party of the proletariat, was to take up the leadership by representing the interests of these rising social strata as well. His 2001 speech, during the 80th anniversary of the CCP, acknowledged these rising social strata as "legitimate" components of the social structure of China under economic reform. This was further elaborated in his report to the 16th National Party Congress in 2002 that one of the policy targets of the government was to enlarge the size of the middle-income group (also see Li, 2010: 10–11).

Unlike those living in a democratic country or a liberal society with minimal state control over ideological matters and political expression, the middle class in China has to look for such official endorsements before feeling certain that the use of the class label, either for self-identification or in their daily conversation, would not be politically sensitive. More importantly, official endorsements facilitated institutional and policy changes to groom a middle stratum. It was observed that "'cultivating' and 'expanding' the middle stratum as an income or consumer group, but not as a social group, has been one of the social development goals that the Chinese government has pursued" (Li, 2013: 15). This was a significant departure from the approach adopted after the Tiananmen Incident in June 1989 when the middle class, given the inclination toward supporting liberalization, was suspected of being subversive to the socialist state. Changes in party ideology and the official discourse on this matter from 2000 onward facilitated policy changes that allowed for the widening of the distribution of material rewards as well as the popularization of a new consumer culture (for example, the acquisition of luxury-brand products as status symbols). Gradually, the middle class, sometimes called the middle stratum and in other occasions the middle-income group, was recognized as a legitimate part of the new social structure in China. The politics of naming and renaming is consequential in terms of institutional change (for the further "cultivation" of the middle class) and the formation of a new ideological atmosphere (so that identification with the middle class would not carry any inconvenient political message). Such a political and ideological construction of the middle class or middle stratum is an important process in the formation of the middle class in contemporary China. As summarized by Guo (2008: 51), "The Party-state may not like the concept of 'middle class', but the 'middle class' by some other name is acceptable." With such a change in the official understanding of the middle class, the socialist state, particularly through housing reform, plays a critical role in engineering the rise of the middle class (Tomba, 2004).

Learning to become middle class

Our extended discussion of the political and ideological uncertainty surrounding the formation of the middle class in China is intended to underline the impact of the institutional setting on shaping middle-class identity and orientation. From the very beginning, the middle class carry with them a sense of insecurity. This was partly an outcome of their ambiguous status in a rapidly changing economic and political environment. On the one side, middle-class professionals' and managers' confidence was growing as they developed stronger command of their economic resources and were able to use these newly acquired economic means to improve their standard of living. On the other, how political and ideological control might impact on their lives remained an open-ended question. Of course, as China's economy has continued to grow, the broader economic and cultural atmosphere has changed accordingly. For most people, the worry of being seen as leading a bourgeois lifestyle has largely become a non-issue. Consumerism is now by and large a part of ordinary people's everyday life.

Indeed, when we returned to Shanghai in 2003–04 and carried out another round of intensive interviews with middle-class informants, responses to our questions on the middle class were rather different. First, respondents were quite relaxed and open in discussing the rising middle class. The negative connotations of the notion of the middle class seemed to be disappearing at that time. Instead of seeing *bailing* simply in the light of their consumption power, it was then recognized by the informants that the professionals and managers had decent jobs, earned respectable salaries, and possessed the required credentials for their top positions on the job ladder. Second, there was a noticeable change in the attitude toward *bailing*. When the *bailing* informants were probed if they belonged to the middle class, those who said no were likely to supplement their answers by saying that they were not qualified, in terms of their salary or consumption practice, to be called middle class (Lui, 2009). Instead of being looked down on (because they were inferior to the intellectuals), *bailing* were looked up to and, to some extent, admired by quite a number of the informants. In a small-scale survey conducted in Beijing and Shanghai in 2004 and 2005 (Wang, 2008: 60–1), similar responses were heard. According to that survey, among the 216 respondents in middle-income occupations, slightly more than one third saw themselves belonging to the middle-income group, 37% "did not think they qualified," and 27% gave a "don't know" answer. The fear of political association of being politically incorrect with the middle class had evaporated. People's concern had changed as the economy continued to grow and the gap between social classes was widening—they began to see the middle class as a social class that they might not be able to enter.[5] Their occupational status and the standard of living were seen as something beyond the reach of the majority. A major change in the perception and attitude toward the middle class was witnessed in the early 2000s.

On the bases of structural changes in employment and attitudinal changes discussed, a middle-class culture and lifestyle was in the process of formation. The term *xiaozi* (petit bourgeoisie) became a popular term referring to the emerging practice of emphasizing style of living, personal taste, authenticity, and probably also cultural distinction. At the beginning, it was a narrower concept highlighting a newly formed attitude toward lifestyle and taste espoused by the educated and high-culture lovers. But then this was gradually changed to a popular expression that covered a way of life and consumption that stood apart from mass culture and fashionable consumption. At the same time, consumption and new forms of material life (say, car ownership, see Zhang, 2017) were no longer taboo topics but had spread from the privileged minority to an expanding "middle stratum." It was to explore whether the rising middle class in China was ready to articulate its culture that an ethnographic study of a middle-class community in Beijing (alias KC) was conducted in 2007 (Liu, 2014). Through participant observation, interviews, and joining intranet communication among the local residents, it was observed that a nascent middle-class community was in the process of formation (Lui and Liu, 2015). At the time of the first observation, it was still premature to say that a middle-class culture and lifestyle was already in place. First, most of the residents in KC were only adjusting to a new living environment that would allow them to enjoy private life in a community setting. This was no longer the kind of collective housing provided by their *danwei*; it was a community based on *jieceng* (social strata) (Zhang, 2010). Second, these residents came from diverse socioeconomic as well as cultural backgrounds and it took time for a relatively homogenous culture to come into shape. Third, they were learning to "live like their well-to-do neighbors" (Zhang, 2010: 123). Home decoration, according less to basic needs but more to personal preference and lifestyle, was a newly found outlet for consumption. For some, it was an expression of their socioeconomic status; for others, they were excited about the freedom of defining their own private space (Liu, 2014).

Drastic changes in the social structure, diverse upward mobility pathways to middle-class positions, and the influx of migrants to major cities were all contributive to the difficulties in crystallizing a class culture among the middle-class informants we observed in Beijing in 2007. Yet, that said, we were aware that the community was developing a moral order that regulated the daily behaviors of the residents. Elsewhere (Lui and Liu, 2015) we discussed how families settled down in KC and through observing discussions via intranet communication it was found the hot topics and issues they shared among themselves were mundane matters like what was the proper way to keep pets and how to utilize the parking space. There were also discussions about whether it was acceptable to be half-naked when on the balcony and thus highly visible to neighbors. There was a strong sense of eagerness shared among the residents to establish some kind of code of behavior for residents to follow in the community. It was our observation then:

> What the KC residents did was more than simply taking into consideration how others felt. They were, in a way, joining a process of constructing a new collectivity. This collectivity was different from the kind of collective unit found in their work unit prior to economic reform in contemporary China. Rather, this was a new collectivity based on homeownership and personal choices. They could choose (through the market mechanism) and yet they were willing to adjust and accommodate other residents' expectations. They were leading a new life in this kind of new collectivity. It was a collectivity built on private property and a chosen way of living. The way of life they were living was their own choice. (Lui and Liu, 2015: 234)

The middle-class informants in KC were adjusting to the way(s) of life in the new community: the new moral order was not supposed to be imposed from above as this was no longer a collective housing unit provided by their *danwei*. Being homeowners, they made their choice to live in the community. They had expectations about the quality of life there. The quality of life they were referring to was not just about the physical structure and the facilities of the community. They had in mind a behavioral code that would guide the residents to enjoy their own chosen lifestyles and to adjust to the expectations of their neighbors. Accommodation, requiring mutual adjustment as well as self-restraint, was the main theme of their discussions. How to respect others and public interests was underlined. Furthermore, how to handle arguments and manage conflicts in everyday life in a civilized manner became a major concern among the middle-class homeowners in KC. All this required the cooperation of their neighbors. While there were rules and regulations governing what would be allowed and what not, more often argument arose when there were violations of sentiments, norms, tacit understanding, or expectation. They were new to this privately owned middle-class community and they quickly found themselves adjusting to this new community environment.

Middle class anxieties

When we returned to KC in 2016–17, many of our former informants had already left the community.[6] Instead of settling down in their newly found privatized community and looking for stability and orderliness, it seems to us that the middle-class professionals, managers, and administrators were still working very hard to find their place in the rapidly changing socioeconomic structure. Some left because they found it necessary to purchase a piece of domestic property whose price would help them hedge the bubbling property market. Differentials in a piece of property's potential of appreciation are one of the major concerns when they make the decision to buy their home. The quality (including the physical structure, facilities, location, and community environment) of the desired property is, of course, important. But for the middle-class professionals and managers, who are living in a city with rapid economic growth and escalating property prices, it is also important to be able to keep up with the skyrocketing real estate prices.

Rapid economic growth and development in China, and particularly in major cities like Beijing, Shanghai, and Guangzhou, has meant that the middle class could not be content to stay where they were. The real estate market was vibrant and apartment prices kept rising. If the appreciation of properties in KC could not match the market average, the homeowners there would feel that they were being left behind. Simply put, they would lose their means to catch up with the rising property prices when they needed to relocate or to move up the housing ladder.[7] Some of our former informants had decided to move back to the city center exactly because they wanted to be strategic in terms of property investment and to possess a piece of property that would continue to appreciate. Despite the fact that the middle class is reasonably well-off, the mindset has continued to focus on survival. One of our informants commented:

> "[In China] everything is about survival. No matter how much money you earn, you don't feel secure. Probably it is because our institutions are not fully established yet. When you reach our age, you feel pressure from your aging parents and your young children. ... So making money is at the top of my priorities."

By survival, our informants were not referring to securing a living at the subsistence level. Rather, they meant the need to keep their place and maintain their current standard of living in the context of rapid changes.

Other former informants had left because they needed to work out their child's schooling arrangements. Indeed, children's education was also a concern for those who continued to live in KC. This touched on another important concern of the middle class—its reproduction (on the middle-class housing strategy for intergenerational social mobility, see Wu et al., 2018). Middle-class families are most nervous about how to ensure that their children will also be able to secure a middle-class position. For them, they will have to assist and prepare their children to enter the right school, to be competitive in examinations, to acquire the right mix of cultural and social capital, and to attain the desired credentials. They invest a lot in all these preparations (Lin, 2018). But still they are uncertain about the outcomes. Thus, they become more eager to invest in various programs and courses that could improve the chance of their children's success in the highly competitive environment. Competition among middle-class parents continues to escalate and further intensifies their anxieties.

People in KC did not look any happier now than ten years ago, despite many of them having significantly improved their incomes. Concerns about food safety, air quality, and other environmental issues frequently popped up in our interviews. Their approach was that "we can only count on ourselves" to deal with these issues. Both the private and public sectors were not trusted for making any significant improvement in these areas. Opportunistic behaviors (for example, food poisoning and unsafe medicines) abound and private enterprises have not effectively developed their internal mechanisms to ensure product quality. And for the public sector, corrupt practices were repeatedly made known to the public and the monitoring system showed limited impact on curbing such misconducts. The informants chose to cope with these problems in an individualized manner. When food safety was a concern, the respondents purchased imported organic food. When one of our informants heard of a report on the use of expired vaccine for kids in a hospital, she "decided to go to a hospital run by foreign investment in order to get an imported vaccine for my son." They dealt with the problem via means they acquired from the market. Some did try to go beyond their own personal response (see Liu, 2018). They collaborated with their friends and neighbors and carried out group purchases. Some even tried to directly source food from farms they had inspected. But such a collective response was not an attempt to bring the issues and concerns to the public domain and to look for an institutionalized arrangement for the purpose of ensuring the supply of safe and quality food. Their collective effort was no more than the sharing of market information and the facilitation of a group-based coping strategy. The more critical issues of, say, food safety in general and the more proper protection of consumers' rights through institutional reform were largely untouched.

The same kind of response was found among the urban middle class on issues closer to their personal interest, like property ownership. The suggestion of the middle class taking up the so-called "double movement," namely to look for a private life (via homeownership) and to engage in public activism because of a need to defend their property (Zhang, 2010: 10), has not been realized in urban China. This postulation is largely based on a rather simplistic depiction of the public role of the middle class in the course of economic development and liberalization.[8] It is believed that as China undergoes marketization and economic reform, its middle class will push for further liberalization and the civil society will become more vibrant. However, observers of Chinese politics have long pointed out that marketization has not really undermined the leadership and authoritarian rule of the Chinese Communist Party. The connection between marketization and the loosening of political control is more of an assumption than an accurate depiction of what is happening in China. Equally important is that the middle class is not necessarily liberal and pro-democracy. Unger suggests that the middle class in China is conservative: "many members of the educated middle class are vaguely pro-democratic just so long as democracy can be put off to a future time. This is not only the case today, but also was true at the time of Tiananmen" (2006: 29). Li (2013: 31), based on the findings of a survey conducted in 2006 on social stability, contends that "members of the middle classes, especially the new middle class, will likely hold conservative attitudes and be resistant to sociopolitical change, as they do not want their standard of living to be negatively affected." It is observed that the middle classes do not adopt favorable attitudes toward state authoritarianism. "The new middle class is the least likely to support an authoritarian state. However, while they prefer a less authoritarian (that is, more democratic) government, this analysis suggests that they do not want change that will bring about sociopolitical turbulence" (Li, 2013: 31).

It was once believed, particularly at the early stage of the rise of the middle class in China, that the new homeowners would be conscious of their property rights and would be ready to take action to defend their property. In the context of rapid urbanization, many of these new homeowners found their community environment jeopardized by road construction and the building of other real estate projects. Also, given drastic changes to urban governance and property management, there were numerous disputes over the handling of management fees, improper use of maintenance funds, and many other issues concerning property management. Quite often, homeowners decided to join a protest because they had the feeling of being a victim of injustice (Rocca, 2013). Being educated and seeing themselves as contributing to the growth and development of the economy and society, the homeowners felt that they were entitled to some kind of protection of the property acquired from the market. They set up *xiaoqu* (community) homeowner committees so that they would have the channel to voice their demands and opinions. These residents' associations did provide middle-class homeowners with the organizational means to arrange action but the scope of their action was often rather restricted. While many middle-class homeowners did become more conscious of their rights as property owners and members of the wider urban community through their participation in organized actions, their contentions were rarely politicized (Guo et al., 2014: 27). Some of them might have thought of organizing a petition to the government. But this would be their last resort; in fact, this rarely happened (Huang, 2014: 73). Rocca succinctly summarized the situation and emphasized that the homeowners' actions were essentially

> limited to the defense of the *xiaoqu* and the construction of a harmonious courtyard … They struggle for "liberalization"— the process of making certain rights that protect both individuals and social groups from arbitrary or illegal acts committed by the state or other forces—and not for democratization—the process whereby the rules and procedures of citizenship are applied to political institutions. (2013: 132)

Cai, in his studies of community action in Guangzhou and Beijing, also found middle-class homeowners moderate. Of course, having spent a large portion of their savings on their property, they were eager to protect their own property rights. But it would be rather hasty to associate such activism and their consciousness of property rights with a desire to articulate demands for political change. In Cai's analysis, they were moderate in the sense that "all wish to advance their interests without threatening the political order" (2005: 798). They lacked organizational resources, particularly in terms of having independent organizations, to confront the state. And it was also important to note that their actions were largely "conducted within the boundaries of the law or government regulations" (Cai, 2005: 794).

When China launched its economic reform and began its course of market transition, there was the suggestion that a marketizing economy and the popularization of property ownership would bring about a new kind of consciousness and politics evolving around property rights protection, with the middle class themselves being property owners, championing the cause of protecting the rights of private property and posing challenges to the socialist state. Since the late 1990s, we have witnessed collective action taken by middle-class owners. Also, given the resourcefulness of the middle-class professionals and managers, these homeowners are often able to articulate and express their grievances. Through collective action, these middle-class property owners have been quite successful in capturing media attention and have impacted on local government, property developers, and/or property management offices. Such collective action is seen as a pressing emerging issue in major cities and the promotion of conflict resolution in urban neighborhoods is now a hot topic in urban governance. To suggest, however, that these scattered actions would, in time, come to form highly organized political efforts to demand for rights protection and freedom of expression of grievances and opinions is not supported by the authors' own observations. More significantly, it is essential to recognize that there are two sides of middle-class homeowners' sense of community interests (also see Xiao, 2016). On one side is their willingness to articulate and speak out for the community (against the infringement of their property rights, against mismanagement, and for environmental protection) and on the other, quite often they also look for exclusivity. Many of the newly developed middle-class neighborhoods in the major cities are, in fact, gated communities (see, for example, Pow, 2009). When these homeowners claim to speak for and represent the community's and residents' interests and rights, they are not referring to people's rights in general. Nor are they about the even higher level of rights to the city. The suggestion that the middle class would be the agent to promote and realize some of those universal values like liberty and justice, needs at least some qualification (Shin, 2013: 1185). As well summarized by Rocca

(2013: 121), "As far as I know, there are no attempts in Beijing to link homeowners' movements with movements against 'pull down and move out' measures, or movements launched by migrant workers." They largely stay out of other people's rightful resistance and/or collective action.

The question is not that the middle class is happy and contented. On the contrary, middle-class professionals and managers, as we found out when we returned to KC, have various issues annoying them. First, they feel insecure (Li, 2016): the cost of living and prices are rising, property prices are particularly challenging and young urban professionals and managers are finding homeownership beyond their reach. Planning for the longer term, say, life after retirement, is getting difficult, basic welfare like decent and reliable medical services is not easily available and children's education is becoming a headache. Their concerns also include food safety, personal privacy, and environmental pollution. Many middle-class managers and professionals, despite securing higher wages and bonuses in the course of economic reform, do not really believe that they can now enjoy the expected standard and style of living of being middle class.

The middle class's response to growing anxiety is not one of organized/ collective effort to demand for institutional changes. Under the present political arrangements, such political attempts are simply too costly and risky (also see Nathan, 2016: 11). Middle-class professionals and managers occasionally do try to find opportunities to voice their grievances. But in major cities, occasions of discontent bursting into open confrontation are rather rare. Nathan (2016: 7) summed it up thus: "Most members of the middle class avoid challenging the regime; when backed into a conflict with authorities, they adopt the strategy of remonstration, proclaiming their loyalty to the regime's principles and policies and aiming criticism at their implementation by lower-level officials."

When we returned to KC, the idea of emigration did come up in our interviews. Indeed, quite a number of respondents interviewed in 2007 had already left and settled overseas. Even among those who stayed, they also brought up the option of emigration. Education was cited as one of the most important considerations in considering emigration. Competition for entering good schools in China is very keen and many informants said they found it easier to obtain quality education abroad. Quality of life was also mentioned as another reason to consider moving abroad. The informants that we could talk to from KC were not necessarily representative and thus we cannot generalize our observations. In our conversations, few directly mentioned migration as a status symbol (because of the ability of being mobile) (cf. Liu-Farrer, 2016). But to be able to afford to leave, and more importantly to make a choice of where to live, was not a strategy available for most people in China. The middle class belonged to the minority that had the resources to make such a choice.

Concluding remarks

The emergence of the middle class is part of the sea change that urban China has been undergoing since the late 1990s. The rise of this social class has brought with them the growing demands of homeownership, car ownership, consumption of high-end products, and a new style of living. Social and cultural changes triggered by middle-class consumption have significant impacts on the urban landscape. The middle class, being a change agent groomed by marketization, is one of the critical factors that facilitate the relaxation of the state's regulation and control of urban life. Liberalization, as evident in the proliferation of different ways of living, has been one of the most important changes in contemporary Chinese cities in this period.

Our discussion highlights the fact that China's middle class has emerged in a highly compressed time frame. They are the babies of market reform. And yet, despite the gradual institutionalization of private property and the emergence of a new system of social stratification, the identity and consciousness of the middle class are still characterized by ambiguity and uncertainty. Middle-class professionals, managers, and administrators remain anxious and feel unsure of what lies ahead. They do look for the means of self-protection and yet their endeavors are, perhaps, very typical of the middle class in many parts of the world, which is to say, highly individualized. That is, they work out their coping strategies and options via their own private and personal means. Instead of becoming a major social force in the public domain and/or the champion for social and political participation in the channels of the establishment, the middle class stays low profile. They do occasionally speak up about their concerns. But so far their voices and actions are far from being adequate to facilitate the constitution of an autonomous civil society in Chinese cities. Indeed, it finds its interests very much embedded in the current state of socioeconomic and political development under the rule of the CCP. The middle class shows no intention to upset this status quo.

The middle-class professionals, managers, and administrators are overwhelmed by senses of ambiguity, anxiety, insecurity, and uncertainty. While they are enjoying the benefits of a vibrant economy, they not very sure of what lies ahead. China has already gone through the early phase of economic take-off (and the concomitant opening of various kinds of opportunity for social mobility) and entered a new stage of socioeconomic development. Many young people go to the leading cities with the hope of becoming the young middle class there. But they quickly realize that the pace of expansion of new positions on the social ladder has slowed down and they encounter fierce competition for the desired openings.

Whereas previously the symbol of the middle class carried the meanings of hope, openness, and newly found individual choice (of career and way of life), now it is increasingly seen as a source of frustration, anxiety, and social pressure.

Notes

[1] The study of global cities (Sassen, 2001) suggests a need to examine the urban social structure. Social polarization is an outcome of a concentration of both high-end positions in finance and business services and low-end jobs in personal services. The study of urban class structure in the context of globalization is expected to be a topic of growing importance. Yet, attempts to analyze social class at the city level are few. A few notable exceptions are Butler et al., 2008 and Bacqué et al., 2015.

[2] Our definition of the middle class is informed by the Weberian perspective developed by Goldthorpe (1980). Occupation and employment status are the key variables in determining class positions.

[3] Rocca (2016: 73) carried out an analysis of Chinese publications with different expressions of the middle class (middle class, middle stratum, and intermediate stratum) in 1980–2013 and showed fluctuations in the frequencies. Apparently, *zhongjian jieceng* (the intermediate stratum), being less politically charged, was the more widely adopted usage. Fluctuations were likely to be results of changing political climate as well as researchers' and commentators' interest in this emerging social class.

[4] Critical observers of Chinese social and political development alert us to the significance of changing party-state discourse on the middle class as well as the usages of *jieji* and *jieceng* in shaping people's responses to new openings in the social structure. See Anagnost (2008), Guo (2012), Goodman (2014b, 2016), and Rocca (2016: 74–80).

[5] Also see Zhang et al. (2017: 129) for a more recent survey showing similar observation on class identification.

[6] Fleischer (2010: 148–9) encountered the same phenomenon of high residential mobility in his study of a suburban community in Beijing.

[7] A similar link between homeownership and securing middle-class positions can be found in other Asian economies (on Hong Kong, see Lui, 1995; on Seoul, see Yang, 2018). Homeownership is a component of the middle class's strategy of keeping up with a booming property market and accumulating wealth.

[8] For a thorough critique of such an analytical framework, see Nathan (2016).

References

Anagnost, A. (2008) "From 'class' to 'social strata': Grasping the social totality in reform-era China," *Third World Quarterly*, 29(3): 497–519.

Bacqué, M.-H., Bridge, G., Benson, M., Butler, T., Charmes, E., Fijalkow, Y., Jackson, E., Launay, L., and Vermeersch, S. (2015) *The middle classes and the city: A study of Paris and London*, Basingstoke: Palgrave Macmillan.

Baumgartner, M. P. (1991) *The moral order of a suburb*, New York: Oxford University Press.

Burgess, E. W. (1970) "The growth of the city: An introduction to a research project," in R. E. Park, E. W. Burgess, and R. D. McKenzie (eds.) *The city*, Chicago: University of Chicago Press, pp. 47–62.

Butler, T., Hamnett, C., and Ramsden, M. (2008) "Inward and upward: Marking out social class change in London, 1981–2001," *Urban Studies*, 45(1): 67–88.

Cai, Y. (2005) "China's moderate middle class: The case of homeowners' resistance," *Asian Survey*, 45(5): 777–99.

Chen, J. (2013) *A middle class without democracy*, New York: Oxford University Press.

Crompton, R. (2008) *Class and stratification* (3rd edn.), Cambridge: Polity Press.

Dong, J. and Blommaert, J. (2016) "Global informal learning environments and the making of Chinese middle class," *Linguistics and Education*, 34: 33–46.

Fleischer, F. (2010) *Suburban Beijing: Housing and consumption in Contemporary China*, Minneapolis: University of Minnesota Press.

Goldthorpe, J. H. (1980) *Social mobility and class structure in modern Britain*, Oxford: Clarendon Press.

Goodman, D. G. S. (2014a) *Class in Contemporary China*, Bristol: Policy Press.

Goodman, D. S. G. (2014b) "Middle class China: Dreams and aspirations," *Journal of Chinese Political Science*, 19(1): 49–67.

Goodman, D. S. G. (2016) "Locating China's middle classes: Social intermediaries and the party-state," *Journal of Contemporary China*, 25(97): 1–13.

Guo, Y. (2008) "Class, stratum and group: The politics of description and prescription," in D.S.G. Goodman (ed.) *The new rich in China*, Abingdon: Routledge, pp. 38–52.

Guo, Y. (2012) "Classes without class consciousness and class consciousness without classes: The meaning of class in the People's Republic of China," *Journal of Contemporary China*, 21(77): 723–39.

Guo, Y., Shen, Y. and Chen, P. (2014) *Juzhu de Zhengzhi* [*The Politics of Dwelling*], Guilin: Guanxi Normal University Press.

He, S. and Qian, J. (2017) "From an emerging market to a multifaceted urban society: Urban China studies," *Urban Studies*, 54(4): 827–46.

Henningsen, L. (2012) "Individualism for the masses? Coffee consumption and the Chinese middle class' search for authenticity," *Inter-Asia Cultural Studies*, 13(3): 408–27.

Hu, J. (2011) *Zhongguo Chengshi Jieceng: Beijing Jingxiang* [*Urban Strata in China: Beijing Image*], Beijing: Social Sciences Academic Press.

Huang, R. (2014) *Congcanyu Daoweiquan* [*From Participation to Rights Protection*], Shanghai: Shanghai Social Science Academy Publications.

Leicht, K. T. and Fitzgerald, S. T. (2014) *Middle class meltdown in America* (2nd edn.), New York: Routledge.

Li, C. (2010) "Introduction: The rise of the middle class in the middle kingdom," in C. Li (ed.) *China's emerging middle class*, Washington D.C.: Brookings Institution Press, pp. 3–31.

Li, C. (2013) "Sociopolitical attitudes of the middle class and the implications for political transition," in M. Chen and D.S.G. Goodman (eds.) *Middle class in China: Identity and behaviour*, Cheltenham: Edward Elgar, pp. 12–33.

Li, C. (2015) "Profile of China's middle class," in C. Li (ed.) *The rising middle class in China*, Milton Keynes: Paths International in association with Social Sciences Academic Press, pp. 87–106.

Li, C. (2016) "Zhongguo zhongchan de buanquangan he jiaoleixintai" ["Chinese middle class's sense of insecurity and anxiety"], *Wenhua Zongheng* [*Beijing Cultural Review*], 4: 32–9.

Lin, X. (2018) "'Goumai xiwang': chengzhen jiating zhongde ertong jiaoyu xiaofei ['Purchasing hope': The consumption of children education in urban China]," *Shehuixue Yanjiu* [Sociological Studies] 4: 163–190.

Liu, S. (2014) "Homemaking and middle class formation in urban China," in H.-H. M. Hsiao (ed.) *Chinese middle classes: Taiwan, Hong Kong, Macao and China*, Abingdon: Routledge, pp. 132–53.

Liu, S. (2018) "Developing sustainable food consumption: A case study of localized food supply in Beijing," *Social Transformations in Chinese Societies*, 14(1): 29–40.

Liu-Farrer, G. (2016) "Migration as class-based consumption: The emigration of the rich in contemporary China," *The China Quarterly*, 226: 499–518.

Lu, X. (ed.) (2002) *Dangdai Zhongguo Shehui Jieceng Yanjiu Baogao* [*Report on Social Strata of Contemporary China*], Beijing: Social Sciences Academic Press.

Lui, T. (1995) "Coping strategies in a booming market: Family wealth and housing in Hong Kong," in R. Forrest and A. Murie (eds.) *Housing and family wealth: Comparative international perspectives*, London: Routledge, pp. 108–32.

Lui, T. (2001) "Shanghai *bailing*" ["Shanghai white collar"], in *Shehui Zhuanbian yu Wenhua Bianmao* [*Social Transformation and Cultural Changes*], Hong Kong: The Institute of Asia-Pacific Studies, pp. 513–29.

Lui, T. (2004) "Bailing: Xinxing de zhongchan jieji" ["White collar: An emerging middle class"], in X. Zhou (ed.) *Zhongguo Shehui yu Zhongguo Yanjiu* [*Chinese Society and Chinese Studies*], Beijing: Social Sciences Documentation Publishing House, pp. 351–74.

Lui, T. (2008) "Fear of falling," in C. McGiffert and J. T. H. Tang (eds.) *Hong Kong on the Move: 10 Years as the HKSAR*, Washington DC: The CSIS Press, pp. 37–51.

Lui, T. (2009) "Jieji fenxi de qinggan zhuanxiang: Shanghai yu xianggang zhongchan jieji de rentong" ["The emotion turn in class analysis: Middle class identification in Shanghai and Hong Kong"], in C. Li (ed.) *Bijiao Shiyexia de Zhongchan Jieji Xingcheng* [*Formation of Middle Class in Comparative Perspective*], Beijing: Social Sciences Academic Press, pp. 167–94.

Lui, T. and Liu, S. (2015) "The moral order of a middle class community," in C. Li (ed.) *The rising middle classes in China*, Milton Keynes: Paths International in association with Social Sciences Academic Press (China), pp. 218–36.

Lui, T. and Liu, S. (2019) "The urban middle class," in R. Yep, J. Wang, and T. Johnson (eds.) *Edward Elgar handbook on urban development in China*, Cheltenham: Edward Elgar, pp. 219–32.

Nathan, A. J. (2016) "The puzzle of the Chinese middle class," *Journal of Democracy*, 27(2): 5–19.

Pahl, R. E. (1989) "Is the emperor naked? Some questions on the adequacy of sociological theory in urban and regional research," *International Journal of Urban and Regional Research*, 13: 711–20.

Park, R. E. (1970) "The city: Suggestions for the investigation of human behavior in the urban environment," in R. E. Park, E. W. Burgess, and R. D. McKenzie (eds.) *The city*, Chicago: University of Chicago Press, pp. 1–46.

Pow, C.-P. (2009) *Gated communities in China: Class, privilege and the moral politics of the good life*, Abingdon: Routledge.

Rocca, J.-L. (2013) "Homeowners' movements: Narratives on the political behaviours of the middle class," in M. Chen and D. S. G. Goodman (eds.), *Middle class China: Identity and behaviour*, Cheltenham: Edward Elgar, pp. 110–34.

Rocca, J.-L. (2016) *The making of the Chinese middle class: Small comfort and great expectations*, New York: Palgrave Macmillan.

Sassen, S. (2001) *The global city* (2nd edn.), Princeton, NJ: Princeton University Press.

Savage, M., Bagnall, G., and Longhurst, B. (2001) "Ordinary, ambivalent and defensive: Class identities in the Northwest of England," *Sociology*, 35(4): 875–92.

Shin, H. B. (2013) "The right to the city and critical reflections on China's property rights activism," *Antipode*, 45(5): 1167–89.

Tomba, L. (2004) "Creating an urban middle class: Social engineering in Beijing," *The China Journal*, 51: 1–26.

Unger, J. (2006) "China's conservative middle class," *Far Eastern Economic Review*, April: 27–31.

Wang, X. (2008) "Divergent identities, convergent interests: The rising middle-income stratum in China and its civic awareness," *Journal of Contemporary China*, 17(54): 53–69.

Whyte, W. H. (1963) *The organization man*, Harmondsworth: Pelican Books.

Wu, Q., Edensor, T., and Cheng, J. (2018) "Beyond space: Spatial (re)production and middle class remaking driven by jiaoyufication in Nanjing city, China," *International Journal of Urban and Regional Research*, 42(1): 1–19.

Xiao, L. (2016) "'Houyuan' zhengzhi: Chengshi zhongchan jieji de 'lingdi' yishi" ['Backyard' politics: Urban middle class 'territorial' consciousness], in Wenhua Zongheng [Beijing Cultural Review], 6: 90–97.

Yang, M. (2018) "The rise of 'Gangnam style': Manufacturing the urban middle class in Seoul, 1976–1996," *Urban Studies*, 55(5): 3404–20.

Zhang, H., Yang, C. and Lai, S. (2017) "Zhongguo tedai chengshi xinshehui jieceng diaoyan baogao" ["Research report on new social strata in Chinese mega-cities"], in Li, Peilin, Chen, Guangjin, and Zhang, Yi. *Shehui Lanpishu 2017* [*Blue Book of China's Society 2017*], Hong Kong: Peace Book, pp. 118–35.

Zhang, J. (2017) "(Extended) family car, filial consumer-citizens: Becoming properly middle class in post-socialist south China," *Modern China*, 43(1): 36–65.

Zhang, L. (2010) *In search of paradise: Middle-class living in a Chinese metropolis*, Ithaca, NY: Cornell University Press.

Zhu, G. (1998) *Dangdai Zhongguo Shehui Gejieceng Fenxi* [*An analysis of different social strata in contemporary China*], Tianjin: Tianjin People's Publications.

12

Conclusion

Everyday Cities, Exceptional Cases

Julie Ren

At first glance, revisiting Robert Park for urban China seems anachronistic, an unnecessarily limiting lens that ignores the vast body of research being produced. Yet, taking Park as a starting point does not dictate the rules about speaking in his terms, nor does it require a retreading of the Los Angeles School critiques of his work. Rather, this volume shows that it can be a valuable approach to reviewing the research on urban China in order to situate this work within greater theoretical debates.

This concluding chapter presents some of the general issues of exceptionalism and methodology haunting the research on urban China. It seeks out scholarship beyond urban studies to look at the way that the entwined issues of Chinese exceptionalism and methodological nationalism can restrict urban research, its interpretations, and broader applications. In short, to address the reasons why the flood of research on cities in China has not resulted in a corresponding deluge of theoretical developments for contemporary urbanism. Finally, in revisiting a critical approach centered on the everyday, it seems Park might in fact prove more relevant than ever, especially insofar as he shifts the focus of urban research away from morphology toward the social. Rather than a research *agenda* like the one Park outlines in his 1915 essay on "The city," however, perhaps the future of research on urban China demands a reconsideration of *approach*.

Theoretical rupture

The current debates around the parochial nature of urban theory often rest on critiques based on who and where. It focuses on "Western academia" as the institutional source of "Western knowledge" and its attendant limitations (see, for example, Edensor and Jayne, 2012). These ideas about the city have traveled and disseminated, imposing canons of thought on places "elsewhere." So entrenched is this process of knowledge production that a theoretical rupture is needed—the question is how (see, for instance, Jazeel, 2016; Robinson and Roy, 2016).

Rather than considering the sources and locations of urban theory-building, a reflection on this volume suggests the need for a consideration of unstated assumptions and a turn toward an analysis of implicit knowledge (Lawhon et al., 2016). For this, revisiting Niklas Luhmann can be helpful for his differentiation of the first- and second-order observer (1995). Most research is focused on the first order, seeking out that which is probable and true (wahr-scheinlich). It seeks to discover something about the world, to evaluate the nature of inequality in Chinese cities, for instance. In contrast, the second-order observer observes both the social scientist observing the social world, the effects this has on the world, and how the forces of the social world shape the outlook of social scientists. This might consider the process of applying for research grants in order to evaluate urban inequality in China, the institutional arrangements that facilitate the policy impact this research may have on certain provinces, and the way these systems of research and policy might reinforce certain kinds of research questions or topics. In this way, the second-order observation enables contingency and possibility rather than finite explanation (Luhmann, 2000: 62). In evaluating the nature of urban theory-building around cities in China, this may prove to generate a more pluralistic approach to theory.

On this point, it might be useful to borrow from the LA School in terms of pluralization, and their allowance for "multiple theoretical frameworks that overlap and coexist in their explanations" (Dear, 2002: x). In other words, the empirical watershed of urban research in China demands a kind of theoretical rupture, but this does not necessitate new hegemonic models of urbanization. On the contrary, the rupture could offer something quite the contrary—a multiplicity of new possibilities.

This potential is largely unfulfilled, however, as the research on urban China consistently reduces itself to its Chinese-ness. For example, with the support of my co-editors for this volume, I surveyed the research on segregation in urban China (Ren, 2016) for a scoping report that sought to understand what kind of research was being generated. It was second-order analysis, studying the research on segregation rather than segregation itself. The report looks at issues around problem definition, objects of study, and methodological approaches. Two dominant research design structures were identified in the course of this work: (1) researchers set up a "Western model" in order to compare and contrast the "Chinese case" and (2) researchers frame the research within the historic economic/urban transition in China. These structures were not mutually exclusive, and served at times to simultaneously provide background context, and to also explain the findings. In other words, the Chinese case is different than the Western model, because it is Chinese.

One example from the report is the research on gated communities, which helps to illustrate some different positions in explaining this residential structure. Introducing the "modern gating phenomenon in contemporary China," Choon-Piew Pow contends that it cannot be explained away as part of an inherited heritage, "the product of immutable cultural tradition or social norm" (Pow, 2009: 5). In a way, Shenjing He agrees about how the phenomenon is also not part of a universal condition that is shared everywhere in the same way (2013). Whereas Pow takes issue with the reduction of urban phenomena to a Chinese tradition, heritage, or legacy, He takes issue with the reduction of the urban phenomena to universal homogeneity. Gated communities in China are thus neither uniquely Chinese, nor the same as everywhere else. Why is the research stuck in these isolating explanatory paths?

At the heart of this enigma are the omnipresent issues of exceptionalism and methodology, relevant for research on urban China, and perhaps also for cities more generally. The next section considers how urban China stands in as an exhibit of Chinese exceptionalism, and explores what exactly Chinese exceptionalism entails.

(Urban) Chinese exceptionalism

The political heritage of Chinese exceptionalism seeks to explain and project the implications of the changing place of China in the world, primarily as a nation-state, but also as a civilization. As such, it is not a specifically urban concept, but rather one that inflects the way that Chinese cities are framed more generally. The concept of exceptionalism is undergirded by a large body of work from policy studies, political science, and international relations. Though it builds on Sinology and area studies, it is less bounded by history, often using exceptionalism to make a normative case for certain kinds of policy. This translates to urban studies and research, limiting the explanatory possibilities of interpreting cities to more or less simply being Chinese.

For instance, some of the research uses history to account for China's place in the world. John Agnew's review of academic and policy research identifies "a striking feature" common in debates. He points out the "versions of the Chinese past," which "have been brought to bear on contemporary questions about China's 'place in the world'" (2012: 302). These include aspects like the institutional characteristics of different imperial dynasties, varieties of Confucianism, and the geographical parameters of previous Chinese polities. Yan Xuetong observes the influential role of China's history of superpower status during the Han, Tang, and early Qing dynasties today (2001). The scholarship posits this legacy as simultaneously giving Chinese people a sense of pride as well as a sense of injustice about its contemporary international standing. Chinese exceptionalism today is in this regard a reaction to the relative decline of China's position in the world, a historical mistake that should be corrected.

An additionally noteworthy characteristic of Chinese exceptionalism is the way that it is tied to a particular form of modernity, characterized by a benevolent pacifism. In synthesizing the views on Chinese exceptionalism, William Callahan draws a stark contrast to American exceptionalism:

> Rather than figure China's modernization as a process of socialization, which they would criticize as "Westernization," books as diverse as Martin Jacques's When China Rules the World (2009), Liu Mingfu's Zhongguo Meng [The China Dream] (2010) and David C. Kang's China Rising (2007) each argue that China has its own modernity, which is not only different from the West but is actually its opposite. According to this view, which is promoted by both academics and policy-makers, China is building its own road, following a model of Chinese exceptionalism that promotes global peace and harmony rather than what they see as Pax Americana's incessant wars. (Callahan, 2012: 34)

Here, Chinese exceptionalism is tied to a political outlook, one that is marked by the pacifism at the heart of its foreign policy. Feng Zhang contends that the emerging exceptionalism that has been witnessed in light of China's rise is seen through Beijing's emphasis on three key components, namely, "great power reformism, benevolent pacifism and harmonious inclusionism" (Zhang, 2011: 319). These characteristics are officially enshrined in proclamations like the Principles of Peaceful Coexistence and the Eight Principles for China's Aid to Foreign Countries (1964), which are built on the Chinese government's interpretation of the 1955 Bandung conference "framework for post-colonial states' responses to the challenges of nation-building in the international system" (Alden and Large, 2001: 28).

This guise of benevolent hegemony is relevant for urban studies insofar as it shifts all research on China (including its cities) to be about this Chinese-ness. Under the guise of benevolent hegemony, this exceptionalism and an attendant essential Chinese identity are constructed in order to establish a kind of "discursive legitimacy for Sinocentric hegemony" (Callahan, 2012: 52). This is a language that "employs a new vocabulary and grammar of naturalized civilization and essentialized identity to describe—and prescribe—China's rejuvenation to greatness" (Callahan, 2012: 50). This Chinese exceptionalism is therefore rendered superior to other exceptionalisms, because of its multiple senses of justice in rectifying China's place in the world, and in its pacifist stance on foreign policy. Politically, it serves as the basis for a kind of Chinese world order.

Similarly, Pow contends that the geography literature also sustains a thesis of exceptionalism (2012). The thesis of exceptionalism arises from the simultaneous confluence of existing urban theories being inadequate in reflecting the urban China experience, and the rise of the nation-state as connected to social science. For Pow, as for the present volume, it is important to consider "what is lost or ignored by framing geographical inquiry and knowledge within such exceptionalist discourses" (2012: 47). As Ray Forrest suggests in Chapter 5 of this volume, perhaps the exceptional is in fact overstated, and reflects the mesmerizing effects of scale rather than a qualitative difference. Chinese exceptionalism clearly has certain political purposes, but for research it is reductive, a handicap to empirical analysis, and it renders its cities incommensurate. In volumes like *Urban China in transition*, the editors ask, "To what do we compare China?" (Logan and Fainstein, 2008: 1).

Methodological issues

To explain the relationship between Chinese exceptionalism and social science, it is useful to return to the second-order observer, and consider the issue of methodological nationalism. Pow argues that methodological nationalism is one of the sustaining mechanisms of Chinese exceptionalism. Originating in the 1970s, with important contributions from Ulrich Beck and Anthony Giddens to underpin some of its main tenets, methodological nationalism may be best known today by Andreas Wimmer and Nina Glick Schiller's critique of methodological nationalism in migration research (2002).

Wimmer and Glick Schiller present three ways that methodological nationalism functions: (1) nation-blind modernities, (2) nationally bounded societies are taken as given or downplaying nationalism in state-building, and (3) "the territorialization of social science imaginary and the reduction of the analytical focus to the boundaries of the nation-state" (2002: 307). For the research on urban China, this implies that research at various scales about a neighborhood in Shanghai, for instance, is reduced to being research about China. Connected to the discursive shifts noted previously on Chinese exceptionalism, it implies that social science serves a nation-building project, to undergird a kind of Chinese nationalism.

In order to transcend the problematic of social science and nation-building working in tandem, however, Daniel Chernilo has argued for a need to better understand the nation-state, its position, and legacy (2006). Wang Hui (2011) would agree, criticizing the "nation-state logic" that inspires much thinking about China as being based on an essentially European experience of state-making. Yet, at the same time, he is aware how much this historical model now permeates elite thought and practice inside China. Wimmer and Glick Schiller describe this permeation as a kind of naturalization:

> Naturalization of the nation state is in part a result of the compartmentalization of social science project into different national academic fields and a process strongly influenced not only by nationalist thinking itself, but also by institutions of the nation state organizing and channeling social science thinking in universities, research institutions and government think tanks ... To the extent that social science is deployed to provide pragmatic solution for "national problems" in economy, politics and the social services. (Wimmer and Glick Schiller, 2002: 306)

Pow echoes this in his analysis of urban research in China, "the national framing of social science research and discourses is especially pronounced in the Chinese context where academic research mostly comes under the auspices (and regulation) of state-funded institutions such as the powerful Chinese Academy of Social Sciences (CASS) and nationalized university systems" (2012: 62). State institutions are currently the main source of big data capture, often providing the technology and supporting the dominance of quantitative sciences. Methodological nationalism functions in part through these state institutions, rendering social science research intrinsically tied to building the nation-state. Charles Gore provides an instructive example of the consequence of this, showing how methodological nationalism explains the misunderstanding that emerges when East Asian economic success is explained in terms of the dominant nation-based paradigm (1996).

Indeed, case-study structures often serve to explain something about China, a particularistic, historical, culturalist, explanation that deals with context. For example, in the aforementioned report on segregation research, the overwhelming majority of studies are situated within China as the contextual frame, with an explicit explanation of the Chinese-ness of the empirical results (Ren, 2016). The city or cities served usually as a case study of a phenomenon that was representative of all Chinese cities (rather than, say, coastal cities or cities of different sizes). Even when the comparative analysis revealed differences, these were evidence of variation rather than any categorical difference among cities in China.

Variation-finding methodology, especially in comparative analysis, is prevalent as a means to explain systematic variation in broadly similar contexts (Tilly, 1984; Pickvance, 1986). It assumes a kind of universal causal explanation, but with slight differences in empirical manifestations. To illustrate, consider framing the Chinese city as a global city; it becomes a variant of the model of Saskia Sassen's (2013) global city. When it serves as a variation of a preexisting model, the researcher then considers in her research the particularities and characteristics that might make the city uniquely Chinese. For instance, in evaluating just how neoliberal China's transition is, Fulong Wu considers the positions that point to China's "particular kind of neoliberalism" in contrast to the positions that categorically reject "neoliberalism" as a possible frame (cf., for example, Harvey, 2007; Ong, 2007; Wu, 2010a: 620). This model of variation-finding analysis is echoed in Wu's study of suburban residential development to show how the experience "in the West" is inadequate to explain the Chinese case (Wu, 2010b; see also Ren, 2016, for more on this approach in segregation research). Significantly, variation-finding methodology acknowledges that the prevailing concepts "neoliberalism" or "suburbia" are sourced elsewhere, but also worth keeping.

The methodological nationalism framing empirical research in terms of its Chinese-ness, and the variation-finding approach relegating the research to an empirical variation of prevailing urban concepts from elsewhere both serve to place the Chinese city in the "urban shadow" of theorization (McFarlane, 2008). The methodological issues render urban China a mere site of borrowed urbanism rather than a source for new theoretical contributions to urban theory in general (Roy, 2011). By elevating the exceptional nature of their Chinese qualities as a mode of explanation, urban research can thus fall victim to the formation of new parochialisms (Ren and Luger, 2015). Rather than enriching theoretical debates, urban China then is relegated to an illustration or a descriptive site. It reifies a kind of "case-studyism" whereby some cities are sites of theory and others as variation (Ren, 2015).

Ironically, the Chinese exceptionalism that is facilitated through these methodological issues serves to delimit the broader theoretical relevance of urban China. The purpose of exploring exceptionalism and methodological nationalism is to understand why the research on urban China does not transcend its borders with new theories, concepts, or models. Like the framing of this present volume, cities in China continue to be understood in terms of its national context. Perhaps what fails us is the imagination to place the city in China elsewhere—in a context of global inequality or neighborhood contestation, in order to better explain the experience of living in cities more generally.

Analytical binaries and the everyday

This kind of conceptual marginalization inspires criticism that tends to resort to reductive binaries. One critique of Park, for instance, was his construction of a rural, traditional, even primitive place in order to contrast the urban and modern space of Chicago. Park's Chicago represented an idea of the city as real, complicated, and rife with contradictions, which stood in stark contrast to the imagined rural space. Jennifer Robinson describes the function of this for urbanism:

> The Chicago School theorists established an understanding of urban experience through a strong contrast with tradition. The account of urban modernity that emerged from their work, which is the workhorse of current urban theory, postulates a modern "here and now" against a traditional "there and then". The past and a haphazard range of other places fulfilled the function of making some urbanites feel very modern. These fantasies enhanced urbanists' sense of elation about what they liked to think of as the novelty of their experiences. (Robinson, 2006: 7)

Notably, however, Robinson herself also resorts to these binary accounts in her parochial/cosmopolitan dichotomization of urban theory. This binary structure is again taken up by Michael Dear in his description of the "beguiling simplicity" of Chicago, which stood in contrast with the "exceptionally complex" Los Angeles (Dear, 2002).

Following Fulong Wu in not categorically rejecting concepts simply because of where they originated, it still seems an approach is necessary that allows for a less determined trajectory of explanation, and a more plural legacy—especially for the research on cities in China. Inspired by Xuefei Ren's empirical insights on informal settlements in Chapter 1 of this volume, it seems one starting point might be to draw on Park's approach rather than the provenance of his work. Rather than thinking about Park in terms of Chicago and the agenda-setting function of the 1915 essay that serves as the starting point for this volume, perhaps there needs to be a focal shift to his approach.

Moving from agenda to approach, it implies a more qualitative, possibly ethnographic, turn toward the experience of everyday life in cities in China. The idea of "everyday life" has been a preoccupation of social and cultural theorists inspiring multiple comparative volumes that include theorists as far-ranging as Michel de Certeau and Georg Simmel, Trinh T. Minh-ha and Dorothy E. Smith (Gardiner, 2000; Highmore, 2002a, 2002b). "Everyday" is broadly situated between the banal (mechanization of life like the assembly line) and the strange (or the making strange of those things that have been taken for granted like Durkheim) (Highmore, 2002a: 12–16).

Everyday practice characterized by inconspicuousness also makes it an important area of potential resistance to institutionalized power in the form of bureaucracy or commercialization (de Certeau, 1984). This, in particular, might be a meaningful inroad for a more critical urban approach in a research setting controlled by state institutions. Building on Lefebvre, this approach is about the possibility of seeing the structure in everyday life. It also stands in contrast to Allen Scott and Michael Storper's view of "the ordinary" as placing emphasis on the particularities of urban places (Scott and Storper, 2015; Storper and Scott, 2016; see also Amin and Graham, 1997). Indeed, much of ethnographic research seeks to investigate the social structures embedded in everyday life. It would be a departure from delimiting the relevance of urban China due to its particularities.

Noteworthy in Scott and Storper's review of urban theory is their primary concern with the concept of the "urban" as such, to establish a universally relevant theory for urbanization as distinct from other social processes (2015). Therefore, they offer a defense of a view about the city as an object, a single narrative of what the city is, from which all other views are "empirical variation over time and space" (2015: 3). The universal process of urbanization echoes the desire to draw on Park's essay on "The city" as an agenda for urban research, for all cities.

Again, it seems important to redirect focus away from the urban agenda or the universal process of urbanization, toward the theory-building possibilities of the everyday experience. Building on Henri Lefebvre's conceptualizations of the everyday (1984, 1991), an everyday approach does not need to make a universal claim nor is it necessarily reduced to the particularities of empiricism. Rather, it can serve to think beyond the morphology of the city, toward the multiple, simultaneous processes that constitute urbanization. As the everyday is tied to experience, it helps integrate the simultaneity of both the objective and subjective. Suzanne Hall's ethnographic work on the street exemplifies how street life can be a means to study notions of multiculturalism, belonging, and the contested process of urban change (2012).

Applying this to research on segregation, integrating both the objective and subjective could better take into account the issues of doublespeak that ethnographers face in conducting interviews or surveys, especially as it pertains to issues like voluntary reporting on housing satisfaction. Indeed the experience of segregation remains largely relegated to satisfaction surveys (Ren, 2016; Cf. Wong and Shaw, 2011 with Song et al., 2008; Du and Li, 2010; Li and Wu, 2013), which does not capture the subjective experience so much as standardize consumption patterns. The value of this is highlighted in Chapter 10 in the present volume, by Zhigang Li, Shunxian Ou, and Rong Wu, building on an ethnographic approach to research the experience of working at Foxconn. It captures individual experience in a way that surveys fail to do. In their chapter, a key finding was the status of "immobility," neither integrated nor able to return home, which would have been impossible to account for without their more open-ended approach to research.

Ethnographic approaches to the everyday experience can also help to transcend the preset scales dictated by available national survey data, often necessary to make claims about "urban China." Available data on households or poverty, for instance, is not uniformly available at different urban or neighborhood scales. With more empirical focus on the everyday experience, researchers could valuably supplement the available research at the municipal or informal scales of spatialization. It would not displace, but rather enrich the limits of available data. Indeed, as Adrian Smith wrote in the *Guardian*, to shift from "big data" toward "thick data" (2018).

In these scalar extensions, another mode of rescaling the research on urban China is to expand "China" as the necessary frame for everything happening in Chinese cities. Returning to Chinese exceptionalism and methodological nationalism, an everyday approach might extend beyond China as the ultimate object, subject, and causal explanation.

The possibilities for this are powerfully espoused by Dorothy E. Smith's work on everyday experiences. Smith contends that dominant, authoritative models of sociological explanation serve to erase the experience of the everyday. She echoes Doreen Massey, in connecting the experience to a place with elsewhere, "how our everyday worlds are organized and how they are shaped and determined by relations that extend beyond them" (Smith, 1987: 121). That is, the experience of the urban is not isolated and bounded to the confines of a neighborhood. Rather, everyday experiences, the way that people experience the everyday, is inherently relational rather than determined and set in place. This relational view is articulated by Massey about places, "places are what they are in part precisely as a result of their history of and present participation in relations with elsewhere" (Massey, 2011: 4).

These accounts for a relational understanding of everyday life and of the significance of place are further echoed by ethnographers. For instance, James Clifford's call for "discrepant cosmopolitans" sought to delocalize anthropology, reflecting anthropological critiques about the misleading nature of village ethnographies and arguing that culture is cannot be reduced to an attachment to a specific location (1997; Gupta and Ferguson, 1999). These ethnographic approaches to studying cosmopolitans also touches on an idea about cosmopolitanism that is not necessarily universalizing, but also goes beyond the nation-state (Cheah and Robbins, 1998). Seeking out these spaces for scales of theory might help disrupt the national enclosure of "China" in framing all urban research being generated there.

One hundred years after Park wrote "The city," it seems that the essay remains an important reminder about the role that ethnographic research can play in epistemological rupture. Rather than transposing Park's Chicago as an iconic agenda-setting place, it is useful to see it from the second-order observer stance and consider it as an approach.

Undergirded by both exceptionalism and methodological nationalism, too much urban research is framed on both ends by China. China serves as the context and the explanation for the results. The troubling political implication of methodological nationalism is to consider the extent to which social science in China is a nation-building exercise, and the extent that institutions for research are complicit in political agendas. And, extending the concern, to consider how the reliance on government data might severely limit not only the nature of research, but also the understanding of life in Chinese cities. The less political, but certainly epistemologically exciting question is: can research on Shenzhen be about the city of Shenzhen without necessarily being about China?

This volume begins to suggest alternative possibilities for framing urban research in China. Connecting the experience of migrant workers at Foxconn to the experience of immobility elsewhere might shed light on emergent forms of urban anomie that transcend the particularism of

Shenzhen's Chinese-ness, and instead focus on the forms of segregation that may connect migrant workers across vastly different national contexts. This is not an exercise of creative thinking, but one that suggests new possibilities for generating theory from urban China.

The rich, vast, varied research on cities in China is an opportunity to not only enrich urban theory, but perhaps also disrupt the way that theorization implies universalization. It suggests the possibility for thinking about cities such as Shenzhen as a lab to investigate "human behavior in the urban environment," rather than as an exemplar of urban China or a new model of urbanism or the next dominant school of thought.

References

Agnew, J. (2012) "Looking back to look forward: Chinese geopolitical narratives and China's past," *Eurasian Geography and Economics*, 53(3): 301–14.

Alden, C. and Large, D. (2011) "China's exceptionalism and the challenges of delivering difference in Africa," *Journal of Contemporary China*, 20(68): 21–38.

Amin, A. and Graham, S. (1997) "The ordinary city," *Transactions of the Institute of British Geographers*, 22(4): 411–29.

Callahan, W. A. (2012) "Sino-speak: Chinese exceptionalism and the politics of history," *The Journal of Asian Studies*, 71(1): 33–55.

Cheah, P. and Robbins, B. (eds.) (1998) *Cosmopolitics: Thinking and feeling beyond the nation*, Minneapolis: University of Minnesota Press.

Chernilo, D. (2006) "Social theory's methodological nationalism: Myth and reality," *European Journal of Social Theory*, 9(1): 5–22.

Clifford, J. (1997) *Routes: Travel and translation in the late twentieth century*, Cambridge, MA: Harvard University Press.

de Certeau, M. (1984) *The practice of everyday life*, Berkeley: University of California Press.

Dear, M. (2002) "Preface," in M. Dear (ed.) *From Chicago to L.A.: Making sense of urban theory*, Thousand Oaks, CA: Sage, pp. vii–xi.

Du, H. and Li, S. (2010) "Migrants, urban villages, and community sentiments: A case of Guangzhou, China," *Asian Geographer*, 27(1/2): 93–108.

Edensor, T. and Jayne, M. (eds.) *Urban theory beyond the West: A world of cities*, Abingdon: Routledge.

Gardiner, M. (2002) *Critiques of everyday life: An introduction*, London: Routledge.

Gore, C. (1996) "Methodological nationalism and the misunderstanding of East Asian industrialisation," *The European Journal of Development Research*, 8(1): 77–122.

Gupta, A. and Ferguson, J. (eds) (1999) *Culture, power, place: Explorations in cultural anthropology*, Durham, NC: Duke University Press.

Hall, S. (2012) *City, street and citizen: The measure of the ordinary*, Abingdon: Routledge.

Harvey, D. (2007) "Neoliberalism as creative destruction," *The Annals of American Academy of Political and Social Sciences*, 610(1): 22–44.

He, S. (2013) "Evolving enclave urbanism in China and its socio-spatial implications: The case of Guangzhou," *Social and Cultural Geography*, 14(3): 243–75.

Highmore, B. (2002a) *Everyday life and cultural theory: An introduction*, London: Routledge.

Highmore, B. (2002b) *The everyday life reader*, London: Routledge.

Jacques, M. (2009) *When China rules the world: The end of the Western world and the birth of a new global order*, New York: Penguin.

Jazeel, T. (2016) "Between area and discipline: Progress, knowledge production and the geographies of Geography," *Progress in Human Geography*, 40(5): 649–67.

Kang, D. C. (2007) *China rising: Peace, power and order in East Asia*, New York: Columbia University Press.

Lawhon, M., Silver, J., Ernstson, H., and Pierce, J. (2016) "Unlearning (un)located ideas in the provincialization of urban theory," *Regional Studies*, 50(9): 1611–22.

Lefebvre, H. (1984) *Everyday life in the modern world*, New Brunswick: Transaction.

Lefebvre, H. (1991) *Critique of everyday life: Foundations for a sociology of the everyday* (Vol. 2), London: Verso.

Li, Z. and Wu, F. (2013) "Residential satisfaction in China's informal settlements: A case study of Beijing, Shanghai and Guangzhou," *Urban Geography*, 34(7): 923–49.

Liu, M. (2010) *Zhongguo meng: hou meiguo shidai de daguo siwei zhanlue dingwei* [*The China dream: The great power thinking and strategic positioning of China in the post-American age*], Beijing: Zhongguo youyi chuban gongsi.

Logan, J. and Fainstein, S. (2008) "Introduction: Urban China in comparative perspective," in J. Logan (ed.) *Urban China in transition*, Malden, MA: Blackwell, pp. 1–23.

Luhmann, N. (1995) *Social systems*, trans. J. Bednarz, Jr., with D. Baecker, Stanford, CA: Stanford University Press.

Luhmann, N. (2000) *Art as a social system*, trans. E. A. Knodt, Stanford, CA: Stanford University Press.

Massey, D. (2011) "A counterhegemonic relationality of place," in E. McCann and K. Ward (eds.) *Mobile urbanism: cities and policymaking in the global age*, Minneapolis: University of Minnesota Press.

McFarlane, C. (2008) "Urban shadows: Materiality, the 'Southern city' and urban theory," *Geography Compass*, 2(2): 340–58.

Ong, A. (2007) "Neoliberalism as a mobile technology," *Transactions of the Institute of British Geographers*, 32(1): 3–8.

Park, R. E. (1915) "The city: Suggestions for the investigation of human behavior in the city environment," *The American Journal of Sociology*, 20(5): 577–612.

Pickvance, C. G. (1986) "Comparative urban analysis and assumptions about causality," *International Journal of Urban and Regional Research*, 10(2): 162–84.

Pow, C.-P. (2009) *Gated communities in China: Class, privilege and the moral politics of the good life*, Abingdon: Routledge.

Pow, C.-P. (2012) "China exceptionalism? Unbounding narratives on urban China," in T. Edensor and M. Jayne (eds.) *Urban theory beyond the West: A world of cities*, Abingdon: Routledge, pp. 47–64.

Ren, J. (2015) "Gentrification in China?" in L. Lees, H. B. Shin, and E. López-Morales (eds.) *Global gentrifications: Uneven development and displacement*, Bristol: Policy Press, pp. 329–47.

Ren, J. (2016) "Segregation research on urban China," scoping report, Urban Research Group, CityU on Cities Working Paper Series, WP No.1/2016, City University of Hong Kong. Available at: www.cityu. edu.hk/cityoncities/upload/file/original/705520160628123959. pdf.

Ren, J. and Luger, J. (2015) "Comparative urbanism and the 'Asian city': Implications for research and theory," *International Journal of Urban and Regional Research*, 39(1): 145–56.

Robinson, J. (2006) *Ordinary cities: Between modernity and development*, Abingdon: Routledge.

Robinson, J. and Roy, A. (2016) "Debate on global urbanisms and the nature of urban theory," *International Journal of Urban and Regional Research*, 40(1): 181–6.

Roy, A. "Conclusion: Postcolonial urbanism: Speed, hysteria, mass dreams," in A. Roy and A. Ong (eds.) *Worlding Cities: Asian Experiments and the Art of being Global*, Hoboken: John Wiley & Sons.

Sassen, S. (2013) *The global city: New York, London, Tokyo*, Princeton: Princeton University Press.

Scott, A. J. and Storper, M. (2015) "The nature of cities: The scope and limits of urban theory," *International Journal of Urban and Regional Research*, 39(1): 1–15.

Smith, A. (2018) "Smart cities need thick data not big data," *The Guardian*, April 18. Available at: www.theguardian.com/science/political-science/2018/apr/18/smart-cities-need-thick-data-not-big-data.

Smith, D. E. (1987) *The everyday world as problematic: A feminist sociology*, Toronto: University of Toronto Press.

Song, Y., Zenou, Y., and Ding, C. (2008) "Let's not throw the baby out with the bath water: The role of urban villages in housing rural migrants in China," *Urban Studies*, 45(2): 313–30.

Storper, M. and Scott, A. J. (2016) "Current debates in urban theory: A critical assessment," *Urban Studies*, 53(6): 1114–36.

Tilly, C. (1984) *Big structures, large processes, huge comparisons*, Russell Sage Foundation.

Wang, H. (2011) *The politics of imagining Asia*, Cambridge, MA: Harvard University Press.

Wimmer, A. and Glick Schiller, N. (2002) "Methodological nationalism and beyond: Nation-state building, migration and the social sciences," *Global Networks*, 2(4): 301–34.

Wong, D. W. and Shaw, S. L. (2011) "Measuring segregation: An activity space approach," *Journal of Geographical Systems*, 13(2): 127–45.

Wu, F. (2010a) "How neoliberal is China's reform? The origins of change during transition," *Eurasian Geography and Economics*, 51(5): 619–31.

Wu, F. (2010b) "Gated and packaged suburbia: Packaging and branding Chinese suburban residential development," *Cities*, 27(5): 385–96.

Yan, X. (2001) "The rise of China in Chinese eyes," *Journal of Contemporary China*, 10(26): 33–9.

Zhang, F. (2011) "The rise of Chinese exceptionalism in international relations," *European Journal of International Relations*, 19(2): 305–28.

Index

Note: Page numbers for tables and figures appear in *italics*.

F

factory enclaves 198–204
Fainstein, S.S. 71, 235
favelas 12, *13*
Fei Xiaotong 2–5, *4*, 7, 25, 26–8, 34
Fincher, L.H. 96
first- and second-order observer 232
Fischer, C. 1
Flusty, S. 64–5, 72
food safety 220
Fordism 105
Foxconn 107, 198–204, *199, 201*
Fu, Q. 91, 94

G

Galea, S. 159
Gamble, S.D. 20
Gans, H.J. 30, 31–2
Garb, M. 86–8
gated communities 42, 71–5, 233
Gaubatz, P.R. 90, 93–4
gentrification 111, 115, 117, 204
ghost cities 96
Giddens, A. 235
Glaeser, E. 111
Glick Schiller, N. 235–6
globalization 67, 68, 104, 107, 127, 200
Goodman, D.G.S. 211
Gore, C. 236–7
Graham, S. 72
Guangzhou 10–11, *11*, 50, 52, 92, 188
Gunn, Selskar 24
Guo, Y. 215

H

Haddon, R.F. 88–9
Hall, S. 240
Halle, D. 67
Handshake 302 projects 130, 131, 132, 133–6, 137
Hartshorne, R. 63
He, S. 69, 70, 85, 233
health of residents *see* subjective well-being

Hendrikx, M. 72
homeownership
  in Chicago 86–7
  as Chinese Dream 90, 97
  in contemporary Chinese city 90–7
  as income generator 83, 84–5, 87, 95–6, 218–19
  and inequality 93–7
  levels of 91–2, 95
  low income 87
  meaning of 85–6
  middle class 45–6, 87–8, 90, 95, 217–18, 220–3
  and modernization 94
  and pathways to urban residency *167, 170*
  as social glue 83–5
  and social status 82, 85–90, 94–5
  and subjective well-being *171, 174*, 178
  see also housing
Hörmann, Bernhard 3
house prices 87, 95, 146
housing
  as a commodity 83, 84–5, 87, 95–6, 218–19
  commodity estates 73–4
  competition for 81–3, 85–6, 88–90, 96
  conflicts around 84
  council housing (UK) 82, 89
  factory enclaves 188, 198–204
  gated communities 42, 71–5, 233
  marketization of 45–6, 86–7, 88–91, 93–6, 218–19
  middle class 45–6, 87–8, 90, 95, 217–18, 220–3
  and migrants 10–11, 50–5, 85–90, 92, 151–2, 187–204
  price of 87, 95, 146
  and redevelopment 10–14, 31–2, 48, 49, 132–3
  renting 31–2, 47, 84, 85, 87, 88, 89, 90
  and shift from socialism to capitalism 93–4
  slums 11–12, *12*, 30–2
  state's retreat from 45
  types of neighborhoods 47–51